Just Sustainabilities: Policy, Planning, and Practice

Just Sustainabilities contributes to understanding, theorizing and ultimately developing strategies toward the development of more just and sustainable communities in both the global North and South. Through a collection of solutions-orientated books, the series looks at policy and planning themes that improve people's quality of life and well-being, both now and into the future; that are carried out with an intentional focus on just and equitable processes, outputs and outcomes in terms of people's access to environmental, social, political and economic space(s); and that aim to achieve a high quality of life and well-being within environmental limits.

Series editor

Julian Agyeman

Other titles in the series

Julian Agyeman, *Introducing Just Sustainabilities: Policy, Planning, and Practice*

About the editors

Karen Bickerstaff is senior lecturer in geography at Exeter University and leads the department's Environment and Sustainability Research Group. Her research interests centre on public engagements with technological risk, innovation and low-carbon transformations. Recent projects have examined nuclear waste policy and controversy in the UK, the efficacy of domestic energy efficiency interventions and the ethical dimensions of low-carbon energy technologies. She led the Interdisciplinary Cluster on Energy Systems, Equity and Vulnerability (InCluESEV), running from 2009 to 2012, which has fostered an international collaborative network developing new ways of thinking about, and researching, energy vulnerability and justice.

Gordon Walker is professor of risk, environment and justice at the Lancaster Environment Centre, Lancaster University. He researches and writes across a wide agenda, including matters of environmental justice, energy demand, social practice, socio-technical transitions, community innovation and renewable energy technologies, and the governance of forms of 'natural' and technological risk. He has led a series of research projects on these themes funded by the UK research councils, the European Union and government departments. His most recent book is *Environmental Justice: Concepts, evidence and politics*, and he is currently co-director of the Dynamics of Energy, Mobility and Demand (DEMAND) research centre.

Harriet Bulkeley is professor of geography at Durham University. Her research interests are the nature and politics of environmental governance, and focus on climate change, energy and urban sustainability. Her recent books include *Cities and Climate Change: Critical introductions to the city* (2013), *Governing Climate Change* (with Peter Newell, 2010) and *Cities and Low Carbon Transitions* (with Vanesa Castan-Broto, Mike Hodson and Simon Marvin, eds, 2011). She has undertaken a number of research projects funded by the ESRC, EPSRC and Leverhulme Trust, and is currently co-investigator for the Ofgem-funded Customer Led Network Revolution project on smart electricity grids (2011–14) and an ESRC project examining the role of China and Brazil in low-carbon transitions in southern Africa. Harriet was appointed an adviser to DECC in 2012, and she has undertaken commissioned research for the Joseph Rowntree Foundation, UN-Habitat and the World Bank.

Energy justice in a changing climate

Social equity and low-carbon energy

EDITED BY KAREN BICKERSTAFF, GORDON WALKER
AND HARRIET BULKELEY

Zed Books

LONDON | NEW YORK

Energy justice in a changing climate: social equity and low-carbon energy was first published in 2013 by Zed Books Ltd, 7 Cynthia Street, London N1 9JF, UK and Room 400, 175 Fifth Avenue, New York, NY 10010, USA

www.zedbooks.co.uk

Set in OurType Arnhem and Monotype Futura by Ewan Smith, London
Index: ed.emery@thefreeuniversity.net
Cover design: www.roguefour.co.uk
Printed and bound by CPI Group (UK) Ltd, Croydon, CRO 4YY

Distributed in the USA exclusively by Palgrave Macmillan, a division of St Martin's Press, LLC, 175 Fifth Avenue, New York, NY 10010, USA

A catalogue record for this book is available from the British Library
Library of Congress Cataloging in Publication Data available

ISBN 978 1 78032 577 4 hb
ISBN 978 1 78032 576 7 pb

Contents

Figure and tables | vii

Acknowledgements | viii

Introduction: making sense of energy justice 1
KAREN BICKERSTAFF, GORDON WALKER AND
HARRIET BULKELEY

1 Household energy vulnerability as 'assemblage' 14
ROSIE DAY AND GORDON WALKER

2 Precarious domesticities: energy vulnerability among urban
young adults. 30
STEFAN BOUZAROVSKI, SASKA PETROVA, MATTHEW KITCHING
AND JOSH BALDWICK

3 Energy justice in sustainability transitions research 46
MALCOLM EAMES AND MIRIAM HUNT

4 Energy justice and the low-carbon transition: assessing low-
carbon community programmes in the UK 61
SARA FULLER AND HARRIET BULKELEY

5 Energy justice and climate change: reflections from a Joseph
Rowntree Foundation research programme 79
KATHARINE KNOX

6 Equity across borders: a whole-systems approach to micro-
generation 91
CHARLOTTE ADAMS, SANDRA BELL, PHILIP TAYLOR,
VARVARA ALIMISI, GUY HUTCHINSON, ANKIT KUMAR
AND BRITTA ROSENLUND TURNER

7 Fair distribution of power-generating capacity: justice, microgrids and utilizing the common pool of renewable energy. . . 116
MAARTEN WOLSINK

8 Framing energy justice in the UK: the nuclear case 139
CATHERINE BUTLER AND PETER SIMMONS

9 Justice in energy system transitions: the case of carbon capture and storage 158

DUNCAN MCLAREN, KRISTIAN KRIEGER AND
KAREN BICKERSTAFF

About the contributors | 182

Notes | 187 Bibliography | 189
Index | 216

Figures and tables

Figures

6.1 Fuel mix for the UK 92
6.2 Schematic representation of the whole-systems approach and cross-cutting themes. .96
6.3 Equity assessment framework. 98
6.4 Fuel mix for Greece 105
6.5 Fuel mix for Japan 109
7.1 'A network of integrated microgrids that can monitor and heal itself' 120
7.2 Three dimensions of social acceptance of renewable energy innovations. 124
9.1 Potential impacts across the CCS development chain 168

Tables

2.1 Percentages of individuals responding affirmatively to different statements in the questionnaire survey 36
4.1 Multiple dimensions of justice 64
4.2 Selected UK low-carbon community programmes 72
4.3 Definition of community in low-carbon community programmes 76
6.1 Output from the SWOT analysis. 97
6.2 Case study detail 100
6.3 Summary of Greek case studies 106
6.4 Summary of Japanese case study 110
9.1 Principles of procedural justice 166

Acknowledgements

The editors wish to acknowledge the UK Research Council Energy Programme for funding the Interdisciplinary Cluster on Energy Systems, Equity and Vulnerability (EP/G040176/1), which was the catalyst for this collection. We would also like to thank the many contributing authors, whose critical engagement with concepts of energy justice has made this such an exciting project. Thanks also go to the 150-plus members of InCluESEV for their support, input and sheer enthusiasm over the three-year period of the network, and to Sue Barker for her superb coordination of many collaborative events. Finally, our thanks to Zed Books, particularly Kim Walker, for patient support throughout the duration of this project.

Introduction: making sense of energy justice

KAREN BICKERSTAFF, GORDON WALKER
AND HARRIET BULKELEY

Human-induced climate change, by its nature, involves the production of injustice. The impacts of climate change impose spatially uneven harms on present and future generations, and the burden of mitigating the causes of climate change is also socially and spatially uneven. Questions of who has the responsibility of addressing climate change or the rights to be protected from the harm it might cause have been central to the efforts to reach international agreement. At the same time, the right to emit greenhouse gases has been fiercely defended within international negotiations by developing countries, which argue that they have contributed proportionately little to the problem and stand to lose significantly from the mitigation costs of addressing climate change.

While these issues of global politics and ethics have been rehearsed over the past two decades, the implications and consequences of addressing climate change in a just manner have barely begun to be considered beyond this global arena. In this volume, it is our contention that the justice dimensions of mitigating climate change, specifically through decarbonizing energy systems, raise significant public, policy and political challenges that require sustained academic attention – empirically and theoretically.

This collection emerges from the activities of the Interdisciplinary Cluster on Energy Systems, Equity and Vulnerability (InCluESEV) – an international network that ran from 2009 to 2012, funded as part of a major Research Councils UK investment in energy research. Our concern in this network, and this volume, lies with the justice challenges presented by efforts to develop and sustain low-carbon energy systems in the UK and internationally. The EU's target of cutting greenhouse gas emissions by 20 per cent by 2020 (with the possibility of increasing this to 30 per cent) has, for instance, generated a substantial body of (supra) national policies and measures. Many of these focus on reducing the carbon intensity of systems of energy production and consumption. In this vein, much has been written about the sustainability of particular (low-carbon) energy systems – with an emphasis on environmental, economic and geopolitical issues. Far less attention has been directed at the social and equity implications of low-carbon policy objectives and decarbonization infrastructures: the spatial and temporal complexity of injustice associated with whole energy systems (from extractive industries, through to innovation processes, consumption and waste) that transcend territorial boundaries; the responsibilities, needs and capabilities of different actors across these systems; and the social, political-economic and material processes driving the experience of energy injustice and vulnerability. In this collection, and taking our cue from what is now a decade of research on 'Just Sustainabilities' (Agyeman et al. 2003; Agyeman 2013), highlighting the ties between a sustainable society and a just one, we argue that energy justice is one of the most critical, and yet least developed, concepts associated with theories and practices of low-carbon transitions, and one that must underpin a sustainable energy future. Energy justice is not as yet a routinely used term,[1] but provides a way of bounding and separating out energy concerns from the wider range of topics addressed within both environmental and climate justice analysis and campaigning. To date, research on energy justice is underdeveloped and rather circumscribed in theoretical and empirical concerns. Work has specifically crystallized around the social and spatial distribution of energy poverty and on the justice dimensions of particular (low-carbon) energy systems.

Current concerns: energy poverty and the politics of consumption

In recent years energy, and the uneven access to energy services, has shot up national and international political agendas (e.g. Provost 2013; Boardman 2010; Wilkinson et al. 2007; Wright 2004). The differential experience of energy-related injustice, and associated claims for rights, has resulted in a breadth of concepts being deployed by academics, activists and political actors alike – including energy poverty, fuel poverty, energy insecurity, energy deprivation, energy vulnerability and energy precariousness (see discussion in Day and Walker, this volume; Bouzarovski et al., this volume). Research and policy activity have been particularly strong in the UK, where the language of fuel poverty has been instrumental in the recognition of problems of access to affordable energy (Walker and Day 2012; Hills 2012). The concept of fuel poverty itself is rooted in UK experience and concerns with access to affordable warmth. Historically, a household has been considered to be in fuel poverty if it needs to spend more than 10 per cent of its income on fuel for adequate heating.[2]

2

While we now have a substantial body of research documenting patterns of fuel poverty and the processes involved, and evaluating associated policy measures, there has been relatively little attention to the impacts of climate change and decarbonization policies on the experience of energy vulnerability – a term which recognizes the variability of circumstances through which problems of energy 'under-consumption' are produced (Day and Walker, this volume). Recent exploratory research (including work funded under the Joseph Rowntree Foundation's Climate Change and Social Justice Programme) has made the case that climate mitigation policies could push increasing numbers of low-income households into energy poverty – unable to spend enough on fuel to achieve the levels of energy services (warmth in particular) deemed sufficient without compromising their ability to meet other basic needs. In the UK context, the majority of climate policies are funded through electricity and gas bills with costs passed on to consumers. This means that funding the costs of climate policies imposes a disproportionate impact on lower-income households (Preston et al. 2013; Stockton and Campbell 2011). Our own work, under the InCluESEV network, has extended thinking on energy vulnerability – how vulnerability is produced in multiple and complex ways, and is dynamic, changing over the life course, seasonally and over longer climatic timescales and in relation to specific events. Through international comparisons, enabled through workshops held in Brussels and North Carolina in the USA, we were able to reveal the different ways in which energy poverty could be experienced and structured, with energy markets, infrastructures and climatic conditions all differentiated between national and regional contexts. The prospect of new forms of energy-related vulnerability opening up with climate change – for example, a greater need for air conditioning to protect householders from the health impacts of heat waves – was also apparent (Fuller and Bulkeley 2013).

Debates around energy consumption, and demand reduction, are also revealing in what they do (and do not) say about justice and fairness. Prevailing approaches to motivating people to reduce the carbon intensity of their everyday lives have been criticized (albeit indirectly) for misrecognition. In other words strategies of behaviour change have tended to focus on constructions of (economically) rational and self-interested consumers. As such they have failed to recognize the fairness or justice dimensions that are critical in public ambivalence towards calls to practise sustainability – notably concerns about others 'free-riding', structural inequalities in the powers of citizens and institutions, and a belief that political institutions and (big) business will not accept their fair share of responsibility for climate mitigation (Horton and Doran 2011; Bickerstaff and Walker 2002).

Indeed, across this energy justice terrain, issues of recognition, and who legitimately should constitute the 'demos', and how, remain a thorny ethical challenge. As Bell and Rowe (2012) point out, geographically many decisions about climate policies are made by a territorially defined democratic community, yet these policies have effects beyond the boundaries of that community as well as into the worlds of future generations.

Bell and Rowe (ibid.) also identify a serious risk that climate mitigation proposals will exacerbate current injustices by further concentrating power in the hands of business interests and more affluent communities. For them, the most just response is to adopt the principle of proportionality – that power in any decision-making process should be proportional to individual stakes – to increase the power of the least powerful. It is a response that creates its own distributional and procedural challenges, but does address some fundamental issues about the recognition of 'affected' voices, of power differentials, and of the geographical and temporal complexity of energy justice problems. Erik Swyngedouw's (2010) challenge to the commodification of carbon through markets raises some broadly connected questions about the ethics and justice implications of political systems for managing carbon that retain a commitment to economic growth, and within which the power to decide (on future energy pathways) is too heavily skewed towards the interests of capital. For Swyngedouw this embracing of neoliberalism, and a drive towards more consensual policy-making, has evacuated the politics of the possible, of alternative – more agonistic, plural and in this sense fairer – ways of determining future socio-environmental arrangements.

Justice and energy systems in transition

With growing political and public interest in the delivery of low-carbon transitions – that is, fundamental changes in the way we provide and access energy services – questions of how such transformations are decided, managed and implemented raise a number of challenges with regard to just processes and outcomes.

In terms of existing justice-oriented research exploring low-carbon energy systems, work has pointed to systematic inequities associated with located energy system components. The bulk of attention has centred on the (social, spatial and temporal) distribution of costs and risks associated with the siting of infrastructures for power generation or for the disposal of waste residues (linked to extraction, generation or other phases of the energy system cycle). The distribution of benefits attached to low carbon generation has also raised some very clear equity concerns. For instance, microgeneration technologies installed at domestic dwellings involve significant upfront capital investment, and are not cost effective today, without a guaranteed fixed price for surplus electricity exported to the grid. The introduction of the UK Feed-in-Tariffs (FiTs)[3] in 2010 is estimated to have cost energy consumers £6.7 billion, with an average increase in electricity bills of £6.50 by 2015 and £10.70 by 2020 (Stockton and Campbell 2011; cf. Preston et al. 2013). Stockton and Campbell (2011) question the distributional outcomes of FiTs; while the costs are levied on all electricity bills, households' access to the payment and the supplementary benefit of free electricity is limited to those that can pay the upfront capital costs. Investing in these technologies is simply not feasible for financially disadvantaged households.[4] As Walker (2008) suggests, the prospect is one of middle classes investing available capital, and realizing returns, while lower-income groups remain dependent on increasingly expensive electricity and gas supplies, making them an 'energy underclass'. The potential for microgeneration to improve access to affordable energy for low-income households will not be realized through a model of development that focuses on households paying upfront for technologies. Varied delivery and governance strategies are needed that recognize the role for local governments, housing associations and energy suppliers (Walker 2008; Stockton and Campbell 2011; Wolsink, this volume) as well as more progressive mechanisms for supporting public investment (Preston et al. 2013).

There has also been a line of critique which centres on the procedural unfairness of decision-making processes around energy infrastructure siting that (in)directly target vulnerable groups such as indigenous and economically marginal communities (e.g. Blowers and Leroy 1994; Gowda and Easterling 2000). Much of the social science engagement with the siting of (low-carbon) energy technologies, in particular carbon capture and storage (CCS) (see McLaren et al., this volume), embeds an implicit or explicit understanding of participation as a key trope of a fair decision-making process and outcome. But too often these efforts to involve publics have centred on the expression of concerns in relation to decisions being made at downstream stages in innovation and policy processes. A particular concern here is the (need for) recognition of alternative cultural understandings of risk, situated knowledges, and the ability of marginalized groups to be heard – to have a voice (Wolsink 2007; Bell et al. 2013) – as fundamental principles underpinning just energy futures. Bell and Rowe (2012), for instance, make a similar point, noting the contradictory political trends in the UK government's responses to the decarbarbonization agenda: while government requires developers to consult local communities over major proposals before planning applications are submitted, the implementation of projects such as wind farms and nuclear power stations is being speeded up, with decisions being taken by ministers rather than local planning authorities. Policies of community volunteerism and compensation are also being pursued in the UK (and internationally) as a corrective to unfair distributional outcomes – particularly linked to the siting of radioactive waste facilities (e.g. Alley and Alley 2013; Bickerstaff 2012). However, concerns have been raised that economically disadvantaged communities are most likely to volunteer and that siting decisions are being made increasingly on social (acceptability) rather than physical suitability criteria – leading to the concentration of risk in socially, politically and economically vulnerable places (see discussion in Butler and Simmons 2010; McLaren et al., this volume).

However, much of this existing literature has tended to focus on the specific geographical contexts of energy system components. Although such analyses are important in understanding the fairness of energy processes, the fragmenting of energy systems does limit our ability to understand justice relations between actors and across time and space. In this respect, the InCluESEV network sought to explore the configuration of justice issues across a number of low-carbon *whole* energy systems (microgeneration, new nuclear power and carbon capture and storage). Although researchers adopted different whole-system concepts, stressing particular spatial, temporal and material relations, all show how the potential for injustice permeates the life of the technology – arguing that these complex impacts need to be more fully acknowledged and debated as part of technology assessment processes and policy decisions about low-carbon energy transition pathways.

Towards energy justice?

We trace through and develop many of the themes discussed above in this volume, drawing on a variety of international case studies, including the UK, the Netherlands, Greece and Japan. Our approach in organizing the collection has been to avoid compartmentalizing the subject matter in terms of extant ideas, as either energy poverty or energy systems, or following particular theoretical perspectives on justice (e.g. distinctions of distributional, procedural and recognition justice). Rather we have structured the chapters into two main sections. The first deals with 'concepts and challenges for energy justice', recognizing that an energy justice agenda is, at present, only partially articulated. This section explores a series of concepts and frameworks that offer distinctive insights into the scope, scale and production of energy injustice. Rosie Day and Gordon Walker open with a (re)conceptualization of energy vulnerability as a dynamic, messy and variable assemblage of (to name but a few) people, things, policies and institutions. Stefan Bouzarovski, Saska Petrova, Matthew Kitching and Josh Baldwick explore the transient and precarious energy vulnerabilities of young adults – perspectives often lost in public policy discourses of fuel or energy poverty. Malcolm Eames and Miriam Hunt offer a critical reflection on dominant models of (low-carbon) innovation and the ways in which they have (and have not) internalized equity issues. Sara Fuller and Harriet Bulkeley extend this thinking, developing a framework for establishing the realization of energy justice through low-carbon community programmes in the UK. Finally, Katharine Knox reflects on the emerging profile of energy justice research within the Joseph Rowntree Foundation (JRF), the evolution of the JRF programme investigating the social justice implications of climate change for the UK and findings emerging from this sustained research effort.

The second section of the book focuses on the justice dynamics of low-carbon transitions, recognizing that transformations in (low-carbon) energy infrastructures and policies may be perpetuating, or producing anew, forms of inequality and vulnerability – or they may be providing opportunities for change for the better.

Charlotte Adams, Sandra Bell, Phil Taylor, Varvara Alimisi, Guy Hutchinson, Ankit Kumar and Britta Rosenlund Turner deploy a distributional justice heuristic to compare the social and spatial impacts of microgeneration projects in a range of international case study contexts. Maarten Wolsink follows with a consideration of novel microgrid and smart grid[5] arrangements, and the distribution of 'common pool' (distributed energy) resources. He considers how such infrastructures, which transform rights and responsibilities in relation to the electricity system, present challenges for energy justice. Catherine Butler and Peter Simmons address the UK debate about nuclear power, examining how justice issues appear within policy and political discourses, and unpacking the consequences for recognizing and responding to the complexity of energy justice. Duncan McLaren, Kristian Krieger and Karen Bickerstaff reflect on the broad sweep of energy justice research addressing low-carbon technologies, though focusing specifically on carbon capture and storage (CCS). They express concerns about an overly instrumental application of participation in downstream decisions about siting and deployment and make the case for a more holistic and joined-up treatment of procedural justice.

It is important to add that we recognize that this collection does not offer a complete analysis of energy justice, its expression and resolution – for instance, there are pressing justice issues surrounding other low-carbon energy sources (e.g. Smith 2010 on biofuels), the links between security of supply and energy justice, the role of decarbonization in employment and well-being, and ways in which decarbonization agendas (in the North and South) are implicated in wider global patterns of energy vulnerability and injustice. That said, this volume provides an important step in defining some of the central debates, problems and challenges, and in offering some genuinely novel ways of thinking about, researching and responding to energy injustices.

Emerging research themes and agendas

For the remainder of this introduction we review the collection of chapters through four thematic lenses which enable us to mark out the contours of an expanding energy justice agenda; the identification of absences and partial understandings; the production of (in)justice; thinking energy justice relationally; and new concepts of energy vulnerability and justice.

First of all, many authors in the volume identify absences in existing energy and justice research. Eames and Hunt point to the very real absence of justice principles within dominant frameworks for conceptualizing and practising low-carbon transitions. They argue that the principal tools for conceptualizing and governing such changes, while offering informative insights into processes of transition in energy systems, neglect issues of distributive and procedural justice. The authors suggest that this deficiency is rooted in an inadequate conceptualization of power; an overly technocratic conception of transition – with a focus on the perspectives of elites – and a neglect of the spatial dimensions of transitions management. Bouzarovski et al. powerfully reveal the absent voices (and experiences) within existing energy deprivation research – which, as they (and others in this volume) note, tends to be focused on traditionally visible groups, such as older people and rural dwellers. Their chapter exposes the precarious and transient nature of energy vulnerability patterns among urban young adults, many of whom are in the private rented sector, emphasizing that issues of recognition are central to understanding and addressing this group's susceptibility to domestic energy deprivation. Katharine Knox offers a reflection on the JRF's Climate Change and Social Justice (CCSJ) programme and the drivers behind this research effort. She reviews the findings of CCSJ projects and 'think pieces' which have in various ways begun to fill out our understanding of the inequalities and justice parameters of climate change mitigation, although much remains to be investigated. She highlights the compounded nature of injustice in relation to carbon reduction policies in the UK, whereby low-income households pay proportionally more of their income and benefit less from energy policies affecting domestic energy bills than wealthier households, while also being least responsible for emissions.

Butler and Simmons articulate a rather different form of absence, which we might read as a restrictive epistemic and political framing of justice issues. Their chapter reflects on the narrowing of conceptions of nuclear justice within UK political discourse, and a closing down of the spaces for articulation of justice-related concerns beyond those related to procedure. They suggest the particular ways in which nuclear energy is framed direct attention away from the multiple justice-related concerns it raises, and underlies a failure to engage properly with justice issues in processes of low-carbon transitions. In a linked way McLaren et al. reflect on the partial reading of procedural justice in the development and deployment of low-carbon innovation generally and CCS technologies specifically – with instrumental goals driving the practice of public participation and engagement in shaping low-carbon energy pathways. The authors note a dominating concern with diagnosing the causes of opposition and, from this, articulating modes of participation that will support socially acceptable siting processes and outcomes. As such the policy and research emphasis on promoting (more) participation remains somehow distant from procedural justice issues such as power, voice, access to early decision-making and recognition of difference in fundamental values and beliefs. McLaren et al. highlight the urgent need for energy research to more fully consider how to provide procedural justice for future generations in the face of pressing present interests.

Our second connecting theme relates to the processes and practices driving the production of injustice. Day and Walker challenge the notion that (energy) vulnerability is an inherent attribute of particular households or individuals – that is, located in the physical body.

Rather they theorize vulnerability as a dynamic process, a coming together, or assemblage, of human and non-human presences and absences, alongside practices, norms and possibilities. Butler and Simmons similarly recognize the socio-material complexity of justice assemblages. They point out that a failure to engage with the 'messiness' of that justice, ethical and equity issues that nuclear energy raises represents a 'closing down' (Stirling 2005: 228) of debate that effectively excludes other energy justice considerations from political and public discussion of energy transitions – both in relation to nuclear and beyond. Adams et al. reflect particularly on the distributional inequities associated with the take-up of microgeneration technologies. They develop a framework for identifying equity issues in specific project contexts and deploy it in case studies in the UK, Japan and Greece. It is an approach that highlights some generic concerns with the distributional impacts of microgeneration that cut across these case studies. Specifically they address the equity challenges of capital funding for (community) micro-generation projects, and stress the need for novel financing and support mechanisms targeted to specific geographical and social groups. Without this, microgeneration will have very little impact in addressing energy vulnerability (cf. Walker 2008). In Wolsink's discussion of the implications of the development of DisGenMiGrid (distributed generation microgrids), he points to the ways in which citizens/consumers and other end users are becoming co-producers of electricity. He sees two particular potential governance pathways: either policies that enhance the autonomy of cooperating end users with the help of smart meters and generated data under their control; or policies that emphasize smart metering – currently framed as meters that generate data to be read and used by power supply companies – and associated (centralized) smart regulation of energy use. In both cases we see a transformation of rights and responsibilities which could raise unexpected challenges around distributive equity and fairness of process. Finally, Bulkeley and Fuller offer an analysis of UK low-carbon community policies and programmes which have been couched in a discourse of supporting a (more) just low-carbon transition. In their analysis of community energy projects they note important differences in the aims and achievements of government, private sector and community-led projects. The authors also reveal some tensions between the distribution of rights and responsibilities to communities and the extent to which participation genuinely recognizes difference and shapes decision-making processes.

A third theme that links many of the chapters is a concern with thinking relationally or holistically about energy justice issues. Adams et al., for instance, propose a heuristic distributional justice methodology for embedding an array of social concerns, related to located microgeneration projects, in policy and decision-making practices for technology development and implementation. Butler and Simmons reflect on the tendency in much social science research on nuclear energy to address specific components of the nuclear fuel cycle and/or particular geographical contexts. As such we see a conceptualization of justice framed primarily in terms of the spatially and temporally located contexts of particular system components (e.g. Bell et al. 2013; Butler and Simmons 2010) – for the most part concentrating on downstream infrastructures of generation and waste management. McLaren et al. draw similar conclusions in relation to CCS technologies. They argue that an understanding of energy justice in relation to (novel) low-carbon technologies must embed an understanding of their relations to a complex set of other infrastructures, physical surroundings, people and procedures, as well as placing value on epistemic diversity and democratizing access to (and power to affect) decision-making. The challenge that both chapters recognize is how we might conceptualize the role of nuclear energy or CCS as part of a just whole-energy system. McLaren et al. respond with a (preliminary) framework for exploring the ways in which injustices are configured across the full life of an energy system and how they impact differentially upon stakeholders at points across that cycle. Here they caution against a reading of equity in terms of the presence (or absence) of participation, and argue for a more joined-up and relational analysis of procedural fairness across whole systems. It's a redrawing of the spatial and temporal boundaries of what constitutes a just transition that demands an institutional engagement with procedural justice principles early in 'upstream' processes of innovation and decision-making. Day and Walker offer a spatially dynamic interpretation of energy vulnerability, as a coming together of disparate social, technological and natural processes. So, energy vulnerability is not just a matter of the juxtaposition or combination of a certain kind of people with a particular kind of building, set of appliances, climatic regime and energy supply and pricing system. It is rather a matter of how these all interact – for example, how specific people want to inhabit their house, at what times and in what rooms; how the type of energy supply constrains the appliances that can be used; who makes household financial decisions; and how they make choices. Wolsink pays particular attention to the role of a diverse array of actors (including consumers) in maintaining the common-pool resource of renewable energy and its distribution through microgrids. Critical here is the role not just of cooperative arrangements between co-producers but also the role of radically different institutional arrangements to ensure recognition, and valorization, of participation. As Wolsink points out, 'if [citizens] are treated as unimportant or irrelevant, they reduce their efforts substantially'.

Our final thematic centres on new ways of thinking about energy vulnerability and justice. In this regard chapters in the collection offer a number of frameworks, concepts and tools for researching, theorizing and responding to energy justice. Day and Walker's reading of energy vulnerability as assemblage brings a dynamism and 'messiness' to a concept that is typically understood as a static quantifiable metric. It is a perspective that demands comprehending vulnerability differently – as displaying varying degrees of fragility or stability – and through this allows a more optimistic outlook, offering numerous points of entry and potentials for change. So, for instance, the authors suggest that by identifying the (constrained) capabilities that create energy vulnerability, we can help develop more inclusive policy approaches and tools in both UK and wider international contexts. Fuller and Bulkeley explore a framework for assessing the justice dimensions of (area-based) communities' low-carbon transition projects. Drawing on the climate change and environmental justice arenas, they develop a 'climate frame' that is structured around the broad distributive–procedural distinction and the principles of rights, responsibilities and recognition. Their analysis reveals a varied picture in terms of project delivery and the extent to which fundamental inequalities at the community level are recognized and addressed. This finding raises questions about whether government, private sector or community-led projects can best realize justice aims, but also points to ways that recognition can find a place in both distributive and procedural aspects of low-carbon communities.

A number of authors develop particular concepts of energy justice. Maarten Wolsink points out that while microgrid systems fundamentally concern involvement of a community right from the start, governance of a 'common pool' energy resource (where it is difficult to exclude potential beneficiaries) brings questions of justice – distributive equity and fairness of process – to the fore; for instance, around the calculation of electricity bills. Wolsink stresses the need to take seriously allocative justice; how a bundle of commodities is to be distributed among various individuals whose particular needs are known to us, and who have not cooperated to produce those commodities. The chapter draws on Common Pool Resource theory to challenge the fairness (and thus efficacy) of imposed markets or centralized command and control policies, making the case for high institutional variety (adaptive governance) and a high level of self-governance. For Butler and Simmons, the concept of capabilities (Sen 2009) offers a means for a deeper, more context-sensitive, analysis of the justice issues associated with new nuclear power and climate change. They argue that an approach that emphasizes capabilities brings focus on to the specifics of different contexts and allows for consideration of the complexity of justice issues. They offer the illustration of communities living in areas where nuclear facilities are already in existence, who often work within those industries; industrial closure can result in rapid decline of those places, with serious consequences for people's capabilities to live healthy lives. McLaren et al. stress the need, at the level of public engagement with CCS, for full recognition and enabling capabilities for those with a stake to not only participate, but to engage in establishing the terms of participation. They argue, like many of the authors in this collection, that energy system decisions need to be informed and interrogated by justice questions in a much more comprehensive and integrated manner. We need to embrace energy justice as a more challenging, variable and contested terrain, recognizing that matters of values and ethics cannot easily be reduced to metrics and direct trade-offs. It is only in such a context that we can nurture a genuinely public debate about different possible low-carbon pathways and the sorts of socio-environmental relations they sustain.

1 | Household energy vulnerability as 'assemblage'

ROSIE DAY AND GORDON WALKER

Introduction

In the profile of current energy justice concerns, those focused on households' access to sufficient and affordable energy are perhaps the most well established. In both developed and developing world contexts the well-being that energy services – such as heat, light and mobility – can bring to people's lives has provided the basis for assertions of energy-related rights and for political mobilization against the inequalities in energy access that are implicated in patterns of ill-health, mortality and diminished life-chances (AGECC 2010; Boardman 2010; Wilkinson et al. 2007; Wright 2004). In the UK, for example, and as discussed in the introductory chapter, the language of fuel poverty has provided a powerful framing for recognizing problems of access to affordable energy and for a range of policy interventions intended to address these (Walker and Day 2012; Hills 2012). Such policy, research and political mobilization is less advanced in other European countries, and elsewhere across the developed world, but is emerging and gradually revealing the prevalence, depth and characteristics of household energy problems in different settings (e.g. Healy 2003; Brunner et al. 2012; Buzar 2007; O'Sullivan et al. 2011; Simshauser et al. 2011; Tirado Herrero and Ürge-Vorsatz 2012).

Partly because research and policy attention has emerged in a quite differentiated manner, different languages have been employed to characterize the problem that is at issue, including those of fuel poverty, energy poverty, energy insecurity, energy deprivation and energy precariousness. To some extent these different terms reflect the underlying understanding or framing of the problem. Fuel poverty, for example, is strongly rooted in the UK experience and its primary focus is on affordable warmth; energy poverty tends to be used in relation to access and affordability problems in the developing world which can take on a quite different character; while energy insecurity can imply a concern primarily with the provisioning and price stability of energy supplies to the household. In this chapter we work with the term 'energy vulnerability' with the intention of following a broad and open framing that does not imply a particular emphasis or understanding of cause and effect. As we explain further below, energy vulnerability is a term that for us better captures the variability of circumstances and processes through which problems of access to sufficient and affordable energy are manifest, and one that has the potential to work across many different national and regional settings.

Having proposed this open terminology, we then seek in this chapter to develop a more theoretically informed account than is typical of work in this field. The bulk of existing research is applied and problem oriented, drawing on different disciplinary traditions, but not engaging very substantially with social or critical theory. There are some exceptions. For example, Buzar (2007: 1908) examines household energy deprivation as an 'innately relational phenomenon', drawing together a range of theory on infrastructure, poverty and everyday life to inform his analysis of the 'socio-spatial arrangements' of energy poverty in post-socialist Europe. Powells (2009) uses actor network theory and notions of entanglement and overflow to examine the complex interactions between fuel poverty and energy efficiency policy in the UK. Harrison and Popke (2011), in a rare examination of 'energy poverty' (their term) in the USA, use the notion of 'assemblage' as a way of setting up and analysing their empirical account of rural household energy problems in North Carolina.

Each of these applications of theoretical ideas has connections with the approach we explore in this chapter, but it is the innovative use of assemblage thinking by Harrison and Popke which we particularly seek to take forward. They argue that 'energy poverty' can be seen as 'a particular kind of techno-social assemblage, made up of an array of networked actors and materialities' and that 'a focus on the networked nature of energy poverty ... can help to highlight its historical foundations and multidimensional character' (ibid.: 950). They go some way to substantiate these claims through their empirical work, but, we would argue, take up only some of the potential of 'assemblage thinking'. In particular they do not go as far as they might to draw out the ways in which assemblage embodies particular understandings of agency, emergence and dynamics. Our specific aim is therefore to explore the value of assemblage thinking to the analysis of energy vulnerability, considering both what it can bring to understanding the basis, formation and dynamics of energy vulnerability, and also what it can less satisfactorily account for.

Before moving on to examine the origin of assemblage as a concept and the core ideas it encompasses, we need to say more about how we understand energy vulnerability. Energy vulnerability is for us a situation in which a person or household is unable to achieve sufficient access to affordable and reliable energy services, and as a consequence is in danger of harm to health and/or well-being. This open definition makes no specific judgement about which energy services are significant, what constitutes sufficient access, how harm may be involved or how substantial that harm needs to be. The notion of vulnerability also conveys a sense of potentiality or precariousness rather than necessarily a situation of demonstrable and existing harm. We understand energy vulnerability as having a number of general characteristics:

- First, as much of the existing literature emphasizes, it is multi-dimensional in character and produced through the coming together of social, technological and natural processes.
- Secondly, the exact nature of this coming together for any particular person or household is locally contingent. Hence energy vulnerability is variable in its production and character over space and time.
- Third, energy vulnerability as experienced exhibits different temporal qualities, sometimes constant and unyielding, sometimes far more dynamic and shifting in cyclical or more unpredictable patterns.

In the following discussion these three key characteristics will be reflected on in the light of assemblage theory, drawing on illustrative cases taken from the review work and extended discussions and interactions within the InCluESEV project. In this respect we draw on varied cases and settings from across Europe and North America (which reflects the scope of work in the project), given, as noted earlier, that we are seeking to provide an analytical framework that is open to the international and regional variability of energy vulnerability experiences. We do not in this chapter extend to specific consideration of energy vulnerability in other parts of the world, but suggest in the concluding discussion that an assemblage framework might be readily applicable to a wider global geography of household energy contexts.

Understanding assemblage

The concept of 'assemblage' as it is used by social scientists is normally attributed in its origins to the work of Deleuze and Guattari, and their notion of '*agencement*', which came to be translated as 'assemblage' (Deleuze and Guattari 1987). While some working with assemblage have attempted to follow Deleuze and Guattari closely, other distinctive versions of the approach have also developed (e.g. De Landa 2006). Also closely related but with distinctive elements is the 'assembling of associations' that is central to Actor Network Theory (Latour 2005; Law 1992; Whatmore 1999).

All of these approaches at their basis view the happening world as coalescing into assemblages, or networks, of heterogeneous entities (sometimes referred to as actants), which include humans, non-human and abstract things. Entities form an assemblage in that they have some kind of relation with each other, such that a kind of collective whole can be discerned. A whole assemblage should be more than the sum of its parts: it is not just a collection of stuff, but a functioning collective, at least for a time. The assemblage, though, need not be self-aware or intentionally formed by any of its members – its function and effect are always emergent and contingent. Although some assemblages may be designed, many are not, and even those that start with a template acquire their own momentum and configuration as they proceed.

The emphasis on the heterogeneity of the constituent entities of assemblages is essential. If we were to take a simple non-energy example and consider a (specific) school classroom as an assemblage, a very simple analysis might reveal it to contain children, a teacher, furniture, building infrastructure involving various material parts, books, clothing, computers and their software, educational theories, curriculum policies, routines, rules, religious beliefs, clocks, artworks, even a cold virus moving from child to child. These and potentially many other entities all shape the 'happening' of that specific classroom.

Viewing things in this way has the effect of decentring the human as the subject. As discussed later, this is an important shift which some social scientists dislike, but which has proved appealing for others, especially geographers, who are centrally concerned with the material world with which humans interact. A core intention for many using assemblage thinking is to make visible the way that non-human (including non-living) entities have a strong role in how situations play out – that is, they are not just props to human endeavours but they assert themselves in significant ways (see especially Bennet 2004, 2010; Callon 1986; Latour 2005).

Another feature of the heterogeneity is that assemblages can also blur spatial and temporal distinctions, bringing together entities that are near with those that are far (Anderson and McFarlane 2011) and entities with different temporal rhythms (Allen 2011). Thus the classroom example is able to include national government educational policy originating in a capital city and with a lifespan of a few years, alongside the daily rhythm of lesson timings, slowly evolving cultural practices and the rapidly changing weather. The existence of an assemblage needn't be in fully concrete or locational terms, but is rather through its working relations and bonds of influence.

Human and non-human entities can of course be involved in many assemblages at once, so defining an assemblage is not a way of separating or bracketing off parts of the world. Assemblages do not always present themselves neatly. Rather, it is the job of analysis to identify and describe them. Deciding what is and isn't an assemblage, where one begins and ends, is therefore an interpretation to be offered and, potentially, contested. This work of identifying and naming an assemblage and its constituents can imply a rather descriptive orientation, and indeed, this is often a criticism of such approaches. Some uses of an assemblage approach do stay in the realms of the more descriptive, and can be productive in doing so. Those drawing on Deleuze and Guattari in particular, though, are often more keen to emphasize the processual aspects of assemblages forming, unforming and reforming, such that the 'time-space of assemblage is imagined as inherently unstable and infused with movement and change' (Markus and Saka 2006: 102).

Because assemblages are characterized as impermanent, unpredictable and in flux, there are always possibilities for alternatives, and this is also an important aspect of the assemblage approach. Rather than describing just what is, the approach is also concerned with fostering imaginative conceptualizations of what may be, of how the world could be reassembled in different configurations and what difference that might make. However, its essential world view of messiness and contingency would militate against precise predictions of outcomes.

Assemblage has been worked with across diverse disciplinary literatures, usually more as an approach, or an orientation, than as the basis of a coherent theory. It is also applied in fairly diverse ways, which is variously regarded as both an advantage and a weakness (see, e.g., Marcus and Saka 2006; Anderson and McFarlane 2011; McFarlane 2011b; Brenner et al. 2011). To give some examples of the varied phenomena that might be conceived as assemblages, the concept has been applied to, among other things, political support movements (Davies 2012), rock climbing (Barratt 2012), flooding (Walker et al. 2011), environmental justice controversies (Bickerstaff and Agyeman 2009) and church buildings (Edensor 2011).

The approach does attract criticism, including over questions of agency and how assemblages come to be (discussed later), and issues around how the boundaries of assemblages are delimited (Allen 2011). Probably the most trenchant criticism is the perceived blindness of assemblage thinking to the structures and uneven power relations within which actants in an assemblage operate. There is thus an inability fully to explain or understand inequality (Brenner et al. 2011; Madden 2010), including how best to overcome it. However, although some believe that assemblage approaches do signify a full alternative to, and potential replacement of, more structural approaches in critical social and political science (Farías 2009), others advocate the combination of an assemblage perspective with other analytical approaches such as political economy or feminism for a fuller analysis and augmented explanatory power (McFarlane 2011b; Rankin 2011; see also Castree 2002). We will return to these questions later in our discussion.

Assemblage and energy vulnerability

Having introduced the concept of assemblage, its underpinnings and the ways of thinking that it draws on and promotes, we can now turn to applying these ideas to energy vulnerability. As noted in the introduction, the use of an assemblage approach has been mooted in this context before (Harrison and Popke 2011), but the ways in which it can inform and illuminate our understanding and conceptualization of energy vulnerability have not been fully explored. To take this agenda forward, we suggest that there are six fundamental features of assemblage thinking which can provide for a distinctive and productive analysis of the basis, formation and dynamics of energy vulnerability. In working through these we will consider the concept of assemblage in more depth, and draw on examples of varied forms of energy vulnerability.

1 *Networks of entities* Assemblage thinking conceives situations (or phenomena more generally) as being constituted by a network or configuration of human, non-human, material and abstract entities in some kind of relations with each other (as noted earlier, a relational ontology it shares with other theoretical traditions). As already discussed, some who use it particularly value the visibility and status that it gives to material, non-human entities, such as buildings and urban infrastructures, in human lives (Bennet 2004, 2010). For example, McFarlane (2011a), drawing particularly on his own work on informal settlements in Mumbai, argues that attention has to be given to how

material environments are both constituted by poverty, and part of the experience of poverty – as well as sometimes having a role in resistance strategies. Others have also seen value in how assemblage brings status and agency to nature in relational networks, from the molecular scale through to forces of earthquakes and global climatic change (Hinchliffe 2007; Clark 2011).

If we consider this open understanding of networks and entities with respect to energy vulnerability, we can see immediate reson-ances with the heterogeneity of entities that come together to create energy vulnerability. This dimension of assemblage thinking is what Harrison and Popke (2011: 959) emphasize most strongly in their 'open and relational account' of 'energy poverty as a geographical assemblage of networked materialities'. An energy-vulnerable household contains people by definition. It also involves a material infrastructure with many constituent parts – a building, a heating system, a supply line perhaps, the fuel itself; cooking and lighting devices, other appliances, insulation. The characteristics and condition of these material com-ponents are vital to the constitution of energy vulnerability, albeit in hugely diverse ways. How efficient are they? How old are they? How big are they in relation to the spaces and needs they service? Are they even there at all?[1]

So we can see the importance of both the human and material elem-ents – energy vulnerability would not exist without both. Non-human nature in the form of the outdoor climate, involved processes of air movement, temperature, humidity and their relation to the indoors are also essentially implicated, particularly in relation to demands on heating or cooling systems and temperature-related threats to health. We can also add in other, more abstract entities – traditions, conven-tions, markets, prices, policy priorities – as each is potentially a part of what comes together to produce vulnerability. Some entities may even be assemblages in themselves – a market is by no means a sim-ple entity – but for our purpose of understanding household energy vulnerability as an assemblage, it would be reasonable to consider markets and other complex entities as a single actant.

Assemblage thinking emphasizes that the nature of the assemblage is made in the *interaction* and association of these diverse elements. So, energy vulnerability is not just a matter of the mere juxtaposition or combination of a certain kind of people with a particular kind of building, set of appliances, climatic regime and energy supply and pricing system. It is rather a matter of how these all interact – for example, how specific people expect to inhabit their house, at what times and in what rooms; how the type of energy supply constrains the appliances that can be used; who makes household financial decisions and how they make choices about their energy supplier and tariff.

Assemblage, then, allows us to be open to, insofar as we can apprehend them, the diverse and varying elements that interact in constituting an energy vulnerability situation. Crucially, the emergence and contingency that are central to assemblage as a process also mean that we do not have to specify a fixed menu of entities involved, or fixed set of relationships between them. While disciplinary silos might often lead us to focus on either the human (for social scientists), material (for engineers and architects) or policy/market aspects (for economists and politicians), with other aspects fading into the background, taking an assemblage approach which insists on a 'principle of generalized symmetry' (Callon 1986; Latour 1993) with respect to human and non-human entities disallows this partial view.

2 *Agency* Developing from the above points, assemblage approaches see agency as distributed between the different entities or actants in the assemblage, not merely lying with the humans involved (although there is some variation across different writers in how this distribution of agency is interpreted). So for example, we might say that a central heating boiler exerts agency in constituting energy vulnerability in a particular situation, perhaps through breaking down, or becoming progressively less efficient as it ages. Pre-payment meters for gas or electricity would be another example of a technical device installed in low-income households (or those with a poor payment record), which disciplines its users to pay for and manage their energy supply in a particular way (OFGEM 2011; O'Sullivan et al. 2011). Bennet (2005) provides a good example of this way of thinking with respect to energy vulnerability in her analysis of the North American blackout of 2003. She shows that while a more conventional analysis might locate the responsibility with human decisions and failings, a convincing alternative case can be made for the agency, and perhaps even the responsibility, being distributed among humans and non-humans.

This blurring of the distinction between human and non-human actants in terms of not just their presence but their agency is essential to the 'symmetrical analysis' referred to above, but thinking in this way is challenging and controversial. Tonkiss (2011), for example, is critical of the status that Bennet seems to give to material objects and argues that human agency is of a different order to that of objects (see also Castree 2002; Kirsch and Mitchell 2004). Fuller, in debate with Latour (Barron

2003), asserts that it is vital to distinguish morally between humans and non-humans. However, it becomes easier to be symmetrical if a distinction is made between agency and conscious intentionality (see Bingham 1996; Whatmore 1999) – so, for example, we can see that a boiler may exercise an effect without it having formulated a plan to do so, similarly a pre-payment meter, or a 'cold snap' in the winter. Latour's response to Fuller (Barron 2003) also indicates that blurring the distinction between human and non-human actors in this way is for the purpose of describing and analysing specific situations, not an all-encompassing world view, and confers the advantage of being able to see the role of the non-human world more clearly.

We shouldn't neglect to think about human agency, however, and this 'distributed agency' analysis presses us to do this as well. Here we can see that in the coming together and functioning of what might be termed an 'energy vulnerability assemblage', humans exert agency in many decisions, preferences, knowledges, practices and ways of interacting with their environment and the material entities around them, such as thermostats, kettles and clothing. This is not to say that the human decisions and choices in such an assemblage are all bad ones or lead directly to energy vulnerability, but they need to be seen as part of the overall situation.

It is also important to note that the assemblage approach, as well as assigning agency to both human and non-human actants, sees the important agency as being that of the assemblage itself – in the inter-actions, and the totality of these – such effect being referred to as the 'milieu' by Deleuze and Guattari (see Bennet 2005; also Law 1992; Whatmore 1999 on Actor Network Theory). With respect to energy vulner-ability, this is clear – the vulnerability which is our ultimate concern is constituted by the overall assemblage; this assemblage goes on to have various, largely negative, effects on the household and its members. There are also ripple effects beyond the household: in the UK context, for example, figures monitoring the number of fuel-poor households gal-vanize campaigners and cause headaches for governments, and there is significant policy activity around the issue with accompanying financial costs. Further, intervening in energy vulnerability assemblages through their material actants, such as building structures, heating systems and insulation, has become a state-supported industry in many places, including the UK and the USA.

3 *Space and scale* As noted earlier, assemblage analyses are able to transcend Euclidean space and cross scale. Entities/actants within the

assemblage can include people, material and decisions that are both near and far in locational terms and which might generally be seen as operating at different scales – for example, the family, neighbourhood, regional and national governments. All such elements can be traced as part of an assemblage without them being arranged into spatial hierarchies (see Marston et al. 2005 and various responses to that paper for seminal debate on such 'flattening' of scale; also Whatmore and Thorne 1997; Bingham 1996). For energy vulnerability, then, the important criterion for inclusion of entities is not their spatial location, but their relevant relations with other entities within the assemblage that as a whole constitutes energy vulnerability. Thus while conventional analyses of fuel poverty might focus on the local social and material characteristics of the home, a relational account could, for example, draw in distant crises in geopolitical relations that destabilize energy prices and impact on the affordability of gas travelling through extended supply networks and pipelines into the home. The gap between the international framing of 'energy security' and the local framing of 'fuel poverty' is thus traversed through a non-hierarchical account. Similar distant tracings might be made with crop harvests and policies to promote biofuels, and with global climate change and its relations both to energy policies and to locally experienced climatic patterns.

4 *Messiness and variety* Those working with assemblage often argue that a crucial characteristic and advantage is the emphasis on 'messiness', on the contingency of any specific assemblage (Dovey 2011; Simone 2011). What might, through other theoretical lenses, be seen as coherent, similar kinds of force being in operation, can through assemblage analysis be revealed to be heterogeneous, quite diverse situations with internal inconsistencies and idiosyncrasies. For example, McFarlane (2011a) has taken this view with respect to neoliberalism, arguing that it should be seen as a set of place-specific contingent assemblages, rather than a coherent meta-narrative that is cleanly reproduced from one context to another with only slight, functional adaptations. We believe that this is one of the most beneficial insights that assemblage thinking can bring to the analysis of energy vulnerability.

Looking again at the UK, the category of 'fuel poverty' has been extremely powerful and instrumental in bringing to light a real problem and injustice faced by millions of households. However, it has become clear that tackling it effectively requires a fuller and more nuanced understanding than the current prevailing models provide. There are stereotypes of the 'fuel poor' or 'energy vulnerable' household that commonly circulate. In the UK, it tends to be the older person on a low income living in a home in poor repair, using outdated, inefficient heating systems and appliances. In other climatic and social contexts there may be other abiding images, perhaps, as in southern Europe and the southern states of the USA, more to do with cooling rather than heating. However, certainly in the UK, those working on the ground know that it can be surprisingly hard to find households that actually fit the stereotype so clearly. That's not to say that the elements of the basic model of energy vulnerability are misconceived – incomes, fuel prices and the energy efficiency of buildings and appliances are highly relevant – but the diversity of actual instances of energy vulnerability is never sufficiently acknowledged. Some energy vulnerability may not even fit the definition of 'fuel poverty'. Within the UK, one energy-vulnerable household could be an off-grid couple on low wages in a detached house in a cold part of the country with an old oil-fired heating system; while another might be a single parent in a rented flat in a large city with a broken gas boiler and an unhelpful landlord. In southern Europe it might be an older person with heart problems in a city flat in summer worried about the safety of leaving windows open and trying to keep cool with electric fans ... the possibilities are extensive.

Can these yet be seen as something that is 'the same'? With so much diversity, should we dispense with the idea of a phenomenon called 'energy vulnerability' altogether? We think not, and don't propose to deny any kind of commonality. The direction that all these assemblages move in may be similar, heading the household towards harm of some kind: ill-health, stress, social stigma – again there may be diversity here, but all would be open to being seen as undesirable situations. Furthermore, in all cases energy is something whose circulation is an essential element of the assemblage. The point is, though, that the configuration of elements, or actants, in the assemblage, apart from energy in some form, may be quite different in each case, and this is important because it follows that the points of productive intervention might also be quite different.

5 *Dynamics and flux* Assemblages are not seen as static, but as entities in flux, forming and unforming, with varying degrees of fragility or stability. Some authors feel that the processes of forming and unforming are a more pertinent focus than rather static conceptions of the assemblage itself (Anderson and McFarlane 2011; Farías 2009;

McFarlane 2011a). We see that both aspects are likely to be relevant to studies of energy vulnerability. As discussed above, what the elements are that constitute energy vulnerability in a specific case is an important question, but we would be perhaps even more interested in how they come together, why, and under what circumstances. We can also see through this approach that some energy vulnerability assemblages will be more stable than others. Elements operate at different temporal rhythms – for example, a chronic illness may span years; a period of unemployment several months, but with longer-term impact on debts; a cold winter or a hot summer a matter of weeks; a broken heating system a day or two. The degree of temporal synchronicity of constituent entities is likely to be one factor that influences the lifespan of the assemblage in a particular form (Allen 2011). Stability may also be conferred by the strength of relationships between different elements or actants, and/or the ease with which some elements may be pulled away or substituted. For example, the relation between a household and their fuel of, say, wood biomass may be one of preferential attachment/tradition (which may be strong or weak), necessity (very strong if choice is limited) or comparative affordability (which again may be strong or weak). To give another example, the relationship between a household and their dwelling building may also be strong or weak, depending on tenure, attachment and so on.

A sense of the dynamism of assemblages is thus important in prompting questions about how the elements come together and become entangled – where was the agency?; what was the context?; what might prevent this happening, and how might the elements come apart? Such analysis can help distinguish between more and less intractable forms of energy vulnerability, revealing those which are easiest and hardest to disrupt, and where the best opportunities for disruption are to be found.

6 *Alternatives* For many, the spirit of assemblage thinking is about conceiving alternatives, and in this sense it can be quite optimistic: seeing the state of things as dynamic and somewhat messy rather eschews any sense of inevitability, offering a prospect where there may be many ways of doing things differently. Although it has been criticized for not offering any roadmap for achieving change (Brenner et al. 2011), which indeed in itself it does not, analysing situations in terms of assemblages, by highlighting the heterogeneous elements, the distributed agency and the varying stabilities of bonds and collectives, does bring into view multiple sites and methods of intervention.

However, the dynamic view means that we need also to recognize that interventions may not produce a consistent, stable or predictable impact. The assemblage may be destabilized but the reconfiguration can be unpredictable, and those intervening actants may themselves be changeable, having their own temporal limits. For example, policy is subject to revision and subsidies can be withdrawn or retargeted. Apparatus such as microgeneration equipment can become damaged or obsolete and financial incentives such as feed-in tariffs reduced.

Discussion and concluding comments

In all, we think that using an assemblage approach has much to offer energy vulnerability thinking. Most obviously, the vantage point it affords exposes an array of heterogeneous actors in energy vulnerability situations that more restricted disciplinary outlooks often don't allow us to see. Revealed are people and their actions and decisions, material entities and their properties, other living organisms and their agendas, abstract entities such as traditions, beliefs, practices and policies, non-human nature and its cycles. The entities whose presence and actions get drawn in may be in different spatial locations and unfolding in different temporal rhythms. Tracing the entities involved and the process of their assembling can be illuminating, demonstrating multiple agencies, with actors perhaps unaware of each other, and each acting according to their own logics and having a role of some kind in the situation.

It also shows the great diversity of situations that, in having the potential for negative and unhealthy experiences for the people involved, might be classified as energy vulnerability. We think this is helpful rather than otherwise, as it allows us to have openness to and clearer understanding of what is involved in real situations in context, rather than expecting a fit to a predefined mould. This in turn can both reveal the complexities of working with interventions that typically work with broad characterizations and expectations, and open up better possibilities for change, finding them in in more numerous places.

Rather than endless diversity, though, the assemblage approach may also be able to reveal commonalities, where energy vulnerability assemblages have similar trajectories or where the particular influence of an entity or relationship between specific entities is similarly critical. The assemblage approach, as Allen (2011) argues, can offer a middle way between seeing the world as infinitely differentiated and contingent on the one hand and constantly reproducing consistent structures on the other. However, the commonalities we find may or may not be the similarities we would expect to see through existing definitions or models of fuel or energy poverty. These existing definitions would lead us to look for energy-inefficient buildings, low incomes, poor access to energy supplies; an assemblage approach may lead us to see, for example, recurring elements of weak social support or liberalized energy markets.

The approach also usefully introduces a sense of dynamism and of situations as evolving. They may evolve at different speeds, however, and in this way we can start to see how some energy vulnerability situations may be fleeting while others are more intractable. Measures of fuel poverty (again most developed in the UK) have traditionally worked with simple 'in' or 'out' categories. A household is either in fuel poverty, and therefore part of the national fuel poverty statistics, or it isn't. A more dynamic understanding would be less absolute, emphasizing that households may be and become more or less energy vulnerable, experiencing harmful impacts to different degrees and over different timescales – maybe seasonally, maybe in response to a particular crisis or sudden shift in household circumstances, energy markets, or geopolitical relations. Recent proposed changes to meas-uring fuel poverty have attempted to capture some measure of the depth of the problem as experienced across the profile of all fuel-poor households (Hills 2012), but it is clear from those involved in grassroots fuel poverty action that the ongoing messiness and flux of on-the-ground experiences cannot be captured by macro-scale measurements.

The assemblage approach does, though, have its limits, and there are two important things it isn't good at seeing. First, the approach doesn't see things that are absent from the assemblage. Because it tends to trace what entities are involved, how they came together and how the bonds operate, it is not good at accounting for absence or lack, a point noted by McFarlane and Anderson (2011) and by Jacobs (2012). In energy vulnerability situations these absences or lacks may be critical, such as the lack of a back-up system in the event of tech-nological failure or the lack of a household's capacity to cope with debt. Secondly, the approach can tend to overlook the wider context and structures within which entities (actants) operate (Brenner et al. 2011; Castree 2002; Kirsch and Mitchell 2004). Some kinds of context might be accounted for analytically in describing the assemblage itself, especially as the elements don't need to be synchronic, for example housing shortages leading to high rents and tenants' constrained budget for services. But on the whole, the limits on the agency of people in particular tend not to be seen, especially structural power relations that constrain people's repertoires of action and their ability to influence an assemblage and its trajectory.

For the first problem, we need to be imaginative in thinking about alternatives, which is what assemblage thinking would encourage us to do. So, in looking for intervention points we can think about not just what is in the assemblage that we might want to exclude, or what decisions might be made differently, but also about what else might be brought in to create an assemblage with a different trajectory that would not push the household towards harm. We might want to use comparisons with other, more successful household energy assemblages (while recognizing that 'success' or indeed 'vulnerability' is not inherent to assemblage analysis, but requires external judgement to be exercised); and we no doubt would find it useful to bear in mind some a priori experience that might lead us to be vigilant for particular absences (e.g. insulation, back-up system, social support network) as well as presences (e.g. illness, cold weather). For the second problem we agree with various authors including McFarlane (2011b) and Rankin (2011) (and Castree 2002 regarding Actor Network Theory) that the assemblage approach can be used in conjunction with other theory (such as Marxist, feminist and other structural theory) that provides the conceptual space to address and explain the context within which actants, especially people, operate, and the limits on their agency. Bringing in strands of normative theory would also be important in using assemblage thinking within a wider pursuit of energy justice.

In this respect the assemblage approach per se does not make judgements about which situations are worse, which should be intervened in or what kinds of interventions are more acceptable than others. In that sense, as noted earlier, our use of energy vulnerability does not inherently imply a state of harm which automatically merits attention and potentially intervention. Vulnerability conveys a sense of potential for harm or diminished well-being, a situation in which the realization of 'necessary' energy services is not necessarily or reliably assured. Any household may be more or less vulnerable in this way. A good analysis should offer the basis for thinking through possible interventions and seeing which would be likely to change the trajectory. It should also give a sense of the stability of the assemblage – whether it is likely to move on with a light push, or whether very stable bonds or interactions need to be broken or substantial new elements introduced. However, any other criteria for deciding which potential interventions to enact or which situations to intervene in would need to be established by recourse to other principles, such as justice theory, ethical principles, societal norms and preferences, political priorities or budgetary constraints. These decisions, though, would necessarily be explicit, as unlike some other framings of energy vulnerability, the approach does not presume any specific remedy ahead of analysis.

As yet, with the exceptions mentioned in the course of this chapter, the assemblage approach has been little applied to the analysis of energy vulnerability, so there is much scope for its development through empirical work. As mentioned at the start, one potential advantage we can see is that the approach can be used in all manner of situations, including those beyond the developed-world contexts that we have largely drawn on in this chapter. Indeed, it would be valuable to have an array of diverse case studies approached in this way for comparison, including situations where vulnerability was less present, each starting without assumptions as to the nature of problems and related responses and looking for dynamics as much as for stabilities. As with research in other domains, such as in the analysis of cities where assemblage has proved quite popular (see McFarlane 2011a; Jacobs 2012; Anderson and McFarlane 2011), we would anticipate variations in how the concept was taken up and applied, theoretically and methodologically. There are certainly challenges to be resolved and limitations to be overcome; we have offered thoughts on some of these but there are no doubt others. However, the essential creativity that is the ethos of the assemblage approach should encourage productive experimentation in future research and potentially in future practice.

Acknowledgements

We are grateful to the insights we have gained from participants in various InCluESEV-funded workshops, seminars and conference sessions, and in particular to Noel Cass for review work which informed our discussion. Thanks also to Conor Harrison for helpful comments on a draft of the chapter. The InCluESEV project was funded by the Research Councils UK Energy Programme.

2 | Precarious domesticities: energy vulnerability among urban young adults[1]

STEFAN BOUZAROVSKI, SASKA PETROVA, MATTHEW KITCHING AND JOSH BALDWICK

Introduction

Even though recent years have seen the publication of a wide body of research on the broad-level relationships between fuel poverty, energy efficiency, poor housing and health (see, for example, Rudge and Nicol 1999; Healy and Clinch 2004) it still remains unclear how these linkages operate at the level of everyday life in the home. What is more, the articulation of the underlying systemic causes of energy vulnerability within the grain of the city is poorly understood, particularly in relation to the rising importance of scientific agendas that see such dynamics as the product of social justice issues of distribution, procedure and recognition (Walker and Day 2012). This becomes especially pronounced once the focus is moved away from issues of energy deprivation among older people – a group that, its objective difficulties notwithstanding, has traditionally attracted the greatest amount of political support, public visibility and assistance from the state – on to more transient and precarious populations.

The almost complete absence of research on fuel poverty among urban young adults exemplifies such research lacunae. While a selected set of social formations that already include this group – especially low-income families with children, and young single parents – have attracted some public, academic and policy attention in the UK fuel poverty debate, households consisting exclusively of young adults, most of whom live in rented accommodation, have generally been excluded from relevant fora (see, for instance, Baker et al. 2003). This situation may have adverse consequences, as, for example, more than 10 per cent of households where the oldest person is younger than twenty-four are likely to fall in fuel poverty, while households living in private rented accommodation – most common among young people – are twice as likely to suffer from fuel poverty as all other households (poverty.org. uk). The importance of studying fuel poverty patterns among young people is further underscored by their specific consumption practices, as this group's low awareness of energy conservation and efficiency measures in the home is well documented in the literature (Clugston and Calder 1999). Furthermore, a significant body of research has found that economic inequalities among young people at school-leaving age are on the rise, while their opportunities for earning an independent income are decreasing (Katz 2004).

This chapter provides some initial insights into the social, spatial and economic underpinnings of fuel poverty[2] among young people. We aim to expose the precarious and transient nature of their energy vulnerability patterns, emphasizing that issues of recognition are central to understanding and addressing this group's susceptibility to domestic energy deprivation. The evidence presented in the chapter is based on quantitative and qualitative research in the Birmingham district of Bournbrook, which houses one of the largest concentrations of flat-sharing young people (mostly students) living in rented accommodation in the country. We explore the extent to which such individuals suffer from fuel poverty as a result of moving out of the parental home, while identifying some of the main housing and social features of households in this group. The chapter also hints at some of the wider mechanisms through which the emergence of fuel poverty among such households is contingent on everyday life practices, behaviours and attitudes. This includes, but is not limited to, issues such as residential energy efficiency, household energy needs, the ability to understand and access energy assistance, and relationships with landlords.

Housing young adults in the UK: unresolved urban and energy policy questions

When talking about young adults moving into independent accommodation, it should be noted that this demographic is characterized by specific housing demand requirements, which set it apart from other social and age groups (Rugg et al. 2000). However, there has been insufficient research on the subject, making it difficult to draw any conclusions on how the UK meets the housing needs of young adults, particularly students. This is despite the fact that over the past fifty years – and in line with the majority of industrialized countries during the post-war period – the UK has seen a consistent growth in student numbers. The expected possession of a university degree has now become commonplace, and despite a commitment of a succession of governments to a growth in higher education opportunities, very little attention has been paid to the housing consequences of expanded student numbers. In particular, there has been a growing reliance on the private rented sector owing to the fact that the student population increase in cities has, in general, surpassed the ability of higher educational institutions to accommodate this group. It has also been recognized that student renting comprises what might be termed a 'niche market' (ibid.): one in which supply has become adapted to meet the needs of a specific, specialized group, and displays a reluctance to meet demand from another source.

The market has a particular characteristic in terms of accommodation type, letting arrangements and type of landlord: letting to a student household is materially different from letting to other types of tenant (ibid.). For example, although student incomes are low, their access to loans means that they are usually able to meet regular rent instalments and thus sidestep difficulties that landlords might anticipate and experience with the processing of payments. The flexibility of student and young adult households places them at an advantage when compared with some other household types that may have more exact specifications (Slater 2002), such as families requiring a garden for their children or wanting to be in a catchment area of good local schools; older couples who may need assistance using the stairs; or couples with young children who may need properties with adequate access for a pram. In contrast with all these groups, student or young adult households can be any size, and have limited specialized requirements. Another aspect of the student (and young adult) housing market is the ability of such households to adapt to any type of property, with perhaps the only requirement being that the dwelling is furnished. This has led to a situation where homes whose original layouts are often not fit for this purpose have been rented out to students.

One of the most marked consequences of the expansion of the private rented sector among students and young adults has been the tendency for large numbers of such households to live in concentrated urban pockets (Rugg et al. 2000). The clear geographic definition of their housing market has made it easy for landlords seeking to make their investment to pinpoint the most appropriate locations in which to buy property. Where pressure for student accommodation is becoming acute, it is likely that properties that come on to the owner-occupied market will be quickly bought up by student market landlords. Student demand has thus been monopolizing the rental sector of particular urban districts (Smith and Holt 2007), often leading to the phenomenon of 'student ghettoization': traditional local retailing has been replaced by an unusual concentration of fast-food restaurants, cafeterias, takeaways, accommodation agencies, second-hand dealers in furniture and kitchen appliances, leisure services and amusement arcades, and discount supermarkets. Other changes have affected the local pubs and clubs, most of which have been reoriented to the student and youth market (ibid.).

One frequent issue relating to student and young flat-sharing accommodation is the poor quality of the properties in which many such households live. The image of 'student squalor' is markedly persistent, and a number of studies of housing conditions among this group have underlined the incidence of dampness, poor electrical safety, overcrowding and inadequate facilities (Humphrey and McCarthy 1997; Nicholson and Wasoff 1989). The poor energy efficiency of rented properties has been one of the key factors behind the poor living conditions in such properties – particularly in relation to issues such as damp and mould.

In order to address some of these issues, the government has introduced the 'Landlord's Energy Saving Allowance' (LESA) so as to provide tax incentives for landlords who make energy-saving improvements to their properties. It allows landlords to claim up to £1,500 against tax every year, and can be claimed for properties rented out in the UK and abroad. LESA can be claimed for costs of buying and installing certain energy-saving products for properties that are being rented out, based on actual expenditure, including: cavity wall and loft insulation, solid wall and floor insulation, draught proofing and hot water system insulation. The allowance can be claimed up to 1 April 2015, when its availability will end. Its scope was recently extended – initially the funding applied per building, which has now been changed to 'per dwelling'. This means that a landlord who makes significant energy changes with a property divided into flats may be eligible for an allowance for each flat. It remains unclear, however, to what extent the LESA has helped alleviate fuel poverty. In general, experts have argued that households living in privately rented housing are arguably the hardest group to reach, while also living in some of the worst insulated and oldest homes (with 45 per cent built pre-1919; see Boardman 2010).

Also of relevance in this context are measures introduced as part of the 2011 Energy Act, and the Green Deal. Given that the rental sector has the largest proportion of least energy-efficient homes (5.8 per cent belong to the category of poorly G-rated properties as opposed to 3.4 per cent in owner-occupied homes) it recently became mandatory that, from 2018, private landlords will need to ensure that their properties either meet a minimum energy efficiency standard, or that they have installed the maximum package of measures under the Green Deal. The broader implications of such policies for the nature of the housing stock and migration patterns within it, however, remain unclear.

These contingencies underline the urgent need to study young people's vulnerability to fuel poverty. Not only can such an endeavour produce new policy-relevant insights into this pressing problem – especially in terms of identifying the kinds of measures that can help raise awareness of energy conservation and fuel poverty among them – but it can also potentially create a new knowledge base about the circumstances of young people more generally, relevant to researchers and activists in the domains of social welfare, environment, housing policy and youth empowerment.

Overarching trends in the case study area

Our study area comprised the western part of the Selly Oak ward, corresponding to seven census areas (Lower Layer Super Output Areas; LSOAs). The index of multiple deprivation places almost all of these locations among the worst 40 per cent in the country. One of the largest contributors to this ranking is the 'Barriers to Housing and Services' component of the index, which categorizes most of the study area in the UK's worst quartile. The study area scores particularly poorly on the 'Income Deprivation Affecting Children Index 2010', which is of special relevance to the circumstances of young people included in our study. A similar situation can be found in the case of the 2007 Child Well-being Index (CWI): nearly all of the LSOAs that constitute the study area are among the 10 per cent most deprived in the UK according to this measure, with one area's rank being an exceptional 2.49 per cent. One of the main contributors to the CWI of these areas is the housing domain of the index, which places most of them among the 5 per cent most deprived areas in the UK (one LSOA is even in the top 0.31 per cent). Overall, therefore, this means that the study area has been characterized by moderate to high levels of multiple deprivation, partly as a result of inadequate housing and low incomes – the main causal factors of fuel poverty.

Quantitative and qualitative methods were employed to achieve the research aims outlined in the introduction. The questionnaire surveys involved seventy-five randomly selected households (containing a total of 320 individuals) undertaken in February 2012. The questionnaire covered the household features and housing history of the participants, their current income, dwelling conditions, thermal comfort circumstances and practices, as well as energy consumption behaviours and patterns.

In addition, semi-structured interviews were undertaken in order to explore some of the questions from the survey in further depth, so as to detect the nuances in household behaviours and expectations.

A total of thirty-six households in Bournbrook were involved in the qualitative part of the research. This included detailed energy diaries, as well as energy consumption and temperature measurements undertaken during one- to two-week periods in 2011 and 2012. The diaries operated on a self-reported basis, including information about the state and use of various energy services in the home, and associated everyday life practices. The diaries and interviews were followed up by thermal camera imaging that allowed us to obtain a better sense of the energy efficiency of the built fabric of the surveyed homes. This method produces an image of the thermal energy emitted by any object (Meola and Carlomagno 2004).

Some of the data from the questionnaire survey made it immediately clear that many of the surveyed households are receiving inadequate energy services in the home. The sample was largely composed of students; 68 per cent of the surveyed households consisted mainly of flat-sharers in this category. A large part of the population in the sample suffered from perceived inadequate levels of warmth in the home (see Table 2.1). The poor energy efficiency of the examined buildings may have contributed to this, alongside the relatively low incomes of the interviewees: approximately 50 per cent of the households in the sample stated that they have been cutting back on appliance use to save energy, and approximately 25 per cent of the surveyed households thought their landlords did not take adequate care of the home (see Table 2.1).

Many of the individuals we interviewed did not live in properties that were well maintained: common problems included ill-fitting windows and poor wall insulation. This was confirmed by the thermal images that we took, as well as by the fact that a large proportion of the surveyed individuals thought that the rooms on the top floor were significantly colder than the rest of the house – thus possibly indicating that there was a loss of useful heat through the roof (see Table 2.1); also, a significant portion (over 50 per cent) reported having mould and condensation in their house. Nevertheless, approximately 40 per cent of the surveyed households 'strongly agreed' that their house had double glazing, and an overwhelming majority felt that they were not living in fuel poverty (see Table 2.1). The results from the survey thus indicated that many of the participants may not be aware that they are living in fuel poverty and poorly insulated homes.

TABLE 2.1 Percentages of individuals responding affirmatively to different statements in the questionnaire survey

Statement	Strongly agree	Agree	Neither agree nor disagree	Disagree	Strongly disagree	No answer	Total
'I am satisfied with the level of warmth in my home'	13	33	15	31	8	0	100
'Our landlord takes care of the house'	8	40	17	14	11	10	100
'The rooms on the top floor are significantly colder'	15	26	11	27	18	3	100
'Our house has double glazing'	41	19	8	2	7	1	100
'There is condensation in the property'	20	31	14	12	1	0	100
'I have observed the presence of mould in the house'	22	17	5	20	14	0	100
'We live in fuel poverty'	1	1	18	32	25	2	100

Note: n ranges between 286 and 310; leading figures are in *italic*

Experiences of fuel poverty

As pointed out above, the quantitative surveys in our study were supplemented with in-depth qualitative investigations, which helped pinpoint some of the everyday articulations and experiences of fuel poverty among households in the study area. In the two sections that follow, we explore these questions in further detail – using a limited number of examples from the evidence base – so as to foreground the broader dynamics of social and infrastructural vulnerability encountered by the surveyed households.

Comparing internal temperature and diary data from some of the surveyed houses demonstrated similar results and trends, with peaks corresponding to heating use. In one of the homes, living-room data indicated a generally higher temperature throughout the period (averaging 19.4°C), which can be explained with the aid of the diaries, which contained frequent comments such as: 'all ate between 6.30 p.m. and 7.30 p.m. and then all stayed in the living room until 10.30 p.m.'.

In contrast, less time was spent, and fewer people resided, in the bedroom of this home, causing a lower average temperature (16.3°C). Still, the highest temperature peaks could be seen in the bedroom data. This is once again detailed in the diaries, where one participant describes 'working from home during the afternoon' during both of the periods when the highest peaks were registered.

This house on the whole used 189.08 kWh of gas throughout the week-long study (roughly costing them just over £8, according to their energy bill – £2 each), which breaks down to approximately 47.2 kWh of gas per person over a week. This appears high when compared to a student house of similar size, where participants used a total of 126.05 kWh over the week; when considering the number of residents this broke down to only 25.21 kWh per person and cost only approximately £6 (ca. £1.20 per person) for the week. The observed gap, however, seems less surprising when the results of the diaries are taken into account. The first house averaged three hours of heating use per day, as a result of which it was possible to see a relatively consistent heating pattern and stable temperatures. In contrast, the second house used only two hours of heating throughout the study – in interviews its residents claimed to be 'tight fisted' with their energy use owing to the fact that 'they had little money and refused to spend it on bills'. This refusal to use the heating was reflected in the thermal images of the building.

Even the house with the highest level of heating use for a privately rented home was characterized by a close relationship between occupancy patterns and heating use, with definite peaks and troughs in line with the information about energy use indicated in the diaries. However, for such a high rate of heating use – on average nearly four hours per day – the average temperature was the lowest of all of the student houses studied (15.8°C – again well below any of the WHO's recommended temperatures). The participants in this house used 189.08 kWh of gas during the study week, or 63.03 kWh per person – the highest kWh consumption per person in any of the private rented homes studied. While the diaries showed that no windows were opened during the study period, the thermal imaging indicated a high rate of energy leakage in the built fabric.

Despite such examples of lower temperatures, many of the interviewees continued to insist that fuel poverty was not a problem for them. Personal choice, university grants, support from parents and the fact that they aren't around during particular months were all highlighted as reasons why they felt that this condition did not impact upon them:

INTERVIEWER: You don't think it is a problem?
EMILY: No, I don't spend 10 per cent of anything on my energy bills. Like I said it was expensive for us but like we must have spent, I don't know, £200 not even that £150 and by the time we have left this house we will have spent £250 and per year I get a ridiculous amount of money like 9 grand it's not a ridiculous amount of money but it is still quite a lot for a student.
INTERVIEWER: You say it is not an issue for you but on the graph over the week there was only one time that the living room was 21 degrees, but it doesn't bother you?
JEMMA: Erm ... I think I should be OK, because my parents help me out quite a lot, so I am going ... well I don't know yet what they are going to do but I think they are going to pay for my rent and then I am going to pay for bills.

Other participants felt that fuel poverty was an issue for them and consequently affected how they used their accommodation. Some commented how particularly cold rooms would be used less, and interestingly, some discussed how they allow themselves to get cold because they don't want to cause an argument with those on tighter budgets who can't afford any more heating:

CHRISTINE: And well I haven't lived here over the summer but I assume that, with the flat roof it might absorb some heat. But I can't turn on the heating without discussing it with the girls so there have been times when I have been really cold.

INTERVIEWER: So though you may be cold, you just put up with it?
CHLOE: Yeah, it is a case of though I may be cold I don't want to do anything that goes against the house decision.

Several participants mentioned that because they cannot afford heating during the day they would go to university or to other people's houses to conduct their daily activities:

INTERVIEWER: Why do you go to uni more this year?
ANNA: Warmth probably [laugh], I mean it would just be too expensive to have the heating on during the day as well, so it is much warmer and you can get far more work done as well. It is generally better all round to go to uni.
GEMMA 2: Well, at first at the beginning of the term when it was quite cold in the house, I started going to the library more. And as well like I thought, you usually get more work done and stuff like that, but the main reason was, it is too cold in the house so I will just go to the library.
NICOLE 2: ... Also, like I go to Rey's house when I get cold, like the other day, so I thought I would go to his house because it will be warm and work there because it will be a lot warmer.

Overall, many of the interviewees did not understand what 'fuel poverty' meant; even when the concept was explained to them, there was an even split between those who felt they were experiencing it and those who felt they were not. The reasons why certain interviewees felt they were not affected by fuel poverty varied considerably, and often centred on the structure of everyday life among such households. For many of them, the active nature of day-to-day movement patterns provided extended periods of time when they did not have to use energy services in the home. Such activities provided an important coping strategy for dealing with the significant 'spatial shrinkage' (Shortt and Rugkasa 2007) in the heating of their homes. However, this also meant that the houses were heated in highly variable ways, over time and space alike.

We also detected the presence of a widespread cultural expectation that living in a cold home is 'a normal part of everyday life when you are young'; this is perhaps one of the reasons why none of the interviewees felt 'shame' for not having a warm home (contrary to, for example, Harrington et al.'s 2005 findings). The lack of reporting of any negative health impacts from living in cold temperatures may also be attributed to the fact that many of the interviewees did not have the impression that they were experiencing a constant exposure to cold temperatures, owing to their mobile lifestyles.

In the case of households that felt they were experiencing fuel poverty, the articulation of everyday life was also affected by additional social dynamics, alongside the conventional questions of income and energy efficiency. Several individuals highlighted the complexities in household relationships: despite paying rent separately, energy bills are collective and therefore, with the household having varying finances, energy use is frequently brought down to a level that can be afforded by the person on the smallest budget. As a result, even those who were relatively well off financially lived in cold temperatures if this was dictated by their household circumstances.

Landlords, housing careers and being 'heard' locally

The qualitative evidence from the case study area indicated that wider political and economic relations also affected the constituent dynamics of energy vulnerability. A number of interviewees indicated that their transitory housing tenure made them poorly involved in local politics, and vulnerable to pressure from landlords. Several of them pointed out that they didn't necessarily feel excluded, but rather were just not interested in getting involved in local community activities. There were a number of individuals, however, who located the reasons for the lack of local involvement in the impression that they were not sufficiently capable or knowledgeable, that they wouldn't be listened to, or that they would not be effective in their activities.

INTERVIEWER: If you had an issue, would someone from like the council do something about it?
BECKY: I think they would listen but not do anything about it, because like we don't really get taken seriously. I don't really know why people would think like that about us. I think people with more life experience will know more about things, I don't know … we don't have that much experience and well I know we are living on our own, but we are still in a bit of a bubble, it is not the same …
INTERVIEWER: So why don't they put in very much effort?
HELEN: I think it is because they think people will just put up with it. I mean I get annoyed by it, but I wouldn't make a complaint to the council or anything. I mean it is quite a lot of effort for a student and we are only here for like a couple of years and it is predominantly students so people are just like 'oh well they are only here for a few years'.

From the interviews it was clear that landlords and estate agents are strongly implicated in the nature of energy consumption. Almost all of the interviewees had obtained their homes through a letting agency, and felt they did not receive very good customer service:

> GEMMA 1: ... Kelly's ceiling leaked and it was literally like water dripping into her room from the outside every time it rained ... she rang them up and it took them like three days to come down. I feel like a lot of estate agents in Selly Oak ... don't take anyone seriously, because everyone is a student and they know that they are not going to do anything. If I ring [estate agent name omitted] up [with a complaint] they will be like 'OK' [sarcasm]. But, if my mum rang up and said you need to do something about it they would do it straight away kind of thing.

In some cases the interviewees felt that they lived in poor-quality housing because the landlords knew the houses would be rented by students and young people, who would be unlikely to be very demanding:

> EMILY: I think they all just see us all as kids still ... they know that people don't actually care that much about where you're living. Everyone just accepts that it is going to be a cold, grimy, disgusting house.
> VICTORIA: But I think the landlords treat these as student homes and they don't repair things properly, because they know students don't care that much.

There was, however, evidence of good practice. A number of individuals thought that they had a good relationship with their landlords, and that it was only the letting agents that were slow to address problems:

> EMMA: Yeah we got the heater straight away, but because we didn't realize it was broken until Friday and they couldn't do anything until after the weekend. On Monday it got sorted out straight away.
> BRIGID: Erm, the landlord we have is actually really nice, we are lucky to have a really good one, because [letting agent name omitted] can be really slow.

The interviewees' comments about the treatment they received from letting agencies highlighted some of the major disadvantages of being a tenant. Some interviewees emphasized that letting agents saw them as 'incompetent and irresponsible', and often failed to provide the necessary information about the quality of the rented house. Still, the efficiency of the housing stock was not considered in many of the interviewees' decisions over their houses. Some of them pointed out that this was particularly true at the point when they entered independent accommodation for the first time – often in the second year of university, having moved out of managed accommodation and halls. Indeed, there is some anecdotal evidence that the average temperature readings in such homes were lower than in the rest of the sample, because the interviewees had selected homes that were less energy efficient. Only one interviewee in this group had a good understanding of what to look for in a house, and even discussed the energy certificate it had been given; the data logger results showed that this was the warmest house in the sample.

The experience of living in independent accommodation did seem to improve the majority of interviewees' knowledge of the energy efficiency of the built fabric, heating system and installed appliances. Many of the interviewees were experiencing another shift in their level of house satisfaction and expectations as a result of this process, and were planning to move, or had already moved, into better-quality accommodation once their contract had ended:

INTERVIEWER: Do you think the house will be OK at keeping the heat?
REBECCA: Well apparently it's quite energy efficient, its rated 'e' or something.
INTERVIEWER: How did you find that out?
REBECCA: We were given it as part of our contract.
INTERVIEWER: Oh right so you got a rating with it.
REBECCA: Yes.
INTERVIEWER: Who did you go through?
EMILY: … we found it through [company name omitted] … Basically in terms of energy efficiency, the downstairs, so the living room and the kitchen are energy efficient, but there is no insulation in the loft which is losing heat, but they are putting it in.
INTERVIEWER: OK, and do you think you have learnt much in like what to look for in a house? And tell me what those things are.
CHRIS: Like check for like double glazing, and ask people what their boiler is like and ask them what they are paying for bills … see if it is gas stove or central heating or whatever. Look to see if stuff is new because like new will be more efficient … like well the girls want a dishwasher but I don't because I think it will use a lot of electricity, plus I would hate unloading it [laugh]. Yeah stuff like that.
RUTH: Well, we are firstly looking at cheaper houses because well like we have got friends … well we have got a really nice house, but there are friends with just as nice houses that are cheaper, we are looking at the size of bedrooms because quite a lot of these ones are quite small … like we are asking whether the house is cold as to why they are leaving

and we are asking about the landlords ... and bathrooms because our bathrooms are really small.

INTERVIEWER: So you talk a bit more, were they not things that you did the last time?

RUTH: No, I mean I think it is just because like you don't really know in the first year, and you just sort of go for whatever.

JO: I guess, probably when you look in student houses you don't pay attention to things you should be looking for, I mean we did not pay attention at all, like we didn't look to see if it would be warm, I mean I didn't even look at the windows. I think next time I will definitely look at stuff like heating and like good insulation.

INTERVIEWER: Why didn't you for this one?

JO: I don't know, when you are with your friends ... we should have really because we have done this for a year already. I think when I leave university I will pay more attention.

Almost all of the interviewees expected that they would stay on the same housing career path in the near future. However, they still insisted they knew what they were looking for and that the quality of the home would be a higher priority in the future. Everyone stressed the importance of flexibility in their living arrangements:

INTERVIEWER: When you moved out what would that be, to rent or buy?

JESSICA: Rent.

INTERVIEWER: Why rent?

JESSICA: I don't know, I just imagine that anything I would have would just be temporary so, I think it is just more ... I mean I know it used to be that you would buy, but I think it is more common that you just rent houses now. I mean my cousin now is in her second house and she has a really good job and could buy it but is renting still for some reason.

INTERVIEWER: Right, do you think you will buy?

JESSICA: Yes, eventually I would buy.

Throughout our field research, it became abundantly clear that for almost all of the surveyed households, it was the area (Bournbrook) rather than the house which made a difference in the choice of living location. In the desire to be close to work, university or friends, many of them were willing to pay more and live in a poorer-quality and energy-inefficient home. This would explain why some of the interviewees are experiencing fuel-poverty-related problems, and also why landlords generally do not improve the quality of the homes.

Not only do tenants fail to see this as a priority, but there is so much demand that houses of the poorest quality can still be rented out.

Conclusion

Although the findings reported in this chapter are of a preliminary nature, they provide some broad insights into patterns of domestic energy deprivation among flat-sharing young people living in privately rented accommodation, especially in relation to broader housing and energy consumption issues. The reviewed evidence in the study area has indicated that many of the surveyed households are living in homes whose temperatures are below what is considered an acceptable standard. Many of them, however, do not acknowledge or recognize that they living in this condition. In addition to the poor knowledge of thermal comfort and energy efficiency standards, their situation is, in part, attributable to the widespread cultural expectation that it is acceptable for individuals to live in poorly heated and low-quality housing at the entry point of their housing career. This means that, in social justice terms, energy vulnerability among young flat-sharing adults is primarily an issue of recognition. Even though this dynamic was shown to be both external and internal to the surveyed individuals, it nevertheless prevented them from fully 'participating in the public realm' and 'unfurling [their] personality's potential in an unforced manner' (Honneth 2004: 351).

In addition to the inadequate knowledge of energy conservation practices and assistance schemes, the emergence of domestic energy deprivation among this group is contingent on a range of specific demographic and housing factors. This includes dynamics internal to the household in situations where bills are shared, as a result of which the level of heat is brought down to the most affordable level. Also of relevance is the constrained and 'niche' nature of the housing market which they occupy, as well as the poor engagement with local politics and communities; this helps increase the power of landlords and letting agencies, and decreases incentives for energy investment. Indeed, most of the individuals whom we interviewed lived in poorly heated and poorly insulated homes. They were keenly aware of energy conservation practices and tried to bring their bills down in every possible way. The level of energy service (particularly heating) varied dramatically in their homes, both diurnally and across the various spaces of the home. To a certain extent, the fluid nature of housing and everyday mobility practices among them helped them address and cope with some of the implications of living in cold homes. It should be noted, however, that these highly temporally and spatially variable energy practices do not lend themselves easily to the binary thinking embedded in current UK fuel poverty and energy efficiency policies.

The results of this chapter make it obvious that flat-sharing young people moving into private rented accommodation represent a part of society that is invisible to fuel poverty assistance. Their highly restricted and time-concentrated energy use patterns mean focusing on capital investment in the housing stock itself could help address the problem. While we did find some evidence that landlords were using the LESA to improve the energy efficiency of rental housing, this was limited and patchy. A more formal and stringent set of obligations to act in this direction may prove more useful. Universities, which are distorting the housing market and indirectly creating some of the conditions that have led to this situation, also need to take a more proactive role; not least given the demonstrated adverse long-term health consequences of living in a cold home.

3 | Energy justice in sustainability transitions research

MALCOLM EAMES AND MIRIAM HUNT

Introduction

Energy touches upon almost every aspect of our daily lives. Innovations in technologies for the extraction, production, distribution, storage and end use of energy have played a central role in transforming human society, underpinning the processes of industrialization, urbanization and international trade which have shaped our contemporary carbon economy and with it humanity's re-engineering of our planetary biosphere. Just as water wheels and then coal-fired steam engines powered much of the first two industrial revolutions, the electric motor subsequently transformed processes of industrial production in the early to mid twentieth century. In transport, first coal (steamships and railways) and then oil (the automobile, heavy trucks, shipping and aviation) have transformed patterns of both human mobility and trade. In the domestic sphere gas and electrical appliances have done much to transform 'housework' and gender relations. In agriculture innovations in the use of energy from fossil fuels underpinned rapid advances in farm mechanization and production of chemical fertilizers, facilitating not just massive increases in agricultural production but processes of mass migration and urbanization as the labour intensity of rural economies declined sharply. More recently we have seen how increasingly pervasive information and communications technologies (ICTs) can result in both widespread improvements in energy efficiency and increased demands for electrical power.

Of course, it is important not to fall into a technologically determinist view of history. Such energy innovations have been intimately bound up with broader social, economic, institutional, political and cultural changes. Moreover, individual energy technologies do not exist to be used in isolation; rather they form part of complex systems of production and consumption. The electric kettle is useless if you cannot plug it into the mains! Much of this chapter is therefore concerned with what may be termed socio-technical systems of energy production and consumption, and the social, economic and environmental impacts of whole systems innovations or 'transitions' within and between such systems.

Taking a long view, we can also see how successive transitions in our energy systems have been associated with 'Schumpeterian' waves of creative destruction, sweeping away old industries and fuelling the growth of the new. Each transition has been associated with particular patterns of comparative advantage, resource exploitation, and social and temporal distribution of costs and benefits. We should expect the prospective transition to 'low carbon' to have no less profound impacts at every level of our economy and society. What is more, we have no reason to assume a priori that a low-carbon economy will necessarily be any more equitable or just.

Processes of innovation and socio-technical systems change are central to the notion of transition. The interdisciplinary field of innovation studies has done much to illuminate our understanding of these long-term historical processes. Moreover, the last decade has seen the emergence of 'sustainability transitions research' as a vibrant and distinct frontier within innovation studies. However, the principal analytical frameworks (Multi Level Perspective and Technological Innovation Systems) and policy-oriented tools (Transitions Management) of sustainability transitions research have relatively little explicit to say about questions of equity and justice.

Given the fundamental role that energy and energy technologies play in structuring socio-economic and socio-ecological relations it is perhaps surprising that greater attention has not previously been paid to exploring the equity and justice implications of energy systems transitions. Framed by the principles of sustainable development and the environmental justice movement, 'energy justice' can be understood as encompassing issues of social, economic and environmental equity, within and between past, present and future generations. That is, like sustainable development more broadly, energy justice deals with issues of both inter- and intra-generational equity. The notion of energy justice is then potentially very wide ranging indeed, taking in concerns ranging from, for example: domestic energy prices and fuel poverty in the developed economies; the plight of those Guruswamy (2011) refers to as the '2 to 2.5 billion energy oppressed poor' in the developing world who are entirely reliant on fire for heating, illumination and cooking; the impacts of fossil fuel extraction on indigenous peoples; the land-use impacts and displacement of peoples associated with 'mega-dams' and large-scale hydropower schemes; the local and regional air quality impacts of fossil fuel power plants; direct and indirect effects on the availability and price of food commodities as a result of biofuel production; through to potential intergenerational impacts associated with nuclear fuel cycles or of anthropogenic climate change resulting from the combustion of fossil fuels. The point here is not simply that the range of energy justice concerns is potentially very wide ranging, but that the framing and prioritization of these issues is inherently subjective and context dependent.

It is of course important to recognize that evidence of inequality does not necessarily mean that an injustice has occurred. So, for example, the fact that solar, wind or marine energy resources are unevenly distributed between different regions and nations is not by itself evidence of an injustice. *A claim for justice requires that evidence of inequality be combined with an argument for fair treatment.* While it is beyond the scope of this present chapter to fully explore the various (and contested) bases upon which arguments for fairness may be posited, it is useful to note the distinction often made in the environmental justice literature that claims for fair treatment may relate to questions of *distributional* and/or *procedural* justice. In this context we understand distributional justice to refer to how the social, spatial or temporal *distribution* of risks and benefits of change are felt across society. While procedural justice relates to both: i) access to and *participation* in decision-making and wider governance processes; and ii) who and what (including what forms of knowledge) are afforded *recognition* in such processes (Walker and Eames 2006).

Moreover, we should acknowledge that 'energy justice', like 'sustainable development' or environmental justice more broadly, is an inherently political and contested concept. That is, competing claims for energy justice will depend upon the often mutually exclusive and incompatible values and interests of different individuals and social groups. Hence, when considering questions of energy justice, we would do well to bear in mind the socio-economic and political processes underpinning unequal distribution of the risks and benefits associated with different energy technologies and systems, as well as the manner in which dominant (or incumbent) groups may use their power and influence to exclude or marginalize particular communities, technologies or forms of knowledge.

This chapter will argue that greater reflexivity is required both with respect to the inherently political and contested character of sustainability, and the core concepts of environmental and energy justice, in working towards an equitable and just low-carbon transition. To do so, it will first offer a brief introduction to the broad and growing sustainability transitions literature, outlining its key tenets, noting some relevant criticisms and considering ways in which these theoretic frameworks have been applied for governing change. Secondly, it will highlight where notions of energy justice are missing from the constructs of sustainability transitions research and suggest some ways of addressing these deficits in relation to both the procedural and distributional dimensions of energy justice. Finally, it will draw some conclusions as to the potential place for energy justice in sustainability transitions research.

Sustainability transitions theory

While looking backward across recent human history one can identify a number of energy-related transitions; it has really only been in the last twenty years or so, with the growing realization of the scale of the systemic social, economic and environmental problems confronting our sustainable development, and the recognition of climate change in particular as an overarching global challenge, that the concept of 'transition' has achieved widespread currency. Indeed as Shove and Walker (2007) noted, '... for those concerned with sustainability, the idea of transition – of substantial change and movement from one state to another – has powerful normative attractions'.

Indeed, the concept of a normatively driven transition to sustainability has achieved particular prominence with respect to the need to transform our global energy systems to mitigate the impacts of climate change. The notion of a 'low-carbon transition' has become a powerful guiding vision, providing a shared narrative and moral imperative around which a broad and diverse range of societal interests – from governments, industry, business and academia to civil society and the environmental movement – can mobilize. However, much of the power of this guiding vision clearly lies in its interpretive flexibility, encompassing as it does competing views of the future based upon nuclear power, fossil fuel generation with carbon capture and storage (CCS) or capital-intensive renewables such as offshore wind, through to visions founded upon smart grids and appliances, distributed microgeneration and demand reduction. Indeed, once we scratch beneath the surface it is apparent that there is not one low-carbon transition but rather many competing and often deeply contested technologies and prospective societal pathways to a range of different low-carbon futures. Each of which will not only entail a different distribution of environmental risks and impacts across their life cycles, but also a differing distribution of socio-economic costs and benefits. More broadly it may be argued that the materiality and political ecology of particular technological systems will be co-produced with particular social, institutional and governance structures (Lawhon and Murphy 2011). For example, the capital intensity and regulatory requirements of nuclear power or fossil fuel generation with CCS serve to align the development of these technologies with centralized forms of government control while simultaneously rendering them incompatible with the decentralized, local and community-scale governance of energy use.

While calls for a 'transition' may, then, mean very different things to, for example, grassroots campaigners within the Transition Towns movement and senior politicians or industrialists who have also adopted the language of transitions, within the field of sustainability transitions research the concept has a quite particular meaning. Calls for a transition to sustainability are understood to imply the need for large-scale socio-technical systems change, rather than simple product or process innovations or behavioural changes: that is, finding radically more (eco-)efficient ways to fulfil societal functions and human needs (e.g. mobility, food, housing, heating, lighting, etc.). Hence, the transition to low carbon is viewed as not 'simply' requiring a transformation of our energy production system, but a systemic restructuring of both the production and consumption of energy goods and services.

Informed by insights from ecology, systems thinking and complexity theory, transitions theory assumes that large-scale societal changes occur in a quasi-evolutionary fashion. That patterns in the dynamics of 'systems innovations', or 'transitions', occur as a result of processes of variation and selection driving the co-evolution of social and technological change. Transitions do not result from a change in a single variable, such as the introduction of a new law, product or even prices signal (such as a change in energy prices). Rather they are complex processes resulting from mutually reinforcing changes involving multiple societal actors, operating across multiple domains (science, technology, economy, ecology, institutions, culture, user behaviours and expectations). Moreover, from work on the history of technology and innovation studies we know that: transitions are long-term (typically spanning twenty to fifty years) non-linear processes; that existing systems resist radical change as a result of processes of lock-in and path dependency; and that, with some important exceptions, many previous transitions have not been planned or managed, but are rather the result of emergent processes (Elzen et al. 2004; Kemp and Loorbach 2006; Kemp et al. 2006; Geels 2005a; Berkhout et al. 2004). Within the academic community at least, the purposive shaping of (low-carbon and sustainability) transitions is therefore seen as requiring the development of new conceptual models and analytical frameworks, as well as novel policy, institutional and governance structures.

Over the last decade sustainability transitions research has emerged as a significant focus of interdisciplinary enquiry. It is beyond the scope of this discussion to attempt to provide a comprehensive review of this rapidly evolving field of research (for a summary of the current state of the art, see Markard et al. 2012). Rather, by critically considering two of the principal analytical frameworks (Multi Level Perspective and Technological Innovation Systems) and one of the key policy-oriented tools (Transitions Management) of sustainability transitions research, we will seek to highlight the limited attention afforded to issues of energy justice within this research field and suggest some ways it can re-enter the debate. However, while these frameworks all offer informative insights into processes of transition in energy systems, they have largely neglected and failed to adequately address issues of energy justice.

Multi Level Perspective The Multi Level Perspective (MLP) has emerged as arguably the dominant heuristic for describing socio-technical transitions. It seeks to conceptualize overall dynamic patterns in socio-technical transitions, taking a 'big picture' approach that crosses domains, scales and actors (Geels 2011). It distinguishes three analytical levels: niche, regime and landscape. The regime level, representing the obdurate status quo of provision and demand in a system, consists of semi-coherent rules that stabilize existing trajectories through routines, regulations and standards, adaptation of lifestyles, sunk investment, infrastructure, competences, etc. (Geels 2002; Geels and Schot 2007). Drawing on roots in evolutionary economics, the MLP conceptualizes these regimes as subject to path dependencies that render current systems resistant to purposive change.

A niche, on the other hand, is a locus of radical innovation, a 'protected space' which supports the learning processes, construction of networks and articulation of institutional requirements needed to support a new innovation in its early stages (Geels 2005b; Smith et al. 2010). These innovations break out of niches when pressures at the regime and landscape levels provide a window of opportunity (Geels 2002). The landscape level, in turn, is something of a residual category, comprising the structural 'gradients of force' exerted by the wider societal and material context, including demographic trends, societal values, political ideologies and macroeconomic patterns (Geels and Schot 2007; Geels 2011). System innovations come about, then, when the interplay between dynamics at these three levels is conducive to change.

The MLP has been widely applied to the analysis of past, present and prospective energy transitions. For example, much of the early MLP literature is concerned with drawing lessons from past transitions, e.g. Geels' (2002) examination of the historical transition from sailing ships to steamships. The MLP has been used to analyse current changes in (often national) energy systems, such as Verbong and Geels' (2007) work on the ongoing energy transition in the Dutch electricity system, and Raven and Verbong's (2007) work on combined heat and power in the Netherlands. It has also been used as an aid to futures thinking, i.e. in structuring foresight scenarios dealing with energy systems transitions (Eames and McDowall 2010; Elzen et al. 2004; Foxon 2013).

As with any heuristic, a number of criticisms have been levelled at the MLP (Geels 2011). When considering questions of energy justice, it is particularly relevant to note that the model maintains a focus on technological processes and artefacts at the expense of social and political relationships. It offers little in the way of exploring the place of agency and power in decision-making and implementation, instead presuming the adoption of unproblematic shared visions around which change is mobilized (Lawhon and Murphy 2011; Markard and Truffer 2008; Shove and Walker 2007). The implication here is that the MLP, in its current form, is not able to (sufficiently) explore the power and negotiation dynamics that occur in transitions. Given that transitions are understood to be multi-actor, multi-domain processes regarding the redistribution of resources, these negotiation processes will have a significant role to play in shaping both the nature and direction of a transition, and also the distribution of costs and benefits emerging from it. Acknowledging that certain types of agency are underdeveloped in the MLP, Geels has nonetheless argued that as a 'middle range' theory the MLP could be adapted to incorporate insights from other theories, such as political science theories of power, cultural sociology, discourse theory and social movement theory (Geels 2011).

A further criticism worthy of note has, until recently at least, been a neglect of geography, with little attention paid to the spaces in which transition occurs. While the MLP has been widely employed in place-specific case studies, the importance of place is often limited to the presence or absence of specific policies (Truffer and Coenen 2012). Hence calls to look beyond the MLP, to fields such as political ecology and economic geography, to explain why geography matters in transitions. Indeed, asymmetric processes of regional development and spatial variety in regional institutions mean that geography will have much to say in determining the 'winners' and 'losers' of a given transition (ibid.; Lawhon and Murphy 2011). Critics have argued that lessons from geography and economic geography will be central in progressing heuristics for transition, focusing on questions such as the role of regions in change, managing subjective and normative aspects of sustainability and characteristics of place, such as susceptibility to climate change and potential for renewable energy (for further discussion of this point see 'Territorial innovation systems' below).

Transition Management Building on insights from the Multi Level Perspective, Transition Management (TM) is concerned with the governance of future sustainability transitions. TM seeks to incorporate a more reflexive, long-term view into short-term policy in order to stimulate transitions towards more sustainable 'regimes'. This is challenging because managing such transitions requires dealing with uncertainties, taking a multi-domain view, stimulating knowledge and technological change and imposing a long-term orientation on short-term policy processes (Kemp and Loorbach 2006).

The TM process is led by a 'transition arena', a core group of experts selected for their particular competences and knowledge (Lawhon and Murphy 2011). The decision-making process is often conceptualized as a four-stage cycle. The first stage is that of establishing this arena of experts and together defining the problem at hand and envisioning potential solutions. The second stage entails building coalitions and an agenda around these problems and visions, recruiting actors and resources. The third phase mobilizes these actors around a series of 'experiments' exploring novel technologies, processes and projects. The final phase then monitors and evaluates the process thus far to support learning, which is in turn fed back in reframing the problems at hand and potential solutions (Rotmans and Loorbach 2008). This focus on reflexivity in decision-making is often vaunted as a defining feature of the TM approach.

TM can be seen in practice in the Dutch Energy Transition Plan, emerging from the 4th Dutch National Environmental Policy Plan in 2001 and running for six years (Geels et al. 2008). The programme sought to address 'system faults in the current social order': that is, societal systems that led to environmental problems such as climate change; it did so through the establishment of transitions 'platforms' consisting of new networks of stakeholders and 'visions' and 'pathways' to sustainable futures. Important outcomes include the formation of networks and the stimulation of learning processes, though regime-level change was impeded by a lack of integration between policy affecting niche and regime levels. (For a more thorough description of the programme, see ibid.)

As the MLP is criticized for neglecting issues of politics and power, so TM has been criticized for underestimating the 'messiness' of political change and paying insufficient attention to issues of contestation, normativity and capture by incumbent interests. Critics note that decisions made throughout the TM cycle will be inherently subjective, raising questions of 'whose' sustainability will be pursued. Indeed, since sustainability remains an inherently contested subject, it is likely that articulations of the problem at hand, visions of future solutions and judgements of 'worthwhile' experiments will differ across actors, meaning that relative power will play a part in what becomes a process of negotiation (Meadowcroft 2011).

A number of authors (e.g. Berkhout et al. 2004; Shove and Walker 2007; Eames and McDowall 2010) have critically addressed the role assigned to shared normative vision(s) within the TM approach. Berkhout et al. (2004: 57–9), in particular, raise two substantive concerns over the centrality afforded to guiding visions in driving the transition management process. First, they highlight a 'disjuncture' between the MLP's 'historically informed niche based model of regime transformation and the normative policy aspirations of transition management', arguing that there are many examples of past transitions where a consensus around a particular guiding vision was largely absent or where a guiding vision has played only a relatively modest role, and that furthermore there are many examples where guiding visions have failed to deliver upon the hype they generated. Secondly, and perhaps more profoundly from an energy justice perspective, they argue that the notion of an unproblematic social consensus around any particular guiding vision is deeply problematic as it ignores confounding issues of incommensurability: in technological performance; divergent social values and interests; interrelationships between social and evaluative context; irreducible uncertainty; the operation of political and economic power; and capture by incumbent interests.

Within the wider discourse of reflexive governance, Stirling (2006) has sought to move this discussion on by arguing for what he terms 'precautionary foresight': using a variety of participatory tools and radical institutional means to facilitate more pluralistic forms of iterative goal formation, and promote greater reflexivity over the role of power in order to 'open up' previously closed processes of strategy development. While others such as Eames and McDowall (2010) and Truffer et al. (2008) have developed and tested hybrid methods combining participatory scenario foresight and sustainability assessment techniques for the multi-criteria evaluation of competing energy futures from a range of societal perspectives.

The TM approach has also been criticized as elitist and exclusive for its formulation of the 'Transition Arena' as a means of bringing together experts and elite stakeholders at the expense of a more inclusive, participatory approach (Hendricks 2008). Here it is suggested that the technocratic arguments for working with elites neglect other forms of knowledge, for example local expertise, as well as other points of view that could better elucidate inclusive societal vision(s) of a sustainable future. A number of authors (see, for example, Lawhon and Murphy 2011) have sought to consider the place for representation and recognition of a plurality of voices in transition procedures. While Eames and Mortensen (2011) explicitly sought to address such procedural justice concerns, through the development of bottom-up community-led foresight processes, intended to provide economically and socially marginalized communities with a voice in setting agendas for urban sustainability research. Participatory and action-research-oriented methodologies of this kind, it is argued, have the potential to contribute to the development of much more socially inclusive and (procedurally) just TM processes (ibid.).

Technological innovation systems Over the last thirty years a variety of systems of innovation approaches have been developed within the innovation studies literature, building upon the early work of Freeman (1987), Lundvall (1992) and Nelson (1993) exploring the role of institutional factors in the comparative performance of 'National Systems of Innovation'. Here the principal concern was to explain patterns of comparative economic development between nations. In common with much of the later (Regional Systems of Innovation, Sectoral Systems of Innovation and Technological Systems of Innovation) systems of innovation literature there is an often implicit assumption that the role of innovation in driving economic growth is an unquestioned social good. More recently scholars have turned their attention to the emergence of sustainability technologies (Coenen and Diaz Lopez 2010). The Technological Innovation System (TIS) framework in particular has been widely employed in analysis of emergent 'sustainable' and 'low-carbon' innovations. PV, wind, hydrogen and biogas technologies have, for example, all been examined with the TIS framework (Dewald and Truffer 2012; Bergek and Jacobsson 2003; Godoe and Nygaard 2006; Markard and Truffer 2008).

Emerging from the innovation systems literature, the concept of a TIS starts from the observation that the innovation and diffusion of technology are both an individual and a collective act: the focus here is on interactions between the actors and institutions involved in a given technology (Hekkert et al. 2007). As the name would suggest, the focus of interest is the system, the components of which are the actors, networks and institutions contributing to the overall function of developing, diffusing and utilizing new products and processes (Bergek et al. 2008). As such, a TIS incorporates not only those involved directly in the development of technological change, but is a multi-actor, multi-domain system that often crosses geographical and sectoral boundaries. Relationships between system components are manifold, and may be complementary or competitive. An important concept here is that of mutual embeddedness: actors are embedded in an institutional context which sets the framework in which they operate, but they also actively shape these institutions (Markard and Truffer 2008).

Policy insights derived from the TIS approach, it is argued, provide a more informed understanding of actor roles and strategies than that offered by the MLP (ibid.). Specifically the TIS approach introduced the concept of system failures, i.e. flaws in the working of an innovation system that prevent innovation and, in turn, transitions. The literature identifies four types of 'structural' system failure: (i) infrastructural, i.e. related to actors and artefacts; (ii) institutional, i.e. related to institutions; (iii) interaction, i.e. related to networks and relationships; and (iv) capabilities, i.e. related to actors (Bergek et al. 2008). The role for policy-makers, then, is to establish whether any of these failures are present and to seek to remedy them. However, assessing the 'health' of a particular structural element within an innovation system is problematic without attention to the innovation processes occurring within the system.

Much of the recent TIS literature has therefore been concerned with developing an understanding of the functional dynamics of such innovation systems, with the aim of improving tools for innovation policy. By this view the functions which must be fulfilled within a 'healthy' TIS include: i) knowledge development; ii) resource mobilization; iii) market formation; iv) influence on direction of search;

v) legitimization; vi) entrepreneurial experimentation; and viii) development of positive externalities (ibid.).[1]

Like the MLP, however, the TIS approach has been subject to a number of criticisms. Key problems relate both to the difficulty of systems delineation and the neglect of 'non-core actors'. Delineating the boundaries of a TIS which may span industries and even countries is a challenging, subjective matter, where the choice of delineation is likely to impact on the results of analysis (Markard and Truffer 2008). Moreover, it is argued that TIS analysis can be rather inward looking (ibid.). System delineation is likely to neglect actors and institutions that have important indirect or blocking effects on system performance: actors that impede change, such as those that comprise the incumbent 'regime' of the MLP, will not be included in analysis since they are not involved with the (sustainable) technological innovation system. From a justice in energy transitions perspective, TIS analysis is also likely to omit or only indirectly acknowledge a range of actors (such as workers, local communities, residents, etc.) who may be impacted upon, be it positively or negatively, by change.

Moreover, it should be noted that as with the MLP and TM, much of the TIS literature naively accepts claims as to the sustainability of the particular technologies as self-evident, rather than as points of societal deliberation and contestation. Hence, for example, sustainability orientation is not considered as a core part of the 'direction of search' or indeed of any of the other functions of the innovation system within the TIS framework: a point which can perhaps be traced back to the normative orientation of much of 'systems of innovation' literature, which, as noted above, views innovation as an unquestioned social good. Again, a better understanding of processes of politics and conflict is needed. Here work by Breukers et al. (2013) suggests one potentially fruitful avenue for future research bringing together TIS case study analysis with more inclusive and participatory methods designed to explore societal controversies from multiple perspectives. Specifically, TIS analysis was combined with a participatory stakeholder dialogue process (employing both Q methodology and Constructive Conflict Methodology) in order to explicitly address the contested nature of 'sustainable' biomass and explore diverse societal perspectives on innovation in biofuels technologies. Noticeable here was that 'opening up' the research process to a range of societal perspectives, through the use of participatory methods, also served to bring the distributive justice concerns of some actors that were not core to the TIS within the remit of the research.

Territorial innovation systems Turning more broadly to how distributive justice concerns might be better explored from an innovation systems perspective, we return to the need to better explore the importance of space and place in transitions. Reflecting on past energy transitions, it is notable that large-scale societal changes across systems have resulted in 'winners and losers', both across and within countries, and that the repercussions of such inequalities have resounded long after the processes of transition are largely complete. It seems reasonable to suppose that a 'low-carbon' transition has the potential to distribute its costs and benefits just as unequally as past transitions without governance mindful of distributional justice. This 'geography' of beneficiaries and risk-bearers will be determined by a wide range of factors, of which two will be discussed here: geographies of innovation, and a rematerialization of energy production.

The nature of renewable energy technologies is such that the capacity to generate and use new knowledge will be a key factor in deciding the success or failure of different places taking part in energy transition. When it comes to regional or national capacity to innovate, a range of 'territorial innovation models' have been suggested for describing the ways in which innovative spaces can work (for a review, see Moulaert and Sekia 2003). Despite differing theoretical backgrounds, all argue that different places will have differing capacities to successfully innovate and, as such, (relational) geography matters. It may be argued that of particular relevance here, given their common theoretical foundations with the TIS approach, are the Regional Innovation Systems (RIS) and National Innovation Systems (NIS) approaches. These argue that innovations are carried out through a network of actors underpinned by an institutional framework (Asheim and Coenen 2006); the territorial aspect, focusing on either the country or region in question, recognizes that localized knowledge and learning can become more competitive by promoting systemic relationships between production and knowledge infrastructures (ibid.). Important here is the observation that positive innovation relationships and infrastructures in a country or region will have pervasive and systemic effects and as such will be cumulative (Doloreux and Parto 2005); similarly, a lack of these networks will risk a vicious cycle of weak innovative performance. The ability to use this innovation will also vary according to institutional context. The existence of strong yet dynamic institutions for governing innovation and energy systems will allow for better diffusion of change, as well as more concerted governance.

Alongside this relational geography of innovation and institutions is a physical geography of resources. The production of energy requires the presence and use of pre-existing, tangible natural resources. In the case of renewable energy in particular this results in a naturally occurring geography of places better endowed with the requisite natural resources, be it wind, solar, tidal, geothermal, etc., for the deployment of particular technologies. As such, the development of (renewable) energy infrastructure will be shaped by a predetermined physical geography.

However, there is still a great deal of politics to the distribution of costs and benefits from the development of this infrastructure. Geography and economics have long since had something to say about the repercussions of natural resources upon a place, with a clear split in opinion between a 'resource curse' and a 'natural advantage' (Eames and De Laurentis 2012). The first group hold the somewhat pessimistic view that resource-led growth cannot lead to sustained growth, and that such a growth model will end in dependency and negative path dependency, while the latter holds that extractive resources provide a comparative advantage that can, if governed appropriately and used to generate rents, underpin economic growth and development (ibid.). The Mediterranean Solar Plan can be considered an example here: it proposes the installation of 20 GW of capacity in the Mediterranean region by 2020 and incorporates the Desertec programme, which aims to provide 15 per cent of European electricity as well as a significant proportion of domestic demand in North Africa by 2050 (Werenfels and Westphal 2010). The scheme cites economic growth and development as one of its goals, alongside renewable energy production and energy security. Indeed, it proposes that its installations, if completed in full, would create 235,280 jobs in producer countries. However, critics argue that benefits to the southern Mediterranean producers will be small while European businesses will receive the bulk of the gains to be had (ibid.).

Integrating energy justice in sustainability transitions research

The aim of this chapter has been to address the absence of justice principles within the dominant frameworks for conceptualizing and practising low-carbon transitions. We have argued that the emerging field of sustainability transitions research, while offering informative insights into the complex, multi-actor and multi-dimensional processes of energy transition, often neglects issues of distributive and procedural justice. Key to addressing these deficits is the need to 'open up' sustainability transitions research to other types of knowledge,

3 · Eames and Hunt

59

drawing upon insights both from other academic disciplines and from wider society. That there is a need for greater inter- and trans-disciplinarity in developing the theoretical and conceptual models, analytical frameworks, research methods and governance-oriented tools within the field.

With respect to interdisciplinarity, a broader, more strategic inter-action with the related disciplines of geography and political ecology would allow fuller consideration of the uneven social and economic consequences of transitions, improving understanding of potential and emerging distributional injustices. Costs and benefits of transitions are distributed unequally across space – and hence society – as a consequence of unequal innovation and institutional capacities and physical geography in processes that are well studied outside of the transitions literature. Such disciplines are well placed to bring the materiality of relational and physical geography into transitions, bring-ing with them a deeper understanding of distributional energy justice. At the same time more broadly based historical, political and economic analysis should also have a role to play in exploring both the role of power and agency in, and the distributive impacts of, transitions. The interdisciplinary field of environmental economics in particular could provide much in the way of deliberative-analytical and multi-criteria appraisal tools with which to reflexively address the distributive im-pacts of prospective transitions.

Looking outwards to wider society, encouraging greater stake-holder and public participation is critical to addressing procedural justice concerns within sustainability transitions. Particular attention is required to how best to engage with vulnerable and marginalized groups. Here community engagement, ethnographic, deliberative and action research methods all have a potential role to play in opening up the field to heterogeneous local knowledges and diverse societal perspectives.

More fundamentally, what is required above all is a clear normative orientation towards prioritizing just sustainability in future energy and low-carbon transitions. This means asking searching questions about who has a voice, and how to ensure fairness, in the distribution of the costs and benefits of such transitions.

4 | Energy justice and the low-carbon transition: assessing low-carbon community programmes in the UK

SARA FULLER AND HARRIET BULKELEY

Introduction

In many countries around the world, (area-based) communities have become seen as one means through which a transition to a low-carbon economy and society should be achieved. With evidence emerging from countries such as Australia (e.g. Moloney et al. 2010) and China (e.g. Zhang et al. 2013), it is clear that the notion of community has become increasingly significant in addressing energy and climate change challenges. In the UK, such approaches place emphasis on the community as a site at which appropriate forms of technology may be developed and deployed alongside a means through which transitions in social practices and behaviours to produce less carbon-intensive lifestyles can be achieved (Heiskanen et al. 2010; Middlemiss and Parrish 2010). While this approach has – more or less implicitly – been couched in a discourse of contributing to a 'just' low-carbon transition, little explicit attention to date has focused on the justice dimensions of such community programmes.

Responding to climate change by and through community raises both conceptual and practical questions for how we might think about the dimensions of justice involved in low-carbon transitions. In particular, the intersection between climate change, communities and energy enables us to consider how existing notions of energy justice – often framed in terms of the 'here and now' in relation to access to affordable energy and fuel poverty – may need to be revisited in the context of climate change. Framing questions of energy in relation to climate change thus brings new spatial and temporal dimensions to the forefront, which in turn raise questions about the adequacy of our fundamental understanding of what being 'just' in energy terms may entail.

In this context, the aims of this chapter are twofold: first to explore how the notion of energy justice might be conceptualized in the context of climate mitigation and low-carbon community initiatives;

and secondly, to use this framework to examine how current UK low-carbon community policies and programmes address issues of justice. Through this exploration of the ways in which notions of justice are being articulated in relation to climate change, communities and energy, we find a wide range of community low-carbon responses and, reflecting this diversity, the manifestation of justice in multiple ways.

Conceptualizing energy justice in the context of climate change

As the Introduction to this book makes clear, the notion of justice in relation to energy is most frequently framed in terms of access to affordable energy and fuel poverty, in terms of the proportion of income dedicated to paying fuel bills. Ever since it entered the policy lexicon, fuel poverty has been regarded as a matter of injustice – that people should suffer cold or discomfort, and that this should lead to ill-health and mortality, has been framed as morally wrong and as requiring collective action to redistribute resources to support those who experience fuel poverty. In their recent work, Walker and Day (2012) seek to build upon and extend this commonsense understanding of justice as it relates to fuel poverty. Retaining the core focus on fuel poverty as an issue for distributive justice that has characterized the field, they seek to extend and deepen our understanding of the ways in which distributive justice comes to matter in shaping fuel poverty. In doing so, they argue that fuel poverty also needs to be regarded in terms of procedural justice, whereby those who are affected ought to have some forms of representation or involvement in decision-making processes, and as concerned fundamentally with the cultural and political recognition of vulnerable and marginalized social groups.

Beyond these concerns with individual experiences of energy and justice, research has also considered the ways in which principles of justice are played out in the politics of energy infrastructures, most notably in relation to siting disputes. For example, environmental justice research around the world has drawn attention to the uneven distribution of energy production facilities, such as nuclear energy or petrochemical plants, in low-income and ethnic-minority communities (Sze and London 2008). Going beyond spatial distributions, procedural considerations have also emerged. In relation to community renewables in the UK, for example, questions about how and by whom such community projects are developed have come to the forefront (Walker and Devine-Wright 2008), as well as the justice implications of the provision of financial and material benefits that might arise from such schemes (Cowell et al. 2011).

This work has done much to develop our understanding of how questions of justice relate to those of energy. To date, however, there has been little reflection about the implications of applying a climate change frame to such analyses. For example, one such consideration is that of how future energy vulnerability might be structured through changing thermal conditions and patterns of future energy demand. UK climate change projections suggest that heatwaves are likely to increase in frequency, intensity and duration in the future (DEFRA 2009). In this context, current seasonal disparities in energy use may become less pronounced as demand for active or mechanical cooling systems increases, meaning summer cooling loads become greater and winter heating demand reduces (Pilli-Sihvola et al. 2010). For example, US studies show that air conditioning in homes, workplaces and vehicles is projected to become nearly universally available by 2050 (McGeehin and Mirabelli 2001), while in Europe research shows continued growth of air conditioning in commercial buildings alongside predictions for rising energy demand due to air conditioning (Levermore et al. 2004; Pout and Hitchin 2009). This prevalence of air conditioning may, in the future, trigger new energy vulnerabilities in dwellings that have poor cooling characteristics or whose residents cannot afford cooling systems (Foresight Sustainable Energy Management and the Built Environment Project 2008; Roberts 2008). As such, increased use of air conditioning means that the problem of fuel poverty under conditions of climate change may shift from one principally of inadequate heating in winter to also feature inadequate cooling in summer.

A second set of considerations lies not so much with the direct impacts of climate change on the experience of energy justice, but instead relates to the ways in which social and policy responses to the problem of climate change may have implications for how we consider and understand energy justice. A significant body of literature has come to analyse how and why the introduction of new energy technologies raises questions of justice, as explored in detail in several of the chapters of this book. At the same time, questions have been raised about the extent to which efforts to reduce energy consumption and support the deployment of energy technologies through the use of subsidies and related charges levied across the population may have important justice elements. In the UK, for example, concerns have been raised that the use of a Feed-in Tariff, supported by charges levied to all consumers, is leading some individuals and organizations to benefit from low-carbon technologies while others pay the price (Stockton and Campbell 2012).

In this chapter, we focus on a third element of the ways in which policies and responses to climate change are taking place – efforts to support and develop 'low-carbon communities'. As noted above, while community-based responses are often seen as a more 'just' response to the climate challenge, we seek to interrogate this notion and develop a framework for assessing the justice dimensions of such programmes. In doing so, we draw on literature from the climate change and environmental justice arenas and consider the broad distinction between concerns about how the costs and benefits of addressing climate change should be shared, often termed *distributive justice*, and an interest in making sure that the processes of decision-making are fair, or *procedural justice*.

These principles have to date been primarily addressed within the international arena, where debates have focused on mitigation, concerned with how *responsibilities* for taking action and *rights* to protection should be distributed, primarily in terms of the role of nation-states in reducing emissions of greenhouse gases and the fair distribution of the burdens of climate change. Alongside distributional justice, concerns for procedural justice – in terms of how, by and for whom decisions are made – have also been central to international debates. However, such discussions over responsibilities and rights in the climate change arena are usually undertaken without explicit *recognition* of the cultural, social and economic basis of inequalities. It is this broad distributive–procedural distinction and the principles

TABLE 4.1 Multiple dimensions of justice

	Responsibility	Rights	Recognition
Distributive	Allocation of duties to mitigate	Share of benefits and costs of climate change impacts and of mitigating its effects	Challenging wider structural conditions that create vulnerability for particular groups
Procedural	Imperatives for participation in climate decision-making	Provision of access to decision-making to relevant groups and individuals	Removing barriers preventing specific groups and individuals engaging with decision-making

Source: adapted from Bulkeley and Fuller (2012)

of rights, responsibilities and recognition which provide our 'climate frame' through which to engage the debate on energy justice and communities.

Energy justice and low-carbon communities

As the discussion above has illustrated, thinking about energy justice in a climate change frame raises different temporal and spatial dimensions to those normally considered. Our account of climate – or energy – justice is based on a broad distributive–procedural distinction across three dimensions: responsibility, rights and recognition (Table 4.1).

While this is a significant simplification of a complex field, it provides a useful framework through which to begin to analyse how issues of justice are being addressed by low-carbon community programmes and the consequent implications. Below, we address each of these dimensions in turn, considering the wider context from which these concepts have been derived and the questions that might be raised when explicitly considering low-carbon communities through each of these lenses.

Distributive justice Once debates about the distribution of *responsibilities* for acting on climate change are moved from the international arena to other sites and scales, the picture of the distributional justice aspects of the climate change problem becomes much more complex (Caney 2005; Harris 2010). While it could be argued that communities, alongside households, nations and regions, have a duty to mitigate climate change, how this responsibility is distributed both within and among communities is fraught with technical challenges. Furthermore, all emissions are not equal – those required for meeting 'basic' needs could be considered to be more necessary than those emitted from 'luxury' pursuits. For example, Middlemiss and Parrish (2010) suggest that responsibility for the community's ecological footprint is held by the community as a collective, and by individuals who constitute that community. However, principles of climate justice suggest that a duty to act should also be related to the ability to take action – again illustrating that significant differences may occur within one community. Achieving a just distribution of responsibility at the community level would therefore require that such issues are taken into account in the design and operation of any initiative.

In relation to *rights*, debates have usually focused on how the burdens of climate change – either in terms of its impacts or in terms of the costs associated with taking action – can be fairly distributed (Caney 2005). While largely played out in international terms, questions of 'rights' also permeate domestic climate change politics, with different groups seeking to ensure that they are not unfairly burdened by climate change policies (Adger 2001; Büchs et al. 2011). Such debates have relevance to low-carbon communities as it is widely advocated that community programmes may result in reduced carbon emissions, economic gain, improved housing conditions and alternative forms of provision, alongside more intangible benefits, such as community capacity-building, skill sharing and citizen engagement (Mulugetta et al. 2010; O'Brien and Hope 2010; Vaze and Tindale 2011). On the other hand, significant risks associated with the emergence of low-carbon communities, such as the implications for energy security and affordability, still exist. How rights to these costs and benefits are distributed within the community is therefore critical for any account of climate justice.

Such discussions over responsibilities and rights are usually undertaken in the climate change arena without explicit awareness of the structural inequalities underpinning these issues that may result in a lack of *recognition* for marginalized individuals or groups. As Young (1990: 8) argues, the distributive paradigm 'obscures other issues of institutional organization at the same time that it often assumes particular institutions and practices as given'. In seeking to address this deficit, Fraser's (1997) work on the need to include recognition of the cultural, social and economic basis of inequalities is useful. In relation to communities, some consider that locally conceived projects are more likely to address such barriers (Peters et al. 2010) and may thus enable the principle of recognition to be put into practice. However, this may be dependent on the scope of activities undertaken within such communities and whether attempts are made to address existing injustices by targeting the needs of the most vulnerable or to recognize and respect specific values. For example, energy efficiency improvements that are accessible to all represent a more effective long-term solution than those that focus on behavioural change in targeting fuel poverty (FPEEG and PRASEG 2011), while distributed generation has potential to improve access to affordable energy for low-income households, but is dependent on the model of development employed (Walker 2008). This suggests not only that any just climate mitigation policy must take into account marginalized and vulnerable groups but also that approaches seeking to address climate change while leaving other issues of social injustice – including forms of exclusion and discrimination, for example – untouched could not be considered a 'just' response. How and why the principle of recognition is deployed at the community level is therefore critical in shaping the extent to which policies intended to enact low-carbon communities can address underlying issues of inequality.

Procedural justice Long-standing concerns have been raised about the access of different interests to the climate decision-making process. Within these debates about procedural justice, questions of *responsibility* have received only limited attention – whether in terms of the duty on particular kinds of actors to participate in making decisions (e.g. those that contribute significantly to the climate change problem or those with a stake in a particular decision – who may or may not be those most responsible) (Bell and Rowe 2012) or in terms of ensuring that those who do participate do so in a responsible manner. This is significant as the expectation underpinning community-based responses to climate change places responsibility on communities to work cooperatively to make decisions about energy and for individuals to take on the role of citizens rather than consumers (Heiskanen et al. 2010; Wolf et al. 2009). However, this expectation may place a burden on communities if they lack control or expertise (Hinshelwood 2001) and give rise to the need for particular skills, characteristics or resources (Seyfang 2010). It may also serve to negate the responsibility of others – including government and industry – who may have more ability to participate in and act on the decisions being reached.

The assumption that every citizen has an equal *right* to participate, as principles of democracy imply, is also contentious in the climate change arena, given that it is known for the complex and often expert-driven nature of the policy process (Aylett 2010). Furthermore, even if principles for providing rights to participate exist, the existence of obstacles, such as lack of capacity, may prevent equal participation between and across levels of decision-making (Paavola and Adger 2006). Therefore involving stakeholders in climate mitigation decisions is a complex task, and barriers to equal participation may exist at all levels.

Furthermore, the ability to participate may be underpinned by a particular set of institutional conditions which inhibit or prevent people from participating in such processes (Young 1990). As discussed above, the principle of *recognition* suggests that there is a need to correct unjust structures and procedures of dominance (Fraser 1997; Shrader-Frechette 2002) and 'identify the strategies through which a more equitable distribution of social power and a more inclusive mode of environmental production can be achieved' (Swyngedouw and Heynen 2003: 914). Underlying structural factors may thus restrict the ability of communities to participate or work collaboratively at community level to implement a low-carbon transition, and may 'serve to prevent citizens from engaging more fully in the wider political debate on sustainable living' (Peters et al. 2010: 7596). Additionally, area-based communities do not immediately imply the ready existence of a 'community' and, as suggested above, recognizing who is and is not part of a community has significant implications for the extent to which such initiatives can address climate justice. This is particularly true given that such communities are built on the expectation of significant commitments to new forms of energy systems and/or to changes in behaviour which may be difficult to achieve (Larsen et al. 2011). How and for whom communities are defined is likely to have implications for how individuals within these communities are able to work collaboratively and participate within decision-making processes, and therefore for the outcomes in terms of climate justice. Furthermore, within area-based communities themselves, there may be multiple overlapping communities of interest. This lack of homogeneity may result in a lack of cohesion with the potential to work in exclusionary ways.

In summary therefore, the move towards community-based responses to climate change as a means of enacting a low-carbon transition raise issues of distributive justice in terms of the duties which are seen to lie with communities, ways in which risks and benefits of low-carbon community programmes are allocated, and whether such programmes can recognize and address more fundamental issues of inequality. Furthermore, issues of procedural justice may be as significant as those of distributive justice at the community level and interconnect in multiple ways. In this context, questions arise about the responsibility of, and rights to, participation within such communities and how recognition for marginalized groups is achieved within low-carbon communities. A climate change frame shifts the focus of such issues from those addressed in relation to either energy vulnerability or specific energy technologies, drawing attention to the ways in which responsibilities and rights may shift over time and space, and requiring more detailed analysis of the ways in which these issues are being addressed in practice. Thus applying these principles of climate justice can provide an alternative way of thinking about justice in relation to energy, and allow us to make use of an 'energy justice' frame through which to assess low-carbon community policies and programmes.

The emergence of low-carbon communities in the UK

The concept of community is increasingly employed in climate governance with multiple meanings and roles; community can be seen as actor, scale, place, network, process and identity (Walker 2011). 'Low-carbon communities', as one manifestation of the role of communities in the low-carbon transition, have emerged over the past few years in the UK as a mechanism for carbon reduction promoted by a range of government, private, civil society and grassroots actors. Underpinning this have been two key drivers: community as a mechanism for behaviour change and community as the site for the development of renewable energy.

First, communities have come to be regarded as a critical site for climate mitigation through achieving behaviour change. Attention has often focused on individual behaviour change and how individuals can not only reduce emissions but also be low-carbon consumers, employees and citizens (Whitmarsh et al. 2011). More recently, the broader context of individual action – such as community – has become important, partly because of a recognition that community action may counter constraints on individual behaviour change such as social dilemmas (where individual efforts are useless unless others participate); social conventions and infrastructure (where behaviour is shaped by conventions and socio-technical infrastructures beyond individual control); and helplessness (where invisibility of the consequences of action leads to a sense of disempowerment) (Heiskanen et al. 2010). In this context, low-carbon communities are seen to enable forms of cooperation and collaboration that reduce the carbon intensity of their members' lifestyles by providing amenable contexts and mechanisms that encourage behaviour change (ibid.). From a government perspective, for example, such a remit for communities as a means of addressing behavioural change was explicitly articulated in the UK Low Carbon Transition Plan. As the Plan notes, 'we often achieve more acting together than as individuals. The role of the Government should be to create an environment where the innovation and ideas of communities can flourish, and people feel supported in making informed choices, so that living greener lives becomes easy and the norm' (HM Government 2009: 92).

Alongside interest in behaviour change, community has also become a site for the development and deployment of renewable energy technologies. Since the late 1990s, and emerging from multiple policy drivers (Walker et al. 2007), a diverse range of approaches towards community energy – in terms of technology, technical configurations and ownership – have emerged. While defining the 'community' nature of such projects is difficult, factors such as the degree of community participation; the manner of governance; whether or not locally gener-ated energy is consumed locally; the structure of ownership; and the technology employed in such a system may all be relevant (Hoffman and High-Pippert 2010). In practice, as Walker and Cass (2007: 461) note, community energy can be seen to encompass 'processes of project development that are to some degree local and collective in nature, and/or beneficial project outcomes (economic and social) that are also to some degree local and collective, rather than distant, individualised or corporate in destination'. As with behaviour change, development of community energy has been an integral part of many policies and programmes aimed at supporting the UK low-carbon transition, in-cluding the Low Carbon Transition Plan, which aims to 'make it easier for local authorities, businesses or community groups to generate electricity at community scale' (HM Government 2009: 96).

In practical terms, alongside government policies, programmes and funding schemes, a plethora of grassroots, civil society and private sector community initiatives are emerging, including initiatives such as Transition Towns, alongside competition-based schemes, such as the Ashden Awards or the NESTA Big Green Challenge, whereby 'competing' for funding is used as a mechanism to support community innovation. This diversity and range of low-carbon community programmes, and the different drivers underpinning their development in the UK, suggests that there may be multiple ways in which notions of justice are being articulated. Understanding how justice principles come to be part of the discourses supporting the development and implementation of these programmes, and act to shape the ways in which they are practised, can therefore provide important insights into how alternative forms of what might constitute 'energy justice' are being established in relation to climate change and the policy imperatives of responding to justice issues through the notion of low-carbon transitions.

Assessing the justice dimensions of low-carbon community programmes

In order to examine the ways in which justice is being articulated through these programmes, we draw from the discussion above to suggest that understanding how issues of climate and energy justice are configured at the community scale requires an engagement with both distributive and procedural justice, and the ways in which notions of responsibilities, rights and recognition structure and comprise these discourses of justice.

For the purposes of this work, we reviewed nine current UK policies and programmes aimed at supporting low-carbon communities. This review aimed to capture the range of activity around low-carbon communities and thus incorporated programmes conducted by government, private and civil society organizations. The review involved analysis of relevant policy and programme literature, such as annual reports and application guidance, with information recorded in a spreadsheet detailing whether and how specific dimensions of justice were explicitly captured in individual programmes. An overview of the programmes reviewed, the lead organization and their key objectives is set out in Table 4.2.

The sections below discuss distributive and procedural justice in turn, assessing how the dimensions of responsibilities, rights and recognition are manifest in different programmes before drawing out some overall conclusions.

Distributive justice As we argue above, community-based initiatives raise issues of distributive justice in terms of the duties which are seen to lie with communities, the allocation of risks and benefits from low-carbon community programmes and whether such programmes can recognize and address more fundamental issues of inequality.

Although the low-carbon community programmes we reviewed originate from a variety of different actors, all of the programmes ultimately place responsibility for climate mitigation on the communities themselves. For example, the British Gas Green Streets programme, the only private sector scheme reviewed, was set up to 'help communities around the UK to save and generate energy' (British Gas 2012). Similarly, the Green Communities scheme, a civil society programme, was designed to help communities to deliver effective carbon savings and sustainable energy projects (Energy Saving Trust 2010). In placing this responsibility for climate mitigation on communities, some programmes are more specific than others. For example, neither the Low Carbon Communities Challenge nor the Climate Challenge Fund articulates specific carbon reduction targets, instead asking communities to decide their own targets, while, in contrast, the London Low Carbon Zones specified a 20.12 per cent target for cutting carbon emissions by 2012 and mechanisms put in place to achieve a further 60 per cent reduction by 2025.

Responsibility is also shared in those schemes where partnership working is required. One example here is the London Low Carbon Zones model, which is led by the local authority but based on a

TABLE 4.2 Selected UK low-carbon community programmes

Programme	Lead organization	Key objective
Government-led		
Low Carbon Communities Challenge	Department for Energy and Climate Change	Financial and advisory support to communities in order to test different delivery packages and capture learning; 22 communities funded.
Climate Challenge Fund	Scottish Government	Funding to help communities in Scotland combat climate change by reducing carbon emissions and increasing their capacity to take action. Funding awarded to 345 communities to date.
London Low Carbon Zones	Mayor and Greater London Authority	To bring together local authorities, private sector partners and community organizations to reduce the carbon emissions and to develop models for carbon-savings measures across and beyond London; 10 zones in different London boroughs.
Civil society		
Big Green Challenge	NESTA	Prize designed to stimulate and support community-led responses to climate change; 10 communities chosen to put their ideas into practice over a year; 3 winners and 1 runner-up received a share of the £1 million prize fund.
Green Communities	Energy Savings Trust	Online support, network of advice centres and consultancy services to help communities deliver carbon savings and move towards a low-carbon future. Around 3,000 community group members.
Ashden Awards	Ashden Awards	Awards for programmes using local sustainable energy to tackle climate change and bring other benefits in an enterprising way. Over 70 UK awards to date.
Grassroots		
Transition Network	Community self-organization	To support community-led responses to climate change and shrinking supplies of cheap energy, building resilience and happiness. Over 400 official initiatives worldwide.
Low Carbon Communities Network	Community self-organization	A network of sustainable communities that offers mutual support, materials and infrastructure for collective action. Over 600 member groups.
Private sector		
Green Streets	British Gas	Competition-based challenge for community groups to lead projects to reduce carbon emissions. Funding for energy-saving equipment awarded to 22 communities in two phases (Green Streets 1 and 2).

consortium of partners. In contrast, several of the grassroots schemes do not explicitly rely on such partnership arrangements, suggesting that they may feel the burden of responsibility more strongly. In order to counter this, sharing knowledge and expertise is often a critical support mechanism. For example, the Low Carbon Communities Network offers mutual support, materials and infrastructure (Low Carbon Communities Network 2008).

The distribution of climate mitigation burdens in terms of rights is addressed less explicitly than other elements of justice. Many of the programmes highlight the positive benefits of low-carbon communities, including local investment, job creation, fuel poverty and climate change (for example, the Low Carbon Communities Challenge). Similarly, the Climate Challenge Fund considers carbon outcomes alongside community outcomes (social, economic and environmental) as criteria for funding, while the NESTA Big Green Challenge aimed to explore how an outcome-based prize could stimulate benefits (particularly innovation) in communities. This is broadly based on an assumption that such benefits will be evenly spread throughout the community. However, there are no schemes that explicitly consider any negative impacts that may arise, such as potential financial implications or the pressure on specific individuals when acting as community leaders, or which consider how the distribution of costs and benefits arising from such programmes may be spread across the community.

It is evident from all of the programmes that the community is recognized as a critical site for addressing climate change. However, the rationale for this approach varies across programmes. Government-led programmes often place priority on policy learning and the ability to test different models of low-carbon community. For example, the London Low Carbon Zones aim to 'bring together local authorities, private sector partners and community organisations to reduce carbon emissions from a local area significantly and to develop a range of models for the delivery of carbon saving measures across and beyond London' (Greater London Authority 2009: 4). Similarly, the objective of the DECC Low Carbon Communities Challenge is to 'find out what works well locally and use this knowledge to inform government policy on what we need to do, as a nation, to enable the UK to reach its carbon reduction targets' (DECC 2010: 3).

At the same time, such government-led programmes also seek to address broader structural issues. For example, while the primary objective of the London Low Carbon Zones Programme is to deliver 'rapid carbon savings from buildings in the zones and the development of models that drive long-term carbon savings', the secondary objectives driving the programme are those of 'mitigation of fuel poverty, promotion of sustainable lifestyles and lower carbon footprints and regional skills development and other positive social outcomes' (Greater London Authority 2009: 16). Similarly, the Low Carbon Communities Challenge has a clear focus on fuel poverty, while also stating in the application guidance that such communities need to be equitable and sustainable. Therefore, in government-led low-carbon community programmes, inasmuch as marginalized groups are recognized, they take the form of the 'fuel poor'. In contrast, the civil society and grassroots schemes take a wider approach and recognition is couched in more general terms. There is often a greater emphasis on building community resilience – for example, the Transition Network aims to 'support community-led responses to peak oil and climate change, building resilience and happiness' (Hopkins and Lipman 2009: 7). Similarly, the Ashden Awards make reference to wider social benefits (including fuel poverty) and the Low Carbon Communities Network has a vision of communities which promote social justice and incorporates a commitment to environmental justice (Low Carbon Communities Network 2008).

In relation to distributive justice, therefore, we find that all programmes ultimately place responsibility for climate mitigation on communities themselves but that the rationale varies across programmes. The distribution of mitigation burdens in terms of rights is addressed less explicitly than other elements of climate justice, and although there is some recognition of difference within communities, this is often focused on fuel poverty.

Procedural justice In the discussion above we acknowledge that issues of procedural justice may be as significant as those of distributive justice. In this context, we need to consider the responsibility of, and rights to, participation within such communities and how recognition for marginalized groups and of diversity within communities is considered.

Turning to assess responsibility for participation, many of the programmes are based on a strong foundation of community capacity-building, implying that there is (an indirect) recognition of the burden of participation. For example, the Transition Network, a grassroots scheme, aims to 'inspire, encourage, connect, support and train communities as they self-organise around the transition model' (Transition Network 2012). Similarly, the Low Carbon Communities Challenge brings together learning, skills and resources while the Low Carbon Communities Network aims to create a network offering mutual support, indicating a commitment to long-term capacity-building on the part of both these programmes.

Similarly, in terms of rights to participate, all of the programmes reviewed had strong criteria for the involvement of all people within communities. For example, the Low Carbon Communities Challenge encourages involvement throughout the community: 'everyone can be involved – local residents, families, school and university students, community leaders and people who work in the area' (DECC 2010: 2). Similar sentiments are found in other programmes, which seek to enable involvement in various ways – for example, through training to facilitate community leadership, as is the case with the British Gas Green Streets and the Ashden Awards. Interestingly, in Scotland, specific mention is made of supporting projects run by and for young people – the Junior Climate Challenge Fund – the only such programme to target this age group.

In relation to recognition, one of the most evident findings is that while there is no fixed definition of what a community should constitute for the purposes of climate change mitigation, as shown in Table 4.3, many of the programmes deploy relatively simple notions of 'community'. As the table indicates, a low-carbon community can be defined by geographic area (for example, British Gas Green Streets or Climate Challenge Fund); by the number of buildings (for example, London Low Carbon Zones); by the number of households or residents (for example, Low Carbon Communities Challenge); or by the communities themselves (for example, the NESTA Big Green Challenge). In terms of recognition, such definitions may not adequately capture the multiple communities – and hence the multiple forms of identity – existing in particular places, which may also pose challenges for the ability of everyone to be involved. Furthermore, for those programmes where community is defined in an arbitrary manner, there are likely to be implications for community cohesion and the ability for collective action on climate change.

Furthermore, many of the programmes are targeted at pre-existing communities and there is little support for initial community development work. For example, the Ashden Awards are targeted at communities that have been delivering local energy savings for at least one year – with start-up, pilot or demonstration projects explicitly excluded. Similarly, the Low Carbon Communities Challenge is targeted at communities that are already trialling approaches rather than those

TABLE 4.3 Definition of community in low-carbon community programmes

Programme	Definition of community
Low Carbon Communities Challenge	Populations of 1,000–20,000 residents but would consider larger/smaller
Climate Challenge Fund	A clearly defined geographical area. Also communities of interest where they can be defined in terms of geography
London Low Carbon Zones	Each zone contains no more than 1,000 buildings, both residential and commercial
Big Green Challenge	Communities defined by entrants and varied by size and in their nature
Green Communities	Not specified
Ashden Awards	Area-based approach but not specified
Transition Network	Scale of activity should be where community feels it can have most influence (likely to be bigger than a street but smaller than a city)
Low Carbon Communities Network	Not specified
Green Streets	One street of houses (Green Streets 1) and community facilities and surrounding houses (Green Streets 2)

starting from scratch, namely 'organisations with the resources and skills to support carbon emission reductions at community level, and who are applying on behalf of communities already instigating or facing change and contemplating what a broader plan for the area might look like' (DECC 2009: 2). A notable exception here is the EST Green Communities Programme, which, until it was disbanded in 2011, had over three thousand members and provided free support for both new and established community groups via online services (such as how-to guides and funding guides), advice centres and free consultancy. Despite this exception, the focus on existing community groups suggests that any structural constraints that may prevent communities working collaboratively are not being addressed through these programmes.

In summary, there are strong criteria not only for the involvement of local communities but also for community leadership in some cases, and many programmes are based on community capacity-building, implying (indirect) awareness of participation burden. However, there is no fixed definition of what a community should constitute and programmes are mainly targeted at pre-existing communities with little support for community development, suggesting structural constraints may not be addressed.

Conclusions

This chapter has explored how the notion of justice can be conceptualized in the context of low-carbon communities, bringing principles of climate justice most often considered at the international scale into the debate on energy justice. In doing so, we suggest that assessing what is 'just' in this context requires an appreciation of distributive and procedural aspects, across three dimensions – responsibility, rights and recognition. Applying this framework at the community scale allows us to examine how current UK low-carbon community policies and programmes address issues of justice while also raising some considerations more broadly for how energy justice within a low-carbon transition might be constituted.

A varied picture emerges when considering how principles of responsibility are being pursued within low-carbon communities. At one level, the allocation of responsibility to communities is clearly addressed within all programmes, although the extent to which such initiatives take account of differential responsibilities within any given community or between such communities appears to be limited. In relation to procedural justice, we find that only two-thirds of the programmes explicitly address the responsibility to participate. Our analysis of the ways in which rights are discussed is in rather marked contrast. While we find that none of the programmes explicitly addresses the distribution of rights within and between communities, in procedural terms all of the programmes consider the right to participate as fundamental.

While all of the programmes recognize communities as critical sites for addressing climate change, we find significant variation in terms of the extent to which fundamental inequalities that shape distributive and procedural aspects of climate justice at the community level are recognized and addressed. Government-led programmes all include recognition of the 'fuel poor' as a marginalized group whose interests need to be taken into account in the pursuit of low-carbon communities. This in turn has led such programmes to seek to ensure that such groups are taken into consideration in the distribution of the costs and benefits of such programmes. However, there is limited evidence that such programmes have sought to involve such groups in decision-making. In contrast, those programmes initiated by private or civil society actors less often consider the distributional impacts of their programmes in this manner, but may adopt more specifically open processes of decision-making. This finding raises significant questions about whether either approach can realize its aims, but also offers the possibility that the principle of recognition can find a place in both distributive and procedural aspects of low-carbon communities.

In seeking to open up questions of how energy justice might be conceptualized, and in particular to consider notions of duty and responsibilities alongside those of rights and recognition in the low-carbon transition, we have highlighted a diverse picture of justice emerging through current UK low-carbon policies and programmes. Understanding how such principles are manifest within these programmes therefore provides important insights for how we might understand energy justice within the UK as well as in the many other countries where community-based responses to climate change are emerging. In conclusion, while recognizing the multiple interconnections between these different forms of justice, it suggests a specific need to consider how recognition might be enacted in practice, which may provide a mechanism for more carefully allocating responsibilities and rights in order to facilitate a move towards a 'just' low-carbon transition.

5 | Energy justice and climate change: reflections from a Joseph Rowntree Foundation research programme

KATHARINE KNOX

Introduction

Energy policy and the way in which energy supply and demand are managed are becoming increasingly critical both in the UK and elsewhere. This agenda is one of both political and economic importance. Energy policy is inextricably linked with supporting a competitive economy, and ensuring secure, clean and affordable energy is an important policy goal. Recent UK governments have been particularly exercised by questions of energy security and ensuring that the UK is not struck by energy blackouts or held to ransom with high prices by being overly dependent on unreliable energy sources from overseas. In addition, there is growing pressure to reassess the composition of our energy supply and to reduce overall energy demand, in order to reduce our reliance on polluting fossil fuels, and to support the transition to a low-carbon economy, deemed critical if we are to reduce both global and UK carbon emissions in efforts to mitigate climate change. The introduction of the Climate Change Act 2008, which had cross-party support and established new statutory targets to reduce emissions and a new governance framework (including independent advice to government through the Committee on Climate Change), heralded a growing political priority being accorded to this policy area. The important interrelationships between energy policy and climate change have also been increasingly recognized politically in the UK, signalled by the introduction of a Department of Energy and Climate Change within the government, which brought together business and environmental policy officials.

With the growing political and economic significance of energy policy, then, the question of how related social justice issues are addressed is becoming ever more important. However, it is not clear that this has been a central consideration of government policy. Social justice is a concept with many associations, linked with notions of rights, equity and fairness for people. There are two primary dimensions to consider here.

First is the idea of distributional justice. This relates to the question of the distribution of income, assets and opportunity, and, in this context, relates in particular to the differential way in which climate change impacts will fall across the population, and the benefits and costs of associated policy and practice responses and how these are shared. An underpinning concern is that the effects of climate change, and of policy responses to it, could create new forms of inequality or exacerbate existing patterns of inequality if they are disproportionately borne by poor or already disadvantaged communities and individuals.

Second is the idea of procedural justice. This relates to issues of governance, participation and democratic decision-making. The enormity of climate change, and its failure to adhere to particular national, political or administrative boundaries, raises particular dilemmas about who is considered to be part of the relevant population for decision-making purposes in tackling the problem. There are many layers to this, from the international negotiations to develop targets to reduce global emissions, to the local decisions made about the location and nature of new energy supply.

Distributive and procedural justice are not independent of each other. If a group is not recognized and cannot participate in planning and decision-making for mitigation policies, its interests are unlikely to inform, and be served by, related plans and decisions. Also, being disadvantaged can create obstacles to recognition and participation in planning and decision-making processes (Bulkeley and Fuller 2012).

The Joseph Rowntree Foundation (JRF), an independent social research funder, has been leading a programme of research to investigate the social impacts and social justice implications of climate change in the UK, and within this has been examining some of the key issues associated with energy policies seeking to mitigate climate change. The programme was initiated in 2009 and was undertaken because the JRF was concerned that the social justice implications of climate change, while increasingly recognized at an international level, particularly in relation to international responsibilities for emissions and carbon reduction, were not sufficiently understood at a national level and within the UK. The JRF programme has involved some seventeen projects funded over the period 2009–13, cutting across a range of topics, from social vulnerability to climate change, and adapting to climate impacts to tackling fuel poverty and developing progressive approaches to reducing carbon emissions. The programme has been supported by an advisory network of policy-makers, practitioners and researchers and has been interdisciplinary in nature, including input from experts in political philosophy, social policy, geography and economics. The project teams have included academics, think tanks, consultants and non-governmental organizations active in delivering practical solutions linked to climate change. See JRF's website for more details on the work programme and publications (www.jrf.org.uk/work/workarea/climate-change-and-social-justice).

JRF's research has identified the following important justice issues in relation to energy and climate change:

- the differential distribution of carbon emissions and questions over the relationships between responsibility for contributing to climate change as well as responsibility for remedial action;
- the distribution of the costs and benefits of energy policy responses and their equity, considering who pays and who benefits from interventions and how to develop fair and progressive policy responses; and
- the procedures used to inform energy policy as a whole and the relative roles and means for different stakeholders to inform strategic planning and decisions and to be affected by policy outcomes, considering what the public might consider to be 'fair' responses to the problem.

The JRF's research points to some important concerns. It provides compelling evidence of a triple injustice in relation to climate change in the UK, whereby households on low incomes, who are least responsible for creating carbon emissions, are facing a disproportionate burden of the costs of policy responses linked to carbon reduction, while also benefiting less from the measures that have been introduced than wealthier households (Preston et al. 2013). There is also concern about this injustice being compounded by the fact that more disadvantaged groups overall, including those in poverty, may also be among those most affected by the direct and negative consequences of climate change – through living in some of the places most likely to be affected by climate change impacts from flooding and heatwaves, while also being least able to prepare for, respond to and recover from these impacts (Lindley et al. 2011). And finally, there is a question about how far those most affected are able to voice their concerns and influence decisions taken by policy-makers and practitioners, which will affect not only their futures, but also those of their children and grandchildren to come, who may find their homes blighted or may become unable to afford costly flood insurance if market forces are left to determine the costs of this protection (O'Neill and O'Neill 2012).

Intergenerational as well as intra-generational justice is a major concern here – the consequences of decisions taken today or, perhaps more significantly, misguided decisions or inaction will have ramifications for years to come. How can we even begin to take account of this justice dilemma?

The issues of distributional justice and procedural justice associated specifically with climate change mitigation are examined and unpicked more fully below, drawing on the findings of the JRF's research programme to date.

Distributional justice issues

The international climate change negotiations have highlighted the fact that responsibility for the creation of carbon emissions (including historically) is a critical consideration in deciding nation-states' responsibilities for action in dealing with the resultant problem and establishing emissions reduction targets. Internationally, there is recognition of the notion of 'common but differentiated responsibility' and also of capability to act, which informs the legal frameworks that have developed to inform climate change policy. Article 3 of the United Nations Framework Convention on Climate Change states that 'parties should protect the climate system for the benefit of future and present generations of human kind on the basis of equity and in accordance with their common but differentiated responsibility and respective capabilities. Accordingly, developed countries should take the lead in combating climate change and the adverse effects thereof' (United Nations 1992). Little explicit consideration of these principles of justice or the idea of common but differentiated responsibility has yet informed UK domestic policy on climate change and emissions reduction.

Carbon emissions have a clear relationship with income. Research by Ian Preston and a team at the Centre for Sustainable Energy (CSE) suggests that the wealthiest 10 per cent of households are responsible for 16 per cent of UK household energy and personal transport emissions, while the poorest 10 per cent are responsible for just 5 per cent. While emissions associated with household energy use by the wealthiest households are double those of people on the lowest incomes, it is transport emissions which are most critical in creating this disparity. The wealthiest households emit seven to eight times as much as the poorest in private travel for leisure and commuting to work. Emissions related to air travel show an even more marked difference – the wealthiest 10 per cent of households emit some ten times as much as the lowest income decile (Preston et al. 2013). Clearly this analysis raises questions about responsibility for contributing to the problem, as well as who should shoulder the costs of remedial action in relation to climate change. It also suggests that, in general, policies which target high transport use may be less regressive than policies targeting high household energy use, as people on higher incomes emit so much more in the course of their travel than those on lower incomes, whereas the distinctions across the income spectrum are less pronounced in housing energy use.

The CSE report also highlights the fact that low-income households will not benefit from the current extensive range of government policies to reduce household emissions and improve energy efficiency to the same extent as higher-income households. Overall, it suggests that the expected impact of policies on household energy bills in England in 2020, compared to a 'no policy' scenario, is an average reduction of 8 per cent on bills, giving a total household bill of £1,180 per annum. However, the wealthiest households on average see a 12 per cent reduction on their bills while the poorest households see just a 7 per cent reduction. The total energy bill also represents a far higher proportion of income for poorer households, equating to over 10 per cent of income for the poorest households compared to just 1.3 per cent for the wealthiest households (ibid.).

The presumed overall average reduction in bills by 2020 is also based on government assumptions about the savings that particular policy measures will deliver, which may not be borne out in practice. Of particular importance is products policy, which seeks to increase the energy efficiency of products, including lighting and appliances. As people shift to using more energy-efficient products, so related carbon emissions should be reduced. The importance of products policy in the overall bill trajectory is considerable. If it is not included in the mix, overall household energy bills are expected to rise by 4 per cent by 2020, with a 9 per cent increase in bills for the poorest households, while the wealthiest households continue to see an average reduction on their bills, though by only 2 per cent. As poorer households are less likely than wealthier households to be able to replace their appliances with newer, more energy-efficient models, and may indeed buy more second-hand goods, these policy assumptions look particularly problematic. The implication is that poorer households may benefit less than projected from product policies in their overall energy bills.

The critical issue CSE's work exposes is the relationship between who pays for and who benefits from current policy measures. Their work suggests that some households will not benefit directly from any current measures (over half of households in their analysis) and yet could still expect to see an increase of £50 on their bill by 2020 owing to government policy. With a whole range of policies in place, funded by different means (varying from general taxation to obligations on energy suppliers passed on to bills which may or may not be linked to rates of consumption), the overall picture is complex and policies do not impact on households in a uniform way.

Some policy measures are clearly more progressive. The Warm Home Discount (www.gov.uk/the-warm-home-discount-scheme/overview) is the policy which sees most benefits going to lower-income households, as it enables energy suppliers to provide discounts on bills to particular priority groups. However, other policies look much more regressive, such as the Feed-in Tariff, which enables households who install small-scale renewable energy to benefit from guaranteed payment from electricity suppliers for electricity generated and used and for unused surplus electricity which can be exported back to the grid. The works require an initial capital outlay which is out of the reach of most low-income households. CSE's work suggests 12 per cent of households are expected to benefit from this policy by 2020, saving a substantial £360 a year on their bills, but this measure is funded by all households, with the majority 88 per cent of households not seeing any benefit – instead these households will see a cost of £10 on their bills.

The Green Deal, which is the government's centrepiece of household energy policy, commencing in 2012 (www.gov.uk/green-deal-energy-saving-measures/how-the-green-deal-works), is also problematic for lower-income households as it relies on households effectively taking out loans to pay for energy efficiency measures. There are no upfront costs to households as the costs of works will be recouped through savings on future energy bills, but this kind of approach is unlikely to be attractive to people on lower incomes, especially as they are already likely to have higher debt to income ratios than other households (Financial Inclusion Centre 2011). As the charge is tied to the home rather than to the individual, the household will not see the full benefit if they move before the total costs of any works have been recouped through savings on bills (although they may get some partial benefit from lower energy bills if the government's Golden Rule is met, under which, every year, savings on bills must equal or exceed costs for measures). The related Energy Company Obligation will provide some funding from energy suppliers to enable lower-income households, including those who face fuel poverty, to benefit from energy efficiency measures, as well as those who live in homes that are hard to treat. However, this will be the only measures-based fuel poverty programme in England from April 2013. Overall, CSE suggest the Green Deal and Energy Company Obligation combined are expected to add £25 to the average bill (Preston et al. 2013).

When looked at as a whole, the mix of policies in place does not seem to offer a particularly equitable approach, nor one which is sufficiently focused on tackling fuel poverty. Other work for JRF suggests fuel poverty can be reduced only by a clearer focus on improving the energy efficiency of homes and reducing the energy bills of those in fuel poverty, especially low-income vulnerable households (Ekins and Lockwood 2011; Stockton and Campbell 2011). Currently fuel poverty is defined as households needing to spend 10 per cent or more of their income on heating and powering their home to a standard sufficient to maintain the health and well-being of household occupants. However, the Hills Review has led the government to reconsider its approach to defining fuel poverty – which is leading to a change in policy. The new approach will be to define fuel poverty as a condition of low-income households with high required fuel costs – thereby moving away from a focus on people's income to a focus on their expenditure (DECC 2013a). Critics of this approach fear that it will not take sufficient account of changing energy prices and, as high energy costs are relative to the median figure, this will mean fuel poverty numbers will change little over time. Such a definition will therefore do little to aid the targeting of practical interventions or to assess progress in tackling fuel poverty over time.

If current policies do not seem particularly fair and are not primarily focused on tackling fuel poverty, there is also a question of how effective they might be in responding to climate change – which in itself will have massive social justice implications if mitigation policies fail.

In order to achieve our climate change targets, the UK's own apparently groundbreaking legislation introduced through the Climate Change Act 2008, the first national legislation to set statutory targets to reduce greenhouse gas emissions internationally, requires us to reduce our emissions by 80 per cent on 1990 levels by 2050. However, CSE's work shows we have a long way to go to achieve that in the residential sector alone, which generates some 31 per cent of the UK's carbon emissions. They suggest that a much more radical programme of housing retrofit works is required, proposing that up to 86 million new measures need to be applied to our homes (from loft, cavity and solid wall insulation to use of renewables) if we are to maximize carbon abatement opportunities in the housing stock. Even applying such approaches will leave us with a shortfall on the 2050 target. The costs will also be enormous – totalling some £293 billion by 2030 (equivalent to around £17 billion per annum from 2012). While this could have a significant impact on reducing, if not fully eradicating, fuel poverty (based on the existing definition), it will still require substantial new investment and finance to be found from a range of sources, although CSE sets out ways to achieve this that will not hit those on low incomes (Preston et al. 2013). However, in the current climate of economic austerity it is hard to see how the finance for this work will be prioritized when welfare reforms are already leading to major public spending cuts.

In another JRF project, Dresner et al. (2013) suggest that as part of our response to climate change, we need to make changes to the tax system to stop providing 'environmentally perverse subsidies'. They suggest one such subsidy is the lower rate of VAT on energy bills of 5 per cent compared to the 20 per cent applied to other goods and services. They also suggest other ideas for developing carbon taxation on energy use for housing and transport through use of the carbon price floor mechanism. These are challenging ideas, particularly in a climate of austerity. Any new taxes will be politically unpopular. But from a social justice perspective, can such taxes be introduced without disproportionately impacting on those on low incomes? Dresner et al. suggest they can. Their research suggests that it is possible provided a revenue-neutral approach is taken so that the money generated through carbon taxes is recycled back to lower-income households in a progressive way. The main route for this is to offer households compensation via universal credit and pension credit, as well as increasing personal income tax allowances for those on low incomes (ibid.). This is a step forward from their previous research on this issue, which found a progressive approach was hard to attain and not likely to be very feasible to deliver. However, it seems unlikely that any government in the near future will countenance such potentially unpopular approaches without wishing to retain a proportion of the revenue. The research suggests billions of pounds could be raised through such carbon taxes. One can only hope the Treasury do not simply see the tax-raising opportunity and apply such an approach without any compensatory measures, which would certainly increase fuel poverty.

There is inevitable tension between the challenges posed by climate change and the costs associated with making the transition to a low-carbon economy, which require us to reconfigure our energy supply and reduce demand. The choice of which mechanism is used to finance investment is critical, as is the design, application and roll-out of policy initiatives and interventions to support this transition. The consequence of increasing energy bills to drive up investment is likely to be an increase in fuel poverty unless policy-makers specifically seek to take remedial action to avoid this. For households in fuel poverty, there may be a need to increase energy use and therefore add to rather than reduce demand in order to ensure adequate warmth, raising further dilemmas about the overall goals of policy and whether carbon reduction and fuel poverty policies can be developed effectively together.

If we are to meet our climate change targets, the evidence suggests the need for major interventions and investment in our energy infrastructure, but also changes in how we live. We also need to take better account of the emissions associated with our consumption patterns in relation to our overall national emissions, rather than just those linked to production. This means taking account of the emissions embedded in products we buy which may be produced elsewhere. This more hidden yet major contribution to emissions is not accounted for in current UK targets and carbon accounting, which allow consumption to be treated as an offshore issue – if we buy goods made abroad which pollute those countries and raise their emissions they are not included in the UK total. This may become an unsustainable position from a justice perspective if we are concerned about the global emissions picture and the relative contribution of different nations to the problem and to remedial action.

Procedural justice issues

While the costs faced by households are fundamental to energy justice, as they generate substantial income to enable carbon emissions reductions to be made and support the shift to a low-carbon economy, this is only one aspect of energy justice.

Another important justice issue relates to the governance underpinning climate change responses. There are a number of important questions here – who participates in decisions which inform policy and practice development? Who decides who participates? What are the rules of engagement? These questions are critical – for who will decide whether the major housing retrofit programme CSE suggests may be necessary or the carbon taxes Dresner et al. outline should be introduced? Bell and Rowe's *Viewpoint* for JRF suggests a number of important principles should be applied in decisions around climate change. In particular they suggest that applying the principle of proportionality is one way of ensuring greater fairness in decision-making. To make things fairer, they suggest we need to consider how much different people have at stake in any decision, and who will be most affected by it. They argue that everyone who is affected by a decision should have some power in the decision-making process and that decision-making processes should be designed to distribute power in proportion to stakes – the more anyone has at stake in a decision, the more power they should have in making that decision. They suggest that since the least well-off people will often be most affected by decisions to do with climate change, they should often have the most power in making climate policies and decisions (Bell and Rowe 2012).

However, in practice, such aspirations are often sidelined in current political processes. Nowhere is this more evident than in spatial planning decisions, which are at the heart of local democratic processes and inform the future shape of the places in which we live. The voice of the vocal minority can often lead choices made by politicians in planning processes. One of the challenges raised by Bell and Rowe here is that local policies and decisions relating to emissions reductions are likely to have impacts on people beyond the local community. Fairness, Bell and Rowe argue, requires that non-locals affected by those decisions should have some power in making those decisions. However, this is highly problematic, as is evident in the politically charged issue of developing new local energy infrastructure, particularly onshore wind farms, where in practice the views of proximate communities can make the difference between the success or failure of schemes in being accepted for development. On this issue, Richard Cowell and colleagues suggest we need to give greater consideration to the community benefits which new infrastructure could provide and enable communities to get a greater share in the financial benefits, not as an incentive for public acceptance of a scheme, but in recognition of the negative impacts that developments can have on communities (Cowell et al. 2012). It appears that the government is increasingly taking this view too, with emerging policies to support financial community benefits from wind farms (DECC 2013b).

As the above example illustrates, a major challenge is the scale at which decisions are made and where responsibilities and the levers for change apply, from the global to the local, and indeed on the household and individual level. It is clear that the individual can feel powerless faced by the scale of the challenge presented by climate change, leading to apathy and inertia – and that assumes people have an interest in taking action in the first place. There can be a tendency for governments to wait for popular pressure to initiate change and for populations to expect governments to lead action through their ability to regulate, enforce, incentivize and disincentivize action. The role of individuals and scope for 'behaviour change' raise many dilemmas, not least the ethics of seeking to 'nudge' people to make choices which are more sustainable. However, a study by the Fabians for JRF suggests that when it comes to climate change, if people understand there are finite resources at play, and a collective dilemma at stake, they are willing to countenance constraints on their use of these resources – based on the idea of 'fair shares' for all (Horton and Doran 2011). While reluctant to face legislation, people nonetheless dislike the notion of 'free-riders' and believe a level playing field is needed. They are therefore willing to consider regulation to support this. If this is the case, perhaps policy-makers need to give more thought to issues of equity and fairness in designing policy solutions to support more sustainable energy consumption, and this could help to underpin approaches more clearly in future.

Nonetheless, responses will also need to grapple with what people consider to be acceptable constraints on their choices. Research by Druckman et al. (2011) for the JRF explored public attitudes to what might constitute a sustainable minimum acceptable standard of living. The work indicated that in many cases people accepted that through adjusting their behaviour they could potentially reduce their fuel consumption in the home by as much as 25 per cent. The adjustments involved were generally seen as being compatible with a minimum living standard. However, reducing the carbon footprint associated with their food consumption, for example through eating less meat, was seen as eroding choice, and people were also more reluctant to travel by more sustainable means without improvements in safety, convenience and costs. These initial findings suggest that efforts to reduce public consumption as part of the drive to reduce overall carbon emissions face real barriers in terms of public acceptability, and perhaps more so in relation to food and travel than domestic energy use.

Conclusion

The issues presented here, as examined in the JRF Climate Change and Social Justice research programme, set out some of the aspects of energy and climate justice that need to be considered in developing policy solutions that address climate change, energy concerns and fuel poverty more effectively together. They lay down a challenge to policy-makers and practitioners involved in making investment decisions, delivering policy and leading practical delivery of energy solutions. There needs to be a clearer connection in a policy domain dominated by economic paradigms and concerns with the social implications and impacts of decisions made. Ensuring fairer outcomes for people from interventions will mean there is more legitimacy for the difficult action that is needed to help respond to the major challenge of climate change through our energy policies. It is critical we do not lose sight of this if we are to achieve the major societal shifts that will be required for the radical transition to a low-carbon economy and society.

6 | Equity across borders: a whole-systems approach to micro-generation

CHARLOTTE ADAMS, SANDRA BELL, PHILIP
TAYLOR, VARVARA ALIMISI, GUY HUTCHINSON,
ANKIT KUMAR AND BRITTA ROSENLUND TURNER

Introduction

Around half of UK CO_2 emissions are attributable to the built environment (DTI 2006). Owing to their scale and suitability for retrofit, micro-generation systems can contribute to meeting UK carbon emissions targets (i.e. a reduction from 2008 emissions of 34 per cent by 2020 and 80 per cent by 2050 (Climate Change Act, 2008). The Energy Saving Trust (Energy Saving Trust et al. 2005) anticipates that domestic micro-generation systems could help to reduce carbon emissions from UK households by 15 per cent per annum by 2050 (DTI 2006) and could meet 30–40 per cent of the UK's electricity requirements by 2050.

This chapter describes the development of an equity assessment tool (EAT) for assessing the equity issues associated with micro and small-scale energy generation projects and demonstrates its application to a range of real and simulated case studies both within the UK and internationally. The EAT has value for a variety of users and applications as a comprehensive analysis technique that focuses upon equity while considering a breadth of socio-technical issues in relation to the installation of micro and small-scale low-carbon energy generation systems.

The UK fuel mix is shown in Figure 6.1. Indigenous production of oil, gas and coal supplies about two-thirds of UK energy demand; however, the UK is moving from being largely self-sufficient in energy to an increased reliance upon fossil fuel imports (House of Commons 2012). The current system of centralized electricity supply is heavily reliant on fossil fuels. Micro-generation offers potential for the generation of decentralized or distributed energy close to the point of use (Walker 2008a) while providing the opportunity for consumers to own and operate their own energy systems, and take responsibility for energy production as well as consumption (Walker and Cass 2007; Lovins 2002). The UK definition of micro-generation covers a range

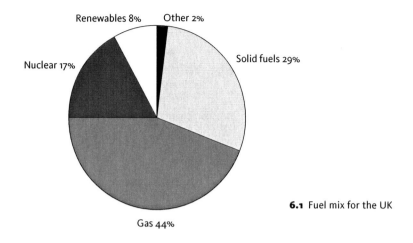

Renewables 8%   Other 2%

Nuclear 17%

Solid fuels 29%

Gas 44%

6.1 Fuel mix for the UK

of heat and power generation technologies rated at up to 45kW^{thermal} or 50kW^{electrical} (UK Energy Act 2004).

Beyond the potential of micro-generation systems for carbon reduction and increased security of supply, the equity aspects of a particular energy system throughout its life cycle (i.e. from manufacture to installation, commissioning and disposal) are important. Assessments of micro-generation technology are often made from the perspective of a singular discipline, using one particular approach, e.g. life cycle analysis (lca), cost–benefit analysis (cba) or multi-criteria decision analysis (mcda) (Burton and Hubacek 2007) or focus upon the carbon savings the micro-generation system offers. For example, Skarvelis-Kazakos et al. (2009) consider a range of micro-generation systems within a micro-grid, but focus mainly on life-cycle CO_2 emissions.

Other authors focus upon a specific technology or application. Rankine et al. (2006) and Staffell and Ingram (2010) focus upon the life-cycle CO_2 emissions associated with a 1.5kW roof-mounted wind turbine and an alkaline fuel cell combined heat and power system respectively to make the case for using these low-carbon technologies, but purely on the basis of their carbon performance when compared to fossil-fired generation. Allen et al. (2010) and Diakoulaki et al. (2001) focus upon domestic solar hot water systems, appraising them upon their environmental and economic performance and embodied energy, while Dalton et al. (2008) use software to model the feasibility of micro-generation systems for a hotel, concluding that a hybrid system comprising micro-generators with a diesel generator is most suitable. The focus of this feasibility study is purely on reducing CO_2 emissions. Bahaj et al. (2007) consider embodied energy, economics and reduction in CO_2 emissions in analysing the building of integrated photovoltaic systems.

The literature also reveals that social, future and unknown factors and more specifically equity issues rarely register in these analyses because assessments may be carried out by researchers from a single discipline or may employ specific modelling packages (containing factors or coding that could become outdated) or make assessments based upon a few criteria such as payback and life-cycle CO_2 emissions. These methods can be too rigid to accommodate social factors such as perceptions about the technology and its appropriate installation or use, even though this can be essential for optimal system performance. Unknown factors, e.g. new and developing technologies and frequent changes in energy policy and pricing, can also be difficult to incorporate into these approaches. Some methods weight the variables, for example Burton and Hubacek (2007) and Afgan and Carvalho (2002), who undertake a multi-criteria assessment of a range of new and renewable energy power plants, weighting each type of plant using sustainability indicators, e.g. CO_2 emissions, capacity factor, cost and space occupied by the plant. However, the use of complex mathematical functions to weight the options could deter certain users. The authors do comment on the potential of non-numerical information in the evaluation process, although their method restricts the use of this type of information. Another major disadvantage of these more rigid, weighted assessment methods is the failure to include other important factors such as stakeholder preferences (Oikonomou et al. 2011) and socio-political aspects – for example, who benefits from and who contributes to Feed-in Tariffs (FiTs), tensions between those who can and cannot afford to install micro-generation systems, and changes in government support for micro-generation and other low-carbon technology. Madlener et al. (2007) consider the social aspects of an energy system but focus upon a specific location and suite of technologies. They demonstrate how stakeholder engagement helped in the development of a whole-systems assessment methodology as part of the ARTEMIS project, which aimed to develop future renewable energy scenarios for Austria.

Whole-systems analysis

The literature identifies a clear need for a whole-systems approach in assessing the equity issues associated with micro-generation projects which is not restricted to a particular technology, application, location or point in time.[1] An interdisciplinary approach is also required in order to include social, technical and economic factors and to accommodate the interests of a wide range of stakeholders. The challenge of this research was to develop a non-numerical assessment tool that facilitates full and careful scrutiny of the distribution of costs and benefits when planning micro-generation projects. The whole-systems concept has been developed as a way of understanding how organizations work internally and collaboratively to improve initiatives in housing, transport, local government and voluntary agencies (Pratt et al. 1999). A whole-systems approach involves identifying the various elements of the system and subsystems being studied and focusing enquiry upon the interactions taking place between them (Meadows 2009). This approach aims to interpret the dynamic attributes of complex systems and to identify and potentially prevent problems that could arise from unseen and unintended consequences. When applied to micro-generation, a whole-systems approach involves taking a wide-ranging view of the many aspects associated with the deployment of micro and small-scale energy generation technology among a range of users who ideally are involved at various stages of decision-making across the whole life cycle of the installation. This approach should ensure that micro-generation has optimal technical efficiency while encouraging citizen engagement and acceptance (Bergman and Eyre 2011).

By incorporating stakeholder participation, whole-systems analysis can facilitate empowerment, improved accountability and transparency by encapsulating the views of stakeholders. One disadvantage of methods that incorporate stakeholder participation is difficulties with mutually resolving disagreement among stakeholders, and reproducibility of output (i.e. a different group of stakeholders may not reach a similar conclusion). The integrated whole-systems methodology described in this chapter provides stakeholders with a framework that encourages constructive discussion. The iterative format allows participants to move away from obstructive topics and revisit them later, building in cooling-off periods if necessary. The assessment can be carried out sequentially by different people at different times and as such can be adapted to a range of situations and circumstances.

Equity in the context of micro-generation

Equity has links with aspects of environmental justice, which has both distributive and procedural dimensions (Walker and Bulkeley 2006). These two concepts have been discussed and mapped by Ikeme (2003). The distributive element of environmental justice is what is normally encompassed by the term 'equity' and essentially relates to the good and bad consequences of social exchanges between different groups of people (Brashear et al. 2004). This definition was adopted for the purposes of this study and, as such, the equity aspects associated with micro-generation technology can be simply described in terms of:

1. the distribution of impacts;
2. the distribution of responsibility;
3. the distribution of costs and benefits associated with its uptake.

Distribution of impacts can be illustrated by considering how the worst consequences of climate change (flooding or drought, for example) are experienced by developing nations, although developed nations are responsible for a higher proportion of emissions (Claussen and McNeilly 1998). For example, a micro-generator could be installed in the UK and create economic returns for the owner/operator and reduce local carbon emissions, but the constituent materials of which the micro-generator is constructed could have been sourced elsewhere (nationally or globally), where the impacts of their exploitation could remain.

Distribution of responsibility can be illustrated by developed nations that have the wealth, technical know-how and capacity to mitigate the impacts of climate change using low-carbon alternatives (Ikeme 2003), but should they have a responsibility to do so? For example, the UK government is supporting the uptake of micro and small-scale generation systems by offering FiTs. Should bill payers subsidize FiTs though their energy bills, which encourages those that can afford it to buy and install micro-generation systems, or should this revenue be used to help low-income groups to access this new technology by assisting them with the capital cost?

Distribution of costs and benefits in relation to fuel poverty is discussed more widely by Walker (2008b). An example of this is the case of early adopters who may pay a higher price for installing micro-generation when markets are less well developed (although this is partly addressed through policy instruments such as FiTs) but will benefit from higher FiTs at an early stage. Their actions are of benefit to wider society by reducing total carbon emissions. This chapter deals with the distribution of costs and benefits associated with micro-generation uptake and uses the EAT to consider this within the context of geographical location and potential future changes in energy systems.

Methodology development

An equity assessment tool (EAT) has been developed with input from thirty energy professionals to fulfil the requirement for an interdisciplinary tool suitable for groups of multidisciplinary decision-makers to assess micro-generation projects (Adams et al. 2012). The framework uses an iterative structure and prompts the decision-maker to promote mutual compromise by discussing the equity implications of proposed energy projects among an interdisciplinary team of decision-makers. It has been tested using synthetic and real case studies and could have value for multidisciplinary groups when planning energy projects.

A whole-systems EAT for assessing the equity aspects of micro-generation projects should include:

1. The technological aspects of micro-generation, e.g. issues associated with the technology such as type, size, nature of attachment to building, power output.
2. The policy and markets issues relating to micro-generation, e.g. government support for certain technology, FiTs, capital cost, payback.
3. The social issues related to the uptake of micro-generation, e.g. public support and acceptance and benefits for people.

These broad themes and the connections between them are considered alongside unforeseen, uncertain and variable cross-cutting factors, such as time, geography, socio-economic group and energy price, while maintaining a focus upon equity and carbon (Figure 6.2).

The EAT was developed by an interdisciplinary team of stakeholders, which consisted of representatives from academia (physical and social sciences), fuel poverty charities, social enterprises, housing associations, technology manufacturers, electricity distribution net-

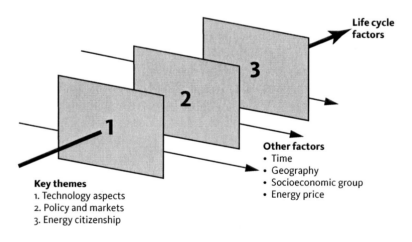

6.2 Schematic representation of the whole-systems approach and cross-cutting themes

work operators, energy researchers, electricity generation companies, education and training providers, energy supply companies, power systems consultants and energy-saving advice centres. The stakeholders also provided insights from the viewpoint of their customers and the communities they interact with.

The development process was initiated by asking stakeholders to undertake a SWOT analysis for micro-generation to help identify the attributes that an EAT framework should possess in order to highlight equity issues (Table 6.1).

TABLE 6.1 Output from the SWOT analysis

	POSITIVE	NEGATIVE
INTERNAL	*Strengths* Could enable benefits of the low-carbon transition to be shared Security of supply Empowerment Increased awareness and sense of responsibility more generally Inclusive – can bring communities together Low risk compared to other mitigation options (CCS and nuclear)	*Weaknesses* Retrofit issues Intermittency Timescales for changes in policy and technology Growth in micro-generation sector could be detrimental to other sectors Capital cost Technological maturity and credibility Shortages of component parts/materials Technology embodied energy/carbon Lack of political support Complex technology rather than simple
EXTERNAL	*Opportunities* Development of new markets Energy storage technology development Feed-in Tariffs and other financial incentives Potential to integrate energy citizenship and environmental citizenship through empowerment Smart metering and monitoring of homes Education opportunities for children and adults	*Threats* Provides secure energy for some and not others New nuclear build and CCS encourage centralized generation to be maintained People don't like being told what to do. Other sectors trying to convey messages at some time – info overkill Potential to enhance marginalization/exclusion and inequalities of wealth and power Economic downturn Poor technology performance Distraction from other priorities, e.g. insulation, double glazing, airtightness

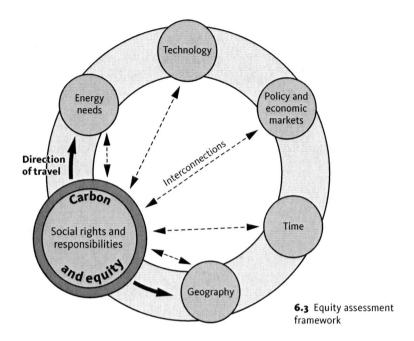

6.3 Equity assessment framework

The group agreed that the framework should be generic, versatile and flexible enough to accommodate future and unknown variables. Other attributes include the need for the framework to be accessible to users from all disciplines and the potential for the framework to be iterative and able to function as a decision-making tool. The group felt that target users of the equity framework would be interdisciplinary teams (e.g. local authorities, housing associations, community groups, consultants) planning energy projects at community or group scale. The stakeholders also agreed that inputs to the equity framework should be readily available and the output should not be numerical in order to allow it to encompass variable and unknown inputs and to render it useful to a wide range of users.

Stakeholders favoured a structure with equity and carbon reduction at its core, using theme entry points with accompanying checklists (Adams et al. 2012) to serve as prompts for discussion under each theme (Figure 6.3). A set of six initial entry points was devised during a stakeholder mapping event. Case studies reflecting the interests and experience of the group were selected as a means for testing several scenarios.

To test and refine the EAT, four case studies were developed by the project team and stakeholders and used to test the methodology during a stakeholder workshop event. Following testing, the utility of the EAT was assessed by the stakeholders, who all agreed that the EAT provided a sound framework for considering the equity issues associated with the selection of micro-generation systems and proved a useful tool in facilitating group consensus with the checklists providing a series of prompts to direct the discussion. This approach has particular value for decision-makers working outside their field of expertise (ibid.).

To improve the flexibility of the EAT and support the iterative approach (one iteration is represented by a complete sweep of all six themes), the participants agreed that themes should be viewed sequentially through a lens, as if using a microscope. Using this approach any single theme could be viewed under high-definition focus while the other related themes provided background and context. The iterative structure prevents sticking points in the discussion as themes can be revisited at a later stage. The EAT is intended to work as a process, with the checklists for each theme providing prompts for discussion, thereby giving users a balanced framework to explore. The EAT is provided as a tool or process with accompanying checklists and therefore allows for comparison with other applications. The output produced is in the form of notes, highlighting pertinent comments and identified inter-theme links.

Using the equity framework to evaluate the equity aspects of the UK case studies

Simulated, prescribed case studies were favoured by participants as a means for comparison between groups working on the same case study. Ten case studies were originally proposed; however, the four chosen were felt by the participants to be representative of the main types of community within the UK and were selected also because some of the stakeholders had experience of working with those types of community and could give valuable insights when assessing the utility of the EAT. The majority of English dwellings (66 per cent) were built more than five years ago and are privately owned or mortgaged. Registered Social Landlords (RSLs) and private landlords control 17 and 14 per cent of English households respectively (DCLG 2011). The number of households represented by each of the four case study scenarios has been estimated in Table 6.2. The number of households in fuel poverty is estimated at 3.44 million or 16 per cent.

Case studies 1 and 2 depict rural housing and housing within the ownership of an RSL respectively. Case study 3 reflects a future scenario (to explore the time dimension of the EAT), looking forward to 2021, when newly built homes will have been carbon neutral for five years;

TABLE 6.2 Case study detail

	CASE STUDY 1	CASE STUDY 2	CASE STUDY 3	CASE STUDY 4
Location	Rural village	Urban block of flats	Future scenario. Suburban estate of similar new build properties	Urban mixed age and types of housing
Access to gas	No	Yes	Yes	Yes
Fuel Poor	Yes and no	No	No	Yes and no
Ownership	Owner occupier, mortgaged, tenanted	Registered Social Landlord	Owner occupier, mortgaged	Registered Social Landlord, private landlord, owner occupier
Housing stock	Mixed existing	Identical	New	1950s semi
Micro-gen mode	Retrofit	New build, integrated	New build, integrated	Retrofit
Disposable income	Some	Low	Medium	Low
Occupiers	Mixed	Mainly families	Young couples, families	Mixed families, elderly
Energy demand	Above average	Average	Average	Above average
Occupancy	Mixed	Mixed	Evenings/weekends	Mixed
Drivers for low-carbon life	Improved comfort, reduced energy bills	Reduced energy bills, good comfort levels	Reduced bills, green interest, income source	Improved comfort, reduced energy bills
Technology choice	Yes	No	Yes	No

Issues	Restricted fuel choice, limitations of housing stock, fuel poverty, planning policy	Low income, age, unemployment, fuel poverty	Occupants affect energy demand, income generation, carbon offsetting, display green values	Fuel poverty, unemployment, housing stock condition and space may affect micro-gen choice
Future	Could be one of first areas to be all electric	Employment opportunities for community, technology replacement issues	Employment opportunities, possible early adopters of electric vehicles	Increased fuel poverty, smart metering and incentives could benefit these people
Opportunities for adjacent large-scale generation	Yes – space and resources suitable	No – space constraints	No – space constraints	No – space constraints
Number of English households in this group[a]	20% 4.3 million	14% 2.8 million	3% 0.75 million	63% 13.6 million

Note: a. England has 21.5 million households with an 80:20 split between urban and rural areas respectively (ONS 2010)

the number of households is estimated using current build rates. Case study 4 represents the majority of English households, the 80 per cent (17.2 million households) which are located in urban or suburban areas. The dominance of this setting throughout the UK offers a key target group to influence, regulate and incentivize. However, the mix of tenure, age and condition of the housing stock and varying energy needs of occupants within this group present many challenges and almost require a case-by-case approach.

Case study 1 Age and condition of housing stock are key factors for these communities, which lack access to the mains gas network (which restricts fuel choice) and are subject to land designations that could affect or preclude the incorporation of micro-generation technology. Equity issues for rural communities include restricted fuel choices for elderly residents who may have to rely upon costly electric heating or struggle to handle solid fuels. Policy measures targeting high emitters would disproportionately impact these communities, because housing stock condition and rural location mean that inhabitants are likely to have above-average energy demands.

Case study 2 RSLs may have bulk buying/bargaining power, meet capital funding criteria and have the opportunity to promote energy literacy and appropriate technologies via regular contact with tenants. New-build and major refurbishment projects offer opportunities for the incorporation of micro-generation. The EAT developed from this research could have a valuable role in assisting the RSL to make good technology choices and consider the future consequences of those choices. Equity issues associated with this case study relate to lack of choice and control – for example, tenants may have little choice in or control over the type of micro-generation installed, but they could benefit from the installed technology through improved comfort levels or lower energy bills.

Case study 3 Research shows that purchasers of low- or zero-carbon homes (represented by this group) are motivated by green values and want low energy costs (Bergman et al. 2009); the installed technology may also be viewed as a status symbol. Householders in this case study will benefit from FiTs, grants, buy-back agreements and reduced imported energy demand. Occupant behaviour is more likely to affect energy demand than building fabric, but the success of such low- or zero-carbon developments relies upon users being conversant with and willing to use the installed technology. Equity issues affecting this group include the effects of installing additional or future replacement micro-generation technology and issues concerning who should pay for any required upgrades of the electrical network.

Case study 4 Policy measures such as the proposed 'Green Deal'[2] (DECC 2010) could be well suited to this group by helping consumers to fund energy improvements from a portion of their annual savings. Those with the most inefficient homes have most to gain. Success depends upon the practicalities of making the required improvements. Using the EAT for this group highlighted a strong case for engagement with private landlords because the private rented sector has the highest proportion of properties that do not meet the 'decent homes' standard (around 680,000 homes). The UK Energy Bill may be amended to prevent private landlords from renting homes with energy ratings F and G. Landlords will be able to finance refurbishments using the 'Green Deal'.

Equity issues arising from the UK case studies Using the EAT with the case studies highlights equity implications associated with micro-generation technology relating to freedom of choice, education, constraints that may limit opportunity and economic status. Most people could reduce their energy demand even if there is a lack of awareness and education. Those who have less choice and control over their energy supply and patterns of use have fewer opportunities.

An appreciation of housing tenure has relevance for this exercise because there are generally fewer opportunities for using micro-generation technology in rented properties unless the landlord is responsible for installing it. Tenants on low incomes, ineligible for benefits and living in privately rented accommodation, generally have least control of all households because they have little control over their housing stock and installed energy arrangements. A significant number of people who have low incomes and are at risk of being in fuel poverty are not homeowners (Walker 2008a) (around 18 per cent of households in private rented accommodation) and are in fuel poverty (this represents one fifth of the total number of households in fuel poverty).

Geographical location can affect opportunities to access micro-generation. In rural areas individual adopters may be charged for upgrades to the electrical network required to support their planned micro-generation system, with clear financial implications. This could be an important future issue if uptake of electric vehicles and heat pumps increases. Land designations and planning issues in rural or urban areas may restrict or preclude micro-generation choice. For example, homes in urban environments may have more restricted technology choice than those in rural areas, although the rural setting may limit fuel choice and restrict technologies such as micro combined heat and power. Households in rural areas are more likely to be in fuel poverty than those in urban areas (18 and 12 per cent respectively), and thus may find it harder to pay upfront capital costs (ibid.).

The age, condition and aspect of housing stock have equity implications. The building fabric or the type of heating system installed can create high energy demands (regardless of occupant behaviour) and offer few opportunities for improvement. Policy measures targeting high energy users (e.g. personal carbon allowances) would disproportionately impact on people living in inefficient housing stock and could exacerbate fuel poverty (Roberts and Thumin 2006).

Climate change policies subsidized by the taxpayer (e.g. the UK's Warm Front and the proposed Green Deal) may be more equitable than measures funded by gas and electricity consumers (e.g. EU Emissions Trading Scheme and Feed-in Tariffs) (Owen 2008), especially for those on lower incomes who pay less tax. Removal of government-funded schemes in favour of levies from energy bills will affect low-income groups and could push more people into fuel poverty (Stockton and Campbell 2011).

The age of occupants also has an equity dimension. The elderly generally have higher hours of home occupancy and may be unable to handle solid fuels, relying upon more convenient yet expensive fuels (e.g. LPG, oil or electricity). Winter fuel payments for the elderly may be insufficient as energy prices rise. Leenheer et al. (2011) found that age may be a factor governing the intention to save energy or install micro-generation with intention decreasing as age increases.

Equity issues are also linked with micro-generation being perceived as a luxury of the affluent that is subsidized (through energy bills) by the less affluent. Between 4 and 10 per cent of the average gas and electricity bill respectively is allocated to environmental costs (Ofgem 2011). This includes funding for energy efficiency initiatives (many of which are not available to higher-income groups), carbon reduction programmes and emissions trading in addition to the FiTs. Therefore only a small percentage of energy users' bills contributes to the FiTs. Purchase of micro-generation systems by early adopters benefits everyone by reducing local carbon emissions while expanding the market for micro-generation.

International case studies – Greece

Greece's fuel mix is strongly dependent upon indigenous solid fuels and imported oil (European Commission 2007) (Figure 6.4). Greece has no nuclear generation and most power is generated from lignite. The Greek islands are either connected to the national electricity grid or are reliant upon diesel generators fuelled by imported diesel and to an increasing extent on renewable energy (especially hydro). Greece is increasing its use of imported gas. The Greek islands have global relevance for other island communities of varying sizes that may or may not have a power grid but are reliant upon fuel imports (regardless of fuel type). Also, the increased reliance of other countries upon imported gas could affect global gas prices, which in turn can affect the economic viability of low-carbon technology options.

The EAT was used for two communities in Greece. Case study 5 depicts the community of Gaidourmadra, comprising twelve residences on the island of Kythnos. Gaidourmadra represents an islanded power system including diesel generators, photovoltaic panels and battery storage. The installation of this system was funded by research programmes (More Micro-grids Project, TF3 2009). Case study 6, Rafina, is a holiday camp of 220 residences on the eastern coast of Attica. This community is connected to the Greek national power grid and has some installed micro-generation also funded via research programmes. These case studies were chosen because they consider communities that are using micro-generation, one in islanded mode

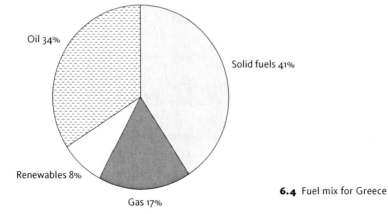

Oil 34%

Solid fuels 41%

Renewables 8%

Gas 17%

6.4 Fuel mix for Greece

and one interconnected with central supplies; they are summarized in Table 6.3.

TABLE 6.3 Summary of Greek case studies

	CASE STUDY 5	CASE STUDY 6
Location	Gaidourmadra, rural, island	Rafina, suburban, holiday camp
Access to gas	No	No
Fuel poor	No	No
Homeownership	Owner occupier and tenanted	Owner occupier
Housing stock	Mixed existing	Single-floor cottages more than 30 years old
Micro-generation mode	Integrated	Retrofit
Disposable income	Medium	Medium to high
Occupiers	Families and elderly	Families and elderly
Energy demand	Average to low	Low during the winter and average during the summer period
Drivers for low-carbon life	Necessity for power supply, green beliefs	Concern about environment, reduced energy bills

Inhabitants of both these areas are predominantly affluent and display transient occupancy during weekends and holiday periods. In the future this situation could possibly change as people sell one of their residences and use their holiday home as a permanent residence.

Case study 5 Issues for this community include enforced demand-side management in order to keep power demand within the limits of the micro-grid system to ensure continuity of supply for all. Improvements to the micro-grid could include the addition of more micro-generation, such as wind that could generate at night and reduce reliance upon diesel imports and storage requirements. Consumers are very aware of the benefits their micro-grid brings; it provides consumers with a tangible link between their domestic energy consumption and local energy provision. System limitations mean that users need to be fully aware about the effect of their activities upon the installed technology and must be willing to make lifestyle changes to support it. This community is energy conscious by default, since irrational energy consumption would pose a supply threat for everyone. Revenues are equal for all households, even if a property is not equipped with micro-generation.

Case study 6 People living within this community are relatively affluent homeowners, with positive views on micro-generation. Energy costs here are subject to national and international resource prices for lignite, natural gas and oil, but this community will have greater supply security with fewer restrictions than the community at Gaidourmadra. Owners of micro-generation in Rafina will benefit from FiTs, whereas those in Gaidourmadra cannot because they are not connected to the electricity grid. The economic situation in Greece could lead to increased occupancy and energy consumption as the population uses their summer residences as permanent ones. Owners of micro-generation systems could be affected by future decrease in FiTs of 5 per cent per year which are to be applied after 2013. The suburban location of this case study and the visibility of the installed micro-generation will positively influence people outside the community to adopt micro-generation.

Comparison of equity issues The EAT has highlighted the fact that residents of the islanded community of Gaidourmadra are more aware of their energy use because system restrictions mean that profligate use of energy by one household could interrupt the supply for everyone. Public attitudes towards micro-generation within the communities are generally positive because of the benefits that improved electricity supply from a low-carbon source brings. Property containing micro-generation would have more value than that which does not. However, in areas more reliant upon tourism, tensions may arise between impact upon visual amenity and the need for low-carbon energy. As in the UK, FiTs in Greece are subsidized through consumers' electricity bills, but not everyone benefits from the FiTs and households without micro-generation subsidize households with access to it. Similarly to the UK, tenants have fewer opportunities with respect to micro-generation uptake, although in Gaidourmadra they may benefit from its use through reduced energy bills.

The reliance of Greece upon imported oil may favour increased uptake of electric vehicles in the future; this will increase electrical demand. Equity issues linked to this include who should pay for the network enhancement and what should be the criteria for evaluation of the applied charges. The anticipated shift of consumers from being two-home owners to using their holiday homes as their primary residence has consequences for electricity supplies as demand shifts to suburban areas. The systems considered in the case studies were intended as demonstration projects and as such funding was provided for their installation. In future, at the end of the system lifespan equity issues could arise linked to who subsidizes replacement and whether the community ultimately loses its supply.

The islanded system offers more opportunities for the development of local energy supply companies as opposed to the interconnected case, where the grid is controlled by large power companies. Both systems provide opportunities for local people to be employed in the installation, maintenance and operation of the micro-generation systems. However, revenues in both cases would also be affected by the declining efficiency of the photovoltaic panels in the future and changes to future FiT structures.

Should a community such as Gaidourmadra become connected to the island grid in future, equity issues could arise as to who would receive revenues from FiTs and who should pay for any required network reinforcements. Consumers on the rest of the island pay higher electricity generation costs but have greater security of supply and fewer usage restrictions. This trade-off may have to be accepted by people from the islanded community if this ever became the case.

International case study – Japan

The EAT was applied to the Kyotango micro-grid project during a study visit. The visit included attendance at the PV 2011 Japan conference, and visits to the New Energy and Industrial Technology Development Organization (NEDO), the smart mobility and motor show, and Tokyo university.

Japan provides an interesting case study because of its energy crisis in the wake of the Fukushima nuclear disaster and because it is an island nation with limited land availability. Since the nuclear disaster there has been renewed focus on domestic energy production, which has enlivened Japan's renewable energy industry and affected the way the Japanese public think about and consume energy.

Energy security is a key driver, with more emphasis placed upon this than climate change. Following the Fukushima disaster, other Japanese nuclear reactors were shut down pending safety testing, causing energy shortages. There is now a political appetite for phasing out nuclear power (current energy policy has abandoned promotion of new nuclear build) while reducing Japan's dependence upon fossil fuel imports and

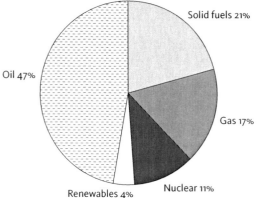

Solid fuels 21%

Oil 47%

Gas 17%

6.5 Fuel mix for Japan

Renewables 4%   Nuclear 11%

increasing the amount of generation from low-carbon sources. Japan's fuel mix is shown in Figure 6.5. Japan is heavily reliant upon imported energy and is the third-largest consumer and net importer of oil. It is also the world's largest importer of natural gas and coal. Japan is also the third-largest consumer of nuclear power globally (US EIA 2011).

Decreased electricity production during 2011 following the Fukushima disaster correlates with increased renewable energy generation over the same period. The IEA reports that, in comparison to September 2010, the share of renewable energy (geothermal, wind and solar) increased by about 200 per cent. This may be an impact of the Fukushima nuclear disaster and part of a planned move towards more sustainable energy.

Case study 7 The Kyotango micro-grid demonstration project (Morozumi 2007) (Table 6.4) occupies an agricultural, predominantly mountainous area of around five hundred square kilometres located approximately ninety kilometres from Kyoto City, 450 kilometres from Tokyo, with a declining population of around sixty thousand. The main industries are agriculture (rice, vegetables and fruit), silk textiles, forest products (timber charcoal and compost), machinery and metal manufacturing, and tourism. The settlement is grid connected. However, NEDO commissioned a virtual micro-grid project in 2003 incorporating five 80kW biogas generators (using local coffee bean waste), 50kW of photovoltaic panels, a 50kW wind turbine, 100kW lead-acid storage and a 250kW fuel cell and municipal loads. PV panels were placed in communal buildings and belonged to the council thereafter.

Equity issues The EAT has highlighted a variety of equity issues relating to the Japanese energy system and the uptake of low-carbon energy and

TABLE 6.4 Summary of Japanese case study

	CASE STUDY 7
Location	Kyotango City Japan, rural
Access to gas	No
Fuel poor	Yes and no
Homeownership	Owner occupier, mortgaged, tenanted
Housing stock	Old housing stock
Micro-generation mode	Retrofit
Disposable income	Some
Occupiers	Mixed
Energy demand	Low to average
Drivers for low-carbon life	Micro-grid demonstration

micro-generation. The Japanese approach to decarbonization has few social drivers at its core. Japanese projects take a top-down, centralized approach, using government-owned facilities, supplying capital infrastructure to validate and showcase technology. Projects focus on addressing technological challenges and industry stimulation with limited community participation. Communities are given energy-saving advice on systems following installation. One representative from NEDO stated, 'We don't have experience in customer focus'; however, its international research programmes are intended to gain knowledge in this area. A representative from the Smart Community Department explained: 'The Japanese people are different from the British. They don't mind living in new houses.' There was a sense of less need to consider the attitudes and behaviours of people in Japan than in the UK, where they might present more of an obstacle.

The Kyotango community were not given any choice about the installed micro-grid system; however, Kyotango City council had some participation in decision-making. The project was a technical demonstration project with little community involvement. Although NEDO financed its installation they have not funded upkeep and repair and, following damage to the wind turbine and PV array by a typhoon, the community have damaged equipment and little incentive for its repair following the removal of FiTs.

The biogas plant consumes more energy than it produces, is unable to supply the local community and does not contribute to increased security of supply, but it uses community waste streams through the incorporation of local residential food waste into the biofuel mix. This may have an impact for awareness-raising and the community perceptions of waste. The plant employs local people and operations are increasing year by year.

Following the earthquake and Fukushima disaster the Japanese government imposed mandatory curbs on energy use (Fukushima et al. 2011). The threat of power cuts has alerted industry and individuals to the significance of energy saving, one survey saying that 90 per cent of respondents would accept slightly inconvenient lifestyle changes and generally displayed high levels of energy-saving consciousness and ecological mindedness (www.japanfs.org/en/pages/031187.html). Time will tell whether such a power crisis instils a permanent culture of energy saving among the people.

Equity issues surrounding future low-carbon energy provision are linked to achieving community consensus for more environmentally sensitive projects, such as the exploitation of geothermal potential within national parks, or where onshore wind farms are planned near settlements. Japan is particularly focused on the potential of large-scale offshore wind using floating turbine technology. However, this resource is distributed in the north and there are equity issues linked to transmission to southern Japan and how this could be funded.

Japan has previously used FiTs to support renewable energy installations (Matsuura et al. 2010). The council at Kyotango benefited from the FiTs which resulted in reduced bills for the whole of the community. However, the energy input from the installed micro-generation was so small the perceived economic effect of micro-generation was not substantially realized. The Japanese government subsequently withdrew its FiT scheme, which led to a stagnation of renewable energy development in the country. A new FiT regime for Japan was approved in June 2012, the tariffs being among the highest in the world. The proposals include the cost of the scheme to be clearly communicated to consumers, visible as a contribution to electricity bills that is paid to generators. Large customers may be exempted.

In Japan, the cost of energy to consumers is communicated clearly: all electricity users pay a surcharge that is distributed to generation owners. Large customers (e.g. energy-intensive industry) may be exempted from the surcharge with government approval; this raises equity issues where intensive users get lower unit prices. The fact that in Japan electricity supply companies are allowed to refuse electricity purchase if there is a likelihood of hindrance to smooth electricity supply increases the risk for installers of micro-generation because they may have no market for power exports. Measures should be put in place to insure against supplier misuse of this provision.

In some countries, natural disasters pose a significant threat of uncertainty, and equity issues surround ownership of the risks and liabilities linked with new developments. A typhoon in 2007 damaged the wind turbine and some of the PV units at Kyotango and thereafter these have not been maintained and do not currently operate. Extreme weather, the risk of earthquakes and induced tsunami and the fact that Japan is mountainous with a restricted land area create a multitude of equity issues and restrict micro-generation technology choice.

Concluding comments

Using the EAT described in this chapter has enabled a comparison of equity issues relating to the uptake of micro-generation technology drawing on case studies for the UK, Greece and Japan. Japan is driving innovation related to energy saving and the provision of alternative energy sources in the wake of the Fukushima nuclear disaster.

The provision of capital funding for community micro-generation projects has many equity implications. For example, the micro-grids examined in Greece and Japan relied heavily upon capital funding for their installation. While such top-down, technology-centric projects are important for demonstration, technology promotion and market development, often no revenue stream exists to cover costs for damage to installed technology, e.g. by adverse weather conditions, or for re-placement at the end of its life. It is essential that when planning such projects either some form of insurance is sought to cover unforeseen damage and/or a proportion of the income generated is set aside for future replacement of equipment.

Micro-generation strategies should be targeted towards reducing CO_2 emissions from more densely populated areas, which may be harder to treat than rural areas that may be more suited (where land designa-tions permit) to large-scale generation, e.g. wind farms and biomass district heating. However, micro-generation policies that focus solely upon increasing system uptake rather than on promoting behavioural change (DECC 2010) and the connection between personal behaviour and energy consumption are short sighted (i.e. fit and forget with no behavioural change, as discussed by Bergman et al. 2009). This is because maximum carbon savings will not be realized if the user does not operate the installed technology and use the energy produced to best advantage.

Similarly, measures for targeting fuel poverty should be aimed prim-

arily at more populated areas, as this is where the greatest number
of households experience fuel poverty. These measures should con-
centrate upon improvements to building fabric in the first instance
before considering the installation of micro-generation. Energy finance
schemes such as the UK's Green Deal could reduce domestic energy
bills while improving comfort levels; however, to maximize national
carbon emissions reduction, funded projects must be mapped against
planned adjacent large-scale generation – for example, favouring thermal micro-generation for suitably sited homes if large-scale electrical
generation is planned near by, or favouring electrical micro-generation
if connection to a biomass-fired district heating system is likely.

Tenants have least access to benefits because they do not own property and micro-generation is normally used in conjunction with the
built environment. This restricts choice, although tenants may benefit
from lower communal bills, can embrace energy-saving behaviour,
and gain familiarity with micro-generation systems and wider energy
issues if their landlord installs micro-generation. Greater costs are
imposed since they pay (through bills) for tariffs. Policy measures that
are funded by the taxpayer are likely to be more equitable than those
funded by consumers, because those on lower incomes pay less tax.

While FiTs are recognized internationally as being supportive of
low-carbon energy generation and valuable for market stimulation,
the global economic climate leads to uncertainty about the level and
longevity of tariffs. This can be illustrated by the lead time of an
energy project (e.g. installation of a wind turbine) where there could
be a period of up to a year between start of works to install and commissioning, with FiTs being agreed only once the unit is producing
electricity. Equity issues relate to who should take this risk during
the interim period.

As observed in Japan and the UK, some intensive energy users pay
less per unit for energy, which contradicts the argument of using less
energy to save more. However, making intensive energy users pay more
for higher consumption has wider economic ramifications that could
affect job security, national income and global commodities costs.

Social perceptions about micro-generation and renewable energy
in general are more positive when framed as being preferable to the
alternative, which in the case of Japan is nuclear power and in Gaidourmadra less or no power. As many countries consider indigenous production of renewable energy or other alternative indigenous resources
to improve their energy security, decisions about the placement of
new energy systems can be emotive and generate tensions between

the need for energy and the visual, economic or environmental impact of the planned development on the host country.

Within the case study communities in Greece and Japan, similar drivers for saving energy have been observed whereby people are more committed to changing behaviour to make energy savings when the alternative is supply interruptions. The mainland UK energy supply system has become a victim of its own success. We have access to and expect limitless, continuous energy. The UK system of highly centralized, convenient energy supply means that for most consumers there is little connection between energy provision and demand, with the need for the future fuel mix to change given reducing fossil fuel stocks and the intention to decarbonize our energy supply. Some individuals then object to planned energy developments, or lifestyle changes, though as consumers the right to object needs to be considered alongside our growing demand on our energy system.

The most equitable system appears to be the island micro-grid system of Gaidourmadra. Although a small community, it demonstrates an equitable, workable energy supply system. The community has clear guidelines about how much they can use, and generated power is shared, as are energy bills. However, the availability of funding for future system replacement and ultimately supply security remains unclear.

The EAT has proved a useful tool for considering the equity aspects of a range of micro-generation deployments from a multidisciplinary perspective. It promotes discourse surrounding the distribution of costs, benefits and responsibilities of planned energy generation projects. Illustrating the distribution of costs and benefits using the UK example, the EAT has highlighted that people who invested in solar PV five to ten years ago will have paid a higher price for less efficient technology that is not eligible for FiTs. People who install approved PV systems now will receive FiTs that are subsidized by electricity consumers. In terms of distribution of responsibilities, private landlords currently have no obligation to improve the energy performance of their properties and their tenants are powerless to make improvements. At the opposite end of the scale, people with disposable income have no obligation to decrease their personal carbon emissions, but these people may generate greater carbon emissions associated with more affluent lifestyles in terms of, for example, foreign travel or increased use of cars and electronic devices.

The EAT is novel owing to the steps taken during its development, its iterative approach and because it offers a comprehensive analysis technique that forces the user to consider a breadth of issues relating to micro or small-scale generation projects. It can be used by decision-makers working outside their field of expertise. A further benefit is that the EAT helps to draw out potentially unforeseen issues (e.g. future arrangements for technology replacement, energy provision and future income) at an early stage.

7 | Fair distribution of power-generating capacity: justice, microgrids and utilizing the common pool of renewable energy

MAARTEN WOLSINK

Introduction

Studies of the issues concerning implementation of renewable energy have shown that institutional factors have proved to be the main determinants of renewables' deployment. The institutional constraints will likely affect the next stage of deployment of renewables even more. This phase concerns the integration of renewables into the energy supply system and the enhancement of these sources by the introduction of so-called 'smart grids' to optimize the exploitation of natural resources. These numerous microgrids mark a revolutionary turn in our system of energy generation that requires many fundamental changes in the social construction of power supply. In this chapter we will discuss the social construction of such smart electricity grids.

Smart grids facilitate 'distributed generation' (DG), geographically dispersed power generation with renewable sources. Citizens/consumers and other end users are increasingly becoming co-producers of electricity, and the option to include 'distributed storage' (electric vehicles) in the system also promises to enhance this role and creates options to increase deployment of renewables. This way consumers become co-producers, who may optimize the contribution of distributed generation by feeding their renewable energy into a cooperative microgrid with mutual delivery. This requires a high level of self-governance and general legislation that allows microgrids and self-governance. However, although such systems fundamentally concern involvement of a community right from the start, and the effective adaptive governance of such systems may be good for renewable energy, self-governance in the 'common pool' brings institutional questions of justice – distributive equity and fairness of process – to the fore. These equity and fairness dimensions of new microgrids and self-governance arrangements are explored in combination with the factors that further distributed energy generation.

Starting point: institutions

Implementation of renewable energy schemes has been largely determined by social acceptance issues (Wüstenhagen et al. 2007), with the result that the transformation of the energy supply system into a low-carbon one, strongly based on renewables, is impeded by institutional lock-ins (Unruh 2002). Institutional factors have proved to be the main determinants of renewables' deployment (Jacobsson and Johnson 2000). The development of smart grids also suffers from a focus on mere 'technology', continuing the neglect of social determinants that creates these lock-ins. This chapter investigates the institutional conditions for further deployment of distributed renewable energy sources in microgrid communities and will raise questions about potential injustice and fairness that may emerge as a result of the development of smart grids. It is argued that the creation of microgrids with substantial amounts of distributed generation – referred to here as 'DisGenMiGrids'– is a problem of collective action which calls for an institutional theory approach such as Common Pool Resources management (CPR; Dietz et al. 2003). Common Pool Resources 'include natural and human-constructed resources in which exclusion of beneficiaries through physical and institutional means is especially costly' (Ostrom et al. 1999: 278). In the case of harvesting renewable energy we are dealing with human-constructed systems. The establishment and the maintenance of such systems in which resources are used and produced requires good governance, which primarily consists of regimes that support and foster cooperation between users and between different levels of regulation. Use, maintenance, monitoring and rules for extraction and contribution to co-production must be institutionalized in such a way that these systems are effectively governed, so the use of the resources can be sustained in the long term. For most Common Pool Resources the difficulty of exclusion is also paramount, and the second component of Common Pools therefore is called 'subtractability', meaning that the 'exploitation by one user reduces resource availability for others' (ibid.: 278).

DisGenMiGrids are socio-technical systems that also aim to optimize the exploitation of natural resources. And this must be achieved in a condition of subtractability as well, because the space that can be allocated to establishing renewable energy generation units and their required infrastructure is limited. Hence, CPR adaptive governance comes to the fore as an obvious concept. Citizens/consumers and other end users are increasingly becoming co-producers of electricity, and the option to include 'distributed storage' (electric vehicles) in the system promises to enhance this role because the storage capacity improves the options for balancing local supply and demand and this capacity is under the control of the consumers. The balance between local supply and demand can also be improved when co-producers feed their renewable energy into a cooperative microgrid with mutual delivery. However, this requires self-governance and regulation that allows micro-grids.

The question of how these new systems are institutionally embedded and socially constructed is relevant for two reasons. First, and primarily, institutional factors like these are going to be important in the shift towards a low-carbon power supply system. Our ability to establish microgrids that locally integrate several renewable sources with each other and with demand is determined by the potential use of space close to end users and therefore the role of these end users in these systems becomes very important. Besides this essential space, the secondary relevant 'institutional' issue relates to whether establishing microgrids based on high involvement of end users creating power supply meets certain standards of equity and fairness.

The significance of smart microgrids for distributed generation

Development of low-carbon energies ranks high on policy agendas. With atmospheric CO_2-equivalent still increasing rapidly, there is an urgent need to switch to low-carbon energy sources. The utilization of renewables (sun, wind, geothermal, biomass, marine sources, etc.), in particular for generating electricity, has become a pressing issue, and most developed countries have put in place policies to promote renewable energy. At the start of the drafting of such policies, general social acceptance issues were not recognized as important and consequently were largely neglected (Wüstenhagen et al. 2007). Country comparisons have demonstrated that institutional factors are due to this neglect, and as a result the use of renewable energy has been developing rather slowly in most countries (Toke et al. 2008; Fischlein et al. 2010).

Some countries started research and development programmes in the 1970s to achieve diversification – as a response to the 1974 oil crisis – and to reduce air pollution associated with conventional power generation. The second phase of deployment started with the adoption of deployment policies for wind in a small number of countries, e.g. Denmark (in the late 1980s) and Germany (from 1991 onwards). Other countries followed with deployment policies, but only in cases with sufficient sociopolitical acceptance of changes in crucial institutional conditions was this second phase of deployment a success. Most developed countries have renewable-energy-supporting policies now, with climate change currently as the most prominent argument, but huge differences in effectiveness still exist. Deployment of renewable energy is innovation, and breaking the 'lock-ins' that prevent such innovation (Unruh 2002; Jacobsson and Johnson 2000) requires the understanding of and the will to change crucial 'rules of the game in a society'. This expression is the shortest definition of institutions (North 1990), which are mutually reinforcing patterns of behaviour and thinking, as reflected in formal and informal rules, norms and procedures. These patterns of thinking and behaviour can be recognized within all realms of society, including governance systems. Substantial deployment of renewable energy requires the socio-political and market acceptance of institutional changes such as crucial reforms of energy market conditions, empowerment of new actors (which implies disempowerment of incumbents in energy supply) and spatial planning systems that effectively support collaborative planning in renewable energy projects.

In the second phase, the start of deployment of renewable energy such as wind and solar power, the new power-generating units could be fitted into the existing power supply system rather easily. Institutional constraints, such as the dominance of incumbent energy companies and spatial planning policies applying hierarchical methods that create mistrust in collaborative project planning, will likely affect the next stage of deployment of renewables even more, as fitting in the new sources will be increasingly hard within the existing infrastructure and the existing organization of power supply. The next crucial phase in the deployment of renewable energy concerns the integration of renewables in the energy supply system and the enhancement of these sources by introduction of so-called 'smart grids'. The way existing supply and demand of electrical power are shaped exemplifies many patterns of behaviour on the part of all kinds of actors. These behavioural patterns are based on formal and informal rules that have emerged over time. These institutions have not emerged to further the integration of new energy sources, as their origin lies in the past, when there were different conditions, and they were serving different ends. The most essential changes in ways of thinking concern modes of thought that are historically rooted in the competent organizations. This phenomenon is called 'path dependency' and reflects the historical roots of existing institutions (Thelen 1999).

Currently, smart grids are a hot topic, but the term is still mainly a buzz-word. Though rapidly gaining attention in the literature and increasingly popular, the 'smart grid' still lacks a precise definition. In

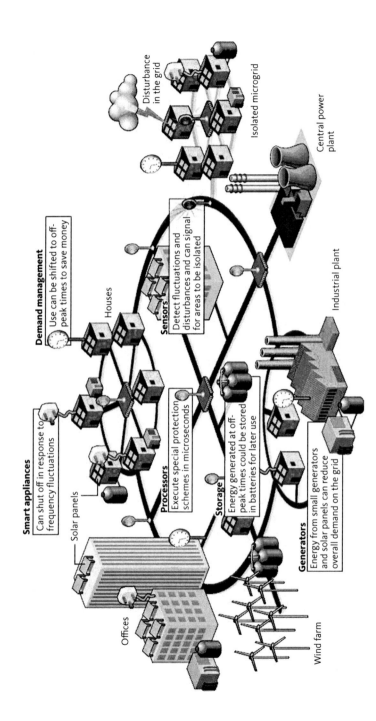

Smart appliances
Can shut off in response to frequency fluctuations

Solar panels

Demand management
Use can be shifted to off-peak times to save money

Houses

Sensors
Detect fluctuations and disturbances and can signal for areas to be isolated

Disturbance in the grid

Isolated microgrid

Central power plant

Processors
Execute special protection schemes in microseconds

Storage
Energy generated at off-peak times could be stored in batteries for later use

Industrial plant

Generators
Energy from small generators and solar panels can reduce overall demand on the grid

Offices

Wind farm

7.1 'A network of integrated microgrids that can monitor and heal itself' (Marris 2008: 570) (*source*: © *Nature*; reprinted by permission of Macmillan Publishers Ltd)

fact, there is no functioning smart grid in existence today. Despite these ambiguities, there is substantial and accelerated technology-driven progress towards developing smart grids (Hammons 2008; Marris 2008). Technically, smart grids are defined as two networks: one for electricity and a parallel information network for data generated by smart metering devices that monitor, analyse and regulate. The focus is on the power grid, but in practice integration with supply and demand of other energies such as heat is also at stake (Lund et al. 2012).

Traditional power plants are large centralized units. Today's trend is towards much smaller, geographically widely dispersed power generation units. These numerous units situated close to energy consumers are called Distributed Generation (DG; Ackermann et al. 2001). Together with improvements in smart grids that serve efficiency and reliability, a system with a large amount of DG is considered an environmentally friendly alternative to the traditional power supply system (Hammons 2008). Because DG is made up of a large number of geographically dispersed generation units – which preferably tap renewable energy sources – it is strongly associated with a more environmentally sound type of electricity consumption. Attuning those multiple generation systems situated close to energy consumers to each other and to the variable loads of end users increasingly requires a 'smart grid'. The most enlightening and comprehensive definition of a smart grid is that it is a 'network of integrated microgrids that monitors and heals itself' (Marris 2008). These numerous microgrids (Figure 7.1) mark a revolutionary turn that requires many fundamental changes in the social construction of the socio-technical system (see next section) of the power supply. As outlined by Wolsink (2012a), this is why DG in smart microgrids goes way beyond development of and application of new technologies. A myriad of new assets, but also of new social arrangements, must be accepted by numerous social actors, so smart grids must be studied through a social science approach as well.

Beyond all the technology development that is still required to establish smart microgrids, important questions remain about the social dimensions and characteristics of DisGenMiGrids. What are the social factors that create opportunities for DisGenMiGrids; and how can institutional constraints that impede the creation of such microgrids be addressed? Central to Marris's definition of smart grids is the recognition of fully changed principles for organizing energy generation and distribution. There will no longer be one centralized public power grid, but many different 'microgrids', in which energy flows from different sources, regulated and fine-tuned to local demand within the same microgrid. With the ongoing splintering of central power grids, there is already a move towards 'Distributed Generation', but there are also several developments towards local adaptive demand and 'distributed storage' capacity. For example, an important new development relates to the social choices made about options for reloading plug-in electric vehicles within DisGenMiGrids (e.g. at home or the workplace). This can become a significant factor in advancing the deployment of renewable energy (Lund and Kempton 2008; Andersen et al. 2009), but this development is determined by the behaviour of many actors. The social choices made by consumers and by other actors, particularly those in the transport sector, with regard to the development and use of electric cars (see 'Future developments'), will have significant consequences for renewables in microgrids.

Smart grid innovation

The overall question of smart grid innovation is a fundamental one about the social acceptability of all social choices that must be made for the social construction of DisGenMiGrids. As elaborated in the following sections, establishing microgrids and implementation of renewables are problems of collective action, requiring forms of self-governance, and institutional conditions that allow such adaptive self-governance (Ostrom 1999; Wolsink 2012a).

Many persistent misconceptions exist about the importance and complexity of social acceptance of renewable energy innovation. For example, the geographical space required for all infrastructure needed to achieve a shift towards a low-carbon energy system, with limited environmental impact, is highly underestimated. In fact, in policy realms there is little awareness of key aspects of renewable power generation. For example, centralized, large-scale developments (e.g. offshore wind, desert solar power, etc.) can provide only a limited amount of all the renewable energy needed for satisfying current energy demand – and in a relatively unreliable and inefficient fashion. All space, particularly close to the energy use, should also be utilized if we want to meet all of our huge energy demand through renewable sources (MacKay 2009). To increase the acceptability of using that space, a good match between energy systems and communities is crucial (Walker and Devine-Wright 2008), and the integration of renewables in DisGenMiGrids is thus essential for further deployment.

Beyond the technological characterization of buildings, power-generating infrastructure, sensors, processors and storage, all potential participants in microgrids shown in Figure 7.1 are social actors. Their participation in creating the microgrid and constructing and utilizing renewable energy-generating facilities is an essential building block in the innovation process. However, the characteristics of participants, their behaviour and their preferences, are not known. Their willingness to support innovation by participating in the new power supply system is questionable, as smart grids imply a drastic departure from the current, predominantly centralized power supply systems.

Innovation is, by definition, a change of ideas that is manifested in products, processes or organizational units being successfully applied in practice. Innovation is not merely the introduction of new technology, but rather of a socio-technical system (STS) (Geels 2004; Jacobsson and Bergek 2004). DisGenMiGrids are socio-technical systems, characterized by the active management of both information and energy flows, and by the community in which members cooperate to construct the microgrid and to manage it. Such cooperating communities should replace the existing social characteristics of the energy supply system. This requires new 'patterns of social practices and thinking'. This expression is the short definition of institutions (North 1990: 4). These patterns of practice and thinking are manifested in the organization of the energy sector as well as other related sectors. They can also be found in regulation, standardization, existing infrastructure, and in existing patterns of thinking ('belief systems', or 'discourses'). Such belief systems concern all aspects of existing power supply systems, for example their (un)reliability; beliefs about the new DG energy sources, for example their variability (or 'intermittency'; Devine-Wright and Devine-Wright 2006); and beliefs about the public interest which the system is supposed to serve, for example 'reliable supply', 'sustainability' and price.

Starting from the perspective of social acceptance, with the concept of institutions at its centre, the general question about the social construction of future power supply based on renewables can be divided into several specific questions. For example: what are the institutional conditions that determine the creation of DisGenMiGrids? Other questions concern which institutional conditions will enable optimal application of renewables in microgrid communities, and how spatial planning and decision-making about infrastructure may affect the creation of DisGenMiGrids. One of the main unrecognized and underestimated factors in the neglect of social acceptance of renewables innovation is the fact that almost all acceptances by all actors are conditional: for example, conditions concerning the distribution of costs and benefits, the sites for building the infrastructure, the control over the installations, the consequences for tariffs, etc. Therefore an essential question for establishing DisGenMiGrids also concerns the geographical and institutional conditions attached to such changes that various actors are willing to accept – and whether policies allow them:

- to install renewables generating units;
- to cooperate in a DisGenMiGrid and mutually exchange energy, regulated by smart metering;
- to adapt their energy behaviour, shaping demand patterns that match the supply of renewables;
- to accept these new configurations and infrastructure of power supply;
- to accept the institutional arrangements that are required to create and maintain DisGenMiGrids.

Acceptance of institutional change for energy innovation

Public acceptance – aggregated individual preferences – is a very poor proxy for social acceptance (Wolsink 2012b). Similarly, the construction of smart grids and the application of renewables are not simply a matter of individual choice. The major shift in the way the

Community acceptance End users, local authorities, residents → decision making on infrastructure, investments and adapted consumption; based on trust, distributional justice, fairness of process

Market acceptance Producers, distributors, consumers, intra-firm, financial actors → investing in RES-E and DG infrastructure, using RES generated power

Socio-political acceptance Regulators, policy actors, key stakeholders, public → craft institutional changes and effective policies fostering market and community acceptance

7.2 Three dimensions of social acceptance of renewable energy innovations (Wüstenhagen et al. 2007; Wolsink 2013: 11)

power supply is organized is determined by institutional change. The dominant approach in consumer choices, as seen in most Demand-Side Management studies regarding energy consumption, may be characterized as the 'ABC account of social change' (attitude, behaviour, choice). This rules out historic path dependencies and it does not reveal relevant social practices, and related infrastructures and institutions (Shove 2010). Similarly, the way policies try to address the social acceptance of renewables seems equally dependent on this limited vocabulary. This is the reason why the topic of acceptance is poorly understood among policy-makers and developers alike. This is also why most problems with social acceptance of innovation in renewables are found in the first of three dimensions in social acceptance: socio-political acceptance (Figure 7.2).

Socio-political acceptance concerns the abilities of policy-makers, governmental agencies and other key stakeholders alike to craft policies and to create frameworks that help to establish conducive conditions for implementing innovations. However, in practice it is often more problematic, as the institutional changes needed for rapid deployment are resisted by key stakeholders and policy-makers (bottom, Figure 7.2). Socio-political acceptance of the institutional changes is needed to create supportive market conditions, and also for furthering collective action at the community level (Sovacool and Lakshmi Ratan 2012). Market and community acceptance are both essential for the emergence of DisGenMiGrids. As is the case in the stagnant deployment of renewables (Sovacool 2009; Breukers and Wolsink 2007), socio-political acceptance could also turn out to be the main barrier to high potential acceptance in the other two dimensions. DisGen-MiGrids run counter to today's highly centralized power grids. For example, Figure 7.1 shows only a peripheral 'central' power plant. The existing organizations in power supply, with their highly centralized infrastructure and their centralized way of operating and thinking, will institutionally impede socio-political acceptance. In innovation in any sector, the close connection between the sector's incumbents and policy-makers induces strong inertia and retards the innovation processes (Walker 2000). According to Lund (2010), for example – among many others – this phenomenon also applies to renewable energy. Working from twelve case studies, he concludes that alternatives, representing radical technological change, have to come from outside organizations representing the existing technologies, where existing incumbents may even make efforts to eliminate alternatives from decision-making processes (ibid.: 4008).

The other two dimensions of social acceptance (community and market acceptance; Figure 7.2) concern the decisions about installation of power-generating units, or about willingness to take part in investing in such installations. The introduction of DisGenMiGrids completely changes the picture of market acceptance relations between incumbents, new firms, consumers and authorities (Figure 7.2, second level) as investment decisions shift to communities. These decisions must be taken at the micro-level, provisionally by actors in the category of 'prime movers' who are crucial for the deployment of renewable energy (Jacobsson and Johnson 2000). These actors, however, have to deal with often suffocating institutional frameworks. At this level the transaction costs of the required collective action are important. The problems with implementation of renewables have shown that high transaction costs are principally determined by institutional conditions and policies at the national level. In terms of justice, the procedures and legal conditions – for example, in spatial planning, grid access, access to subsidies, etc. – may create problems of lack of recognition, according to Schlosberg (2004; also see section 'Justice as fairness' below), one of the three essential components of environmental justice. The important role of consumers in establishing renewables' capacity should be recognized in policy, as well as within the existing energy supply sector. Lack of such recognition may easily result in constraints on ability to exploit the local options for establishing renewables' capacity. For microgrids, a crucial issue is how the institutional frameworks can be changed in order to create optimal conditions for positive decisions – investments and siting – at the meso level of communities. The social costs involve not only transaction costs for individual investors; they also involve changes in the mutual position of consumers and the related distributions of costs and benefits. As consumers may also become producers, some become involved in production while others remain consumers only. How does this affect their social relations and equity?

The community and collective action perspective

The territorial acceptability of decisions on energy infrastructure is strongly determined by the connections between the energy system and the community in which it is sited. This acceptability may be particularly low in cases of 'exogenous and invasive projects that are disconnected from the socio-economic and environmental local context' (Bagliani et al. 2010). With DG located close to end users, the literature on the deployment of renewables shows the importance of securing a good fit between the energy schemes and host communities (Walker and Devine-Wright 2008). This can be achieved by means of collaborative decision-making and by effective involvement and participation in the management and/or ownership of the new energy systems (Toke et al. 2008; Wolsink 2012b). Projects initiated by community outsiders (e.g. energy companies) are much more likely to face resistance from the community. Solid commitment in implementation of renewable energies requires trust among the relevant actors, and lack of recognition and ignorance of how to establish and maintain such trust is the main reason why renewable energy policies have been ineffective in most countries. Community members must have a strong conviction that the new energy system will be to their benefit as well as that the organization that is facilitating this process will act in their best interests. 'Trusting social relationships support and enable cooperation, communication and commitment such that projects can be developed and technologies installed in ways that are locally appropriate, consensual rather than divisive, and with collective benefits to the fore' (Walker et al. 2010: 2657). With this trust many people are willing to invest in renewables, even without immediately optimizing their personal financial gains. However, they prefer to invest on their own terms without obstruction by regulatory conditions imposed by grid managers and power-distributing companies, the likely preferred condition being 'plug-and-play' (Sauter and Watson 2007; Wolsink 2012a). This implies that property and ownership regimes for the various assets in DisGenMiGrids therefore become an important issue in terms of trust and social acceptance.

Within the broader approach of the DisGenMiGrid as a social-technical system this question is not only about formal ownership, but about different kinds of property. For governance regimes within common pools systems, Schlager and Ostrom (1992) have developed four distinctive types of property rights: 'owner'; 'proprietor' (unlike owner, without the option to alienate the good from others); 'claimant' – without the proprietor's rights of exclusion; and 'authorized user' – without the claimant's rights of management. These different types of property rights include all goods that determine access to the resource. The important point here is that access for one may be dependent upon the property rights of others – for example, when buildings or trees may impede the free flow of the resource (wind or solar radiation) and disrupt the generation of energy units for others. 'Access' can be defined as the right to benefit from things, or more broadly as the ability to derive benefits from things. Following this definition, access is about a bundle of powers rather than the narrower notion of property as a 'bundle of rights' (Ribot and Peluso 2003). Within newly emerging microgrids, who will hold these powers, and how are they distributed within the community, and among different communities? This is a real issue of distributive justice as well as of fairness of process. These issues are formulated as questions, because there are not many answers yet.

Justice as fairness

The socio-technical system of renewable power generation within a smart microgrid requires high levels of involvement of energy end users. However, the participation of those users in the new system will probably be unequal, as it may require investments that cannot be made by all. The obvious variable determining the options for investments is financial capital, but equally important may be the amount of space that users can offer for installing renewable capacity and 'harvesting' the energy to supply to the microgrid.

So neither the costs nor the benefits of participating in microgrid developments will be distributed equally, which immediately leads to questions of equity. The establishment of DisGenMiGrids is an environmental issue, and therefore it has consequences related to environmental justice. When we try to assess these justice issues relating to smart microgrids and distributed generation, which are largely in the hands of all kinds of end users, we start where almost all reflections on justice start. Rawls (1972) proposes two principles of justice: 'First: each person is to have an equal right to the most extensive basic liberty compatible with a similar liberty for others. Second: social and economic inequalities are to be arranged so that they are both (a) reasonably expected to be to everyone's advantage, and (b) attached to positions and offices open to all' (ibid.: 60). Together with the 'principle of fairness' for individuals, this leads to priority rules for institutional as well as individual principles. According to Rawls (ibid.: 108) these aspects of fairness imply 'priority rules for assigning weights when principles conflict'. In the case of DisGenMigrids, for example, this means that general justice needs rules that assign priority to both rights of individuals to generate their own power, and rights of consumers who are not in a position to generate that power themselves to derive a reliable amount of electricity for living needs.

'Justice as fairness' is the issue of how the basic structure is shaped in a scheme of institutions to create a fair, efficient and productive system of social cooperation that can be maintained over time. Contrasting this with 'the very different problem of how a bundle of commodities is to be distributed, or allocated, among various individuals whose particular needs, desires, and preferences are known to us, and who have not cooperated in any way to produce those commodities' ... 'is the problem of allocative justice' (Rawls 2001: 50).

This allocative justice resembles fairness in the process of decision-making as it is recognized as a crucial dimension in the concept of environmental justice. Within this framework, currently three dimensions are recognized. The original concept focused on distributive justice (Capek 1993) but soon a broader conceptualization emerged (Young 1990; Fraser 2000). Two dimensions were added. The first is so-called 'procedural justice', with a focus on decision-making and participation (Schlosberg 2004). Usually the focus is upon inequalities and injustices in the distribution of environmental quality, but in his conceptual elaboration of environmental justice Schlosberg joins Harvey (1996) in emphasizing that 'the achievement of environmental justice will come only with confronting the fundamental underlying processes (and their associated power structures, social relations, institutional configurations, discourses, and belief systems) that generate social injustices' (ibid.: 534). In the end, Schlosberg distinguishes three dimensions: distributional justice, procedural justice and the 'interactional' dimension of 'justice as recognition'. The latter refers to the fundamental human need that feelings of dignity and integrity are supported by the treatment by others (Honneth 1992), which also applies to the support for such feelings by institutional conditions, for example the recognition of the fundamental stakes that people hold in decisions about energy supply.

DisGenMiGrids for all?

Studies of renewables implementation indicate significant justice factors, particularly associated with the community perspective. Translated to DisGenMiGrids, this knowledge can be applied to many issues related to all three justice dimensions.

The perceived equity and fairness issues associated with the energy systems When we consider equity and fairness combined as an umbrella for all of Schlosberg's environmental justice dimensions, the important factors as perceived by community members are:

- The ownership of the assets in the energy system. This concerns equipment like the power-generating units; the transmission infrastructure within the microgrid; the smart meters, etc.

- All aspects of distributive justice in 'ownership' of resources and benefits. On the one hand this is about access for any participant to options of generating power with renewable sources, but also on the other hand the access to supplied energy yields and the associated economic benefits.
- The perceived fairness of the process of decision-making about anything related to the infrastructure that is opening up or closing down opportunities for participating in the establishment of distributed generation in microgrids. In terms of environmental justice, this is a combination of 'procedural' and 'interactional' justice.
- Openness of decision-making processes: access to all information available, as well as access to the arena of decision making.
- Institutional constraints on participation in decision-making as a result of policies and regulation. Some of such constraints are paradoxically associated with the legitimization of spatial planning decisions as created by legal procedures. Such procedures often reduce the options for adaptive governance, as they legitimize powers exercised by higher tiers of government. For all kinds of siting decisions, for example, this mainly concerns hierarchical and procedural rules within planning legislation. In several countries these options have been limited during the last decade by national governments with the introduction of so-called 'speed up' legislation relying on the argument of 'streamlining' decision-making (Cowell and Owens 2006; Wolsink 2003).

The level of trust/distrust and the conditions that may create such (dis)trust The collective action required for the establishment of a microgrid, renewable energy generation capacity and a system of mutual supply and demand of power requires trust.

- Mutual trust among the community members that cooperate in a microgrid.
- Trust in the investors in the new energy system. These can possibly be investors from within the community itself, but also optionally outsiders investing in it. Most previous research on renewables suggests that trust in community outsiders' investments is generally not high; when it is associated with energy companies it is particularly low (Walker and Devine-Wright 2008). The key issue here is the role(s) for such actors that would be considered fair and trustworthy by the participants in microgrids.

- The level of trust in actors managing and regulating the system, again either from within the microgrid community or from outside the community. Here the role of public grid managers in the microgrid is a key issue, in particular when the grid infrastructure within the microgrid is still owned by a public grid manager.
- Trust in authorities that may have procedural powers in decision-making governing how the microgrid is managed and how the electricity is generated and distributed.
- Trust in national authorities and their policies. Governments have created the regulatory frameworks that set important conditions for operating microgrids and distributed generation, and the regulations have a strong component of institutional path dependency as they mainly support the centralized model of power supply. These regulations are a strong building block of the institutional lock-in (Unruh 2002; Lehmann et al. 2012).
- Trust in the amount of support or obstruction created by procedures and legal frameworks. Many legal obstructions may exist to establishing microgrids, to generating power and supplying the energy not only to oneself but to others within the microgrid. The existence of such obstructions depends upon existing national legislation, which is an essential building block of the institutional lock-in for energy innovation.

The match between identity characteristics of the community and the energy system The identity of the community is determined by a wide variety of variables. Many of those can be relevant for establishing a good fit with the new energy system. In order to achieve such new systems with large amounts of renewables the existing identities of communities should be recognized as extremely relevant. Hence, the recognition (third dimension of justice) of the importance of that identity is at stake, as well as the recognition that the best way to achieve a good match between the identity and the new system is to let the members of the community define that identity themselves. In fact this is why self-governance in CPR management is so important, as it creates the opportunity to shape the new system according to the identity that the community members know better than anyone else.

- The physical identity of landscape and environment, which includes variables determining the geomorphology, the character of the soil, and diverse variables related to wildlife and biodiversity, such as flora, fauna, and water.

- The symbolic meaning of the landscape and environment factors, as similar characteristics in different places can have varying significance for the members of communities, according to historic and cultural values.
- The socio-economic composition of the community, which is an important factor in the characteristics of energy demand as well as the capacity and the willingness to invest in energy innovation and self-supply.
- The community members' identities, with a huge variety of socio-cultural factors and lifestyles.

Renewable energy: a Common Pool natural resource

The identity factors of the community are connected to the location as well as to the profile of people in the community. Place attachment to a particular location, and the symbolic values held by the people, plays a significant role in shaping people's responses to any proposed changes to their surroundings (Devine-Wright 2009). The identity of the actors in the community is important in determining such variables as the possible location of new renewable energy-generating capacity (rooftops, farmland, underground, etc.) as well as patterns and flexibility of electricity consumption (including the potential of using electric cars and recharging them with renewables in the microgrid). However, the identity of the partners in the DisGenMiGrid may be varied to such a degree that their contribution to the establishment of the microgrid may also be very different. This unequal contribution has immediate consequences for what distribution of the benefits among these partners is perceived to be equitable and fair.

All actors in electricity production and consumption will play entirely different roles. All actors can become co-producers, but co-production must be supported by institutions. 'Citizens are an important co-producer. If they are treated as unimportant or irrelevant, they reduce their efforts substantially' (Ostrom 2010: 10). This relates to the recognition issue in the justice concept, but this observation is also in accord with the recognition that a DisGenMiGrid is a socio-technical system that must be classified as a Common Pool Resource (Sauter and Watson 2007; Wolsink 2012a). Common Pool Resources (CPRs) are characterized by difficulty of exclusion and subtractability of resource units. CPR studies show that simple governance strategies that are applied in the name of efficiency and rely on imposed markets, or on centralized command and control, tend to fail – which is in line with the failing governance of renewables implementation in many countries. CPRs ask for high institutional variety (Dietz et al. 2003) and that is why the establishment of DisGenMiGrids requires adaptive governance based on institutional variety and a high level of self-governance.

As DisGenMiGrids will become a significant cornerstone of the power supply system, a properly designed CPR management approach – adaptive management – should provoke societal initiatives to invest in distributed generation. The presumption that a shift towards low-carbon energy provision is needed requires such initiatives, but an important follow-up question is what the social consequences of this development may be. The rules and norms studied in institutional CPR research include penalties imposed by formal and informal authorities for non-compliance. Norms are social prescriptions on compliance without formal or informal consequences (Ostrom 2010). In CPR lit-erature there is some attention paid to environmental equity (Pero and Smith 2008; Smith and McDonough 2001) but there has also been a critique that economic and political trade-offs are overemphasized, and that the research question about institutional conditions for en-vironmental governance should be reformulated as a justice question (Paavola 2007). The considerations are significant in terms of genera-ting power with renewables in microgrids. From studies on CPRs and renewables implementation, the following factors have come to the fore as essential for adaptive governance (Dietz et al. 2003; Ostrom 1999; Wolsink 2012a).

- *System boundaries:* What constitutes a 'community'? Walker (2011) recognized such various meanings of community as (1) identity, (2) an actor, (3) as scale, (4) a network and (5) as a process. The definition of a community is complex, but in this case the socio-technical system is formed by all potential participants in the microgrid. Some factors that determine the feasibility of the system, but also the options to establish justice within it, are the appropriate size, the relationship between the microgrid and the public grid, and the space that is used for the power generation and the power supply infrastructure.
- *Ownership and control* of the various assets of distributed genera-tion and the microgrid (Brown et al. 2010). Who owns the power-generating units, all different types of sensors and regulating units (smart meters), the grid infrastructure, the sites where all these assets are located, and possible storage capacity? First of all, this is a matter of who has invested in these assets, but also of

the location. For PV panels on rooftops, a clear model is that they are owned by the homeowners, but this model may become more complex when not all rooftops of participants are equally available for efficient generation, or when districts consist primarily of rental housing. Other partners in or outside the microgrid, such as ESCOs (energy service companies) or housing associations, may participate in investing in these assets. Eventually, financial actors such as banks will play a significant role as well.

- *Management:* Ownership does not necessarily equal management, as specialized actors, for example ESCOs or new bodies created by the community, may become important. In fact the emergence of such new actors is essential for innovation (Jacobsson and Johnson 2000). Obviously, engineering capabilities are essential in building microgrids and installing renewable-energy-generating units, but these can be outsourced to different types of companies. The issue eventually is who decides about the allocation of control over assets, which companies are enabled and under what conditions. Crucial is who controls the smart meters and, hence, who can use the data generated by all the sensors and for what purpose. The microgrid model assumes that the application of the smart meters as well as the data are primarily used to optimize the production and demand within the microgrid community.
- *Access rules*: The resource, renewable energy, is free, but the space needed to build the infrastructure for generation as well as distribution is limited. How can the availability of land, rooftops and resource rights be regulated in the community? In particular, the rights to catch the sun and wind are complex and as yet far from crystallized (Vermeylen 2010). Important for the establishment of microgrids, and optimal conditions for citizens to become co-producers, are a wide variety of opportunities for self-governance that are not restricted by uniform regulations (Dietz et al. 2003).
- *General standardization/regulation:* Mutual delivery to neighbouring consumers (currently legally blocked in most countries) and standardization of equipment, e.g. 'plug-and-play' for solar panels (Sauter and Watson 2007), require regulation at higher levels. Simultaneously adaptive governance in CPRs requires strong limits on interference by central authorities, utilities, (public) grid managers and tax agencies (Wolsink 2012a). Some general principles of recognition and procedural justice may demand general frameworks that create options for participants who cannot contribute essential resources – e.g. finances, space for siting generating units

– to become part of the microgrid community. They may not be in a position to contribute to the production of the common good but allocative justice would mean that they nevertheless should have rights to participate (Rawls 2001). At the same time, general principles of regulation must be available to create frames of self-governance that avoid free-riding, which would imply that participants who are in a position to contribute can be forced to do so.

- *Compliance rules:* What should the architecture of internal regulation be? This issue includes the regulation of energy flows, of information flows, of financial transactions regulated in the internal tariff system, as well as simple and easy rules for joining a microgrid community – for all kinds of actors. The right to co-produce and to deliver power to the microgrid, and the right to meet demand with internally produced power, demands an internal system of self-governance that is tailor made to create an optimal match with the geographical identity of the microgrid community.

Future developments

Obviously the framework of energy regulation is among the primary institutions and practices that determine whether DisGenMiGrids will further renewables' deployment. However, there are other relevant domains, such as transport – e.g. with regard to infrastructure for vehicle-to-grid (V2G) development – see below – and spatial planning with regard to land use for infrastructure and housing, with high relevance for ownership and management issues. In particular the energy framework aims to establish a harmonized regulatory platform, consisting of European energy efficiency directives as well as the EU member states' national legislative and regulatory conditions to secure and enforce the energy supply in Europe.

The institutional frameworks within these other domains include legislation, knowledge frameworks and organizational structures. They all show patterns that are shaped by norms and values that are relevant for the implementation of smart grids and DG, according to the institutional categories that are distinguished in Ostrom's theory of CPRs (Ostrom 1999, 2010; Dietz et al. 2003). These are norms and values concerning ownership relations, for example the regulatory conditions between existing and future licence holders of local energy distribution networks, local production capacity, and all other assets in DisGenMiGrids (e.g. smart metering devices). Crucially in the current policy frame there are basically two possible paths of development. Policies might either enhance the autonomy of cooperating end users to further their options to install renewable DG by managing local generation and use (hence, to create their DisGenMiGrid), or they might further the construction of smart metering and smart regulation of energy use, primarily aiming for increased surveillance of consumers by energy companies. The latter option is in line with centralized goals, usually not DG, and may be associated with values representing a 'technocratic fix'. The first option provides a wider scope of possibilities for applying renewables in DG (Hammons 2008).

In policy this cooperation choice is hardly recognized, while the incumbents in the energy sector are heading towards maintaining the centralized option. Indeed, current policies seem to opt for heavy infrastructure and centralized scenarios. This is illustrated by discussions about 'intelligent grids' and developed scenarios – see, for example, the UK Ofgem/LENS (www.ofgem.gov.uk/LENS), though a striking suggestion from the latter study is that the DG and microgrid scenario requires far less investment in heavy infrastructure, such as high-voltage transmission and large-scale generation, than the centralized scenarios.

Closely linked to the centralization/decentralization debate is the issue of authority with regard to 'smart applications'. This concerns the access and use of data generated from 'smart metering': is it collected primarily for energy providers and/or grid managers, or primarily for consumers/'prosumers' balancing their own energy demand and supply? This involves the system services' access to the distribution network, which is currently a particular responsibility, allocated exclusively to national transmission system operators. The functions required for smart grids may prove problematic for distribution systems operators at the local level.

A crucial issue in centralization, with strong relevance for justice, is tariffs. In all frameworks for smart grids tariffs are considered the key element of demand response, and tariffs systems are a major element in how current centralization has been established (Houthakker 1951). Existing systems of demand management are usually based on static time-of-day variability, with occasionally options for fees for switching off loads during periods of peak demand. In smart grids the variability of tariffs will sharply increase. Tariffs may become increasingly variable in size and timing once adequate two-way smart meters and load control devices have been developed. For acceptance the important issue is who will control this variability and for what purpose. The two basic paths of development are likely to show large differences for acceptance, as the continuation of centralized power supply will also imply centralized control. Tariffs systems with variability aiming at optimizing deployment and utilization of renewables would imply control within the microgrid community. In both cases, however, there is a strong justice dimension to demand response. 'Any type of tariff or direct control will affect people differently according to their ability and willingness to change daily routines, adopt new technology, invest in efficiency measures or participate more actively in energy markets' (Darby and McKenna 2012: 767). Microgrid optimization implies invoicing and settlement of energy supply: between various local (market) actors, between the microgrid community and the individual members, and between microgrid communities and public grid managers, and with authorities. An interesting topic, with huge relevance for the feasibility of renewables deployment and mutual supply of power within microgrids, will be the systems that are implemented for taxing energy flows and how they affect tariffs.

CPR theory explains why institutional arrangements addressing questions of collective action in managing CPRs and of social acceptance must be layered, with diverse complex institutions that provide some degree of redundancy (i.e. repetition of function) (Dietz et al. 2003). In power supply, currently the layer of national institutions and the 'installed base' of existing infrastructure is dominant, but for adaptive management directed at efficient use of natural resources the shape, management and decision-making about the infrastructure in which the microgrids must become integrated must be reconsidered (Marris 2008). This primarily concerns decisions on the structure and infrastructure of power supply, but it also includes structures and infrastructure in related domains. In smart grid development this concerns IT, for example, but new directions in transport infrastructure and in the transport sector also become particularly important.

Electric cars create extra load and storage capacity in households (Andersen et al. 2009; Lund and Kempton 2008). This vehicle-to-grid (V2G) application increases the feasibility of renewables and microgrids. Currently electric vehicles are recharged with the 'dirty mix' of public power generation. Recharged by renewables in DisGenMiGrids, they would reduce transport GHG (greenhouse gas) emissions significantly. Furthermore, flexibility in time-of-loading is inherent in the energy storage of the cars. This enhances the opportunities for smart applications of renewables. The aggregated load of V2G is important for levelling demand and supply imbalances by means of absorption of power – 'regulation down' – as well as the provision of power – 'regulation up' (Green et al. 2011).

However, the institutional question with regard to transport is whether these opportunities will actually be utilized to promote Dis-GenMiGrids. What kind of infrastructure will be developed for recharging cars: will consumers be recognized as important co-producers and will the storage techniques in cars support recharging at home and at the workplace – in the event that employers are also connected to a microgrid? Or will they be designed to fit large on-the-road recharging stations? The latter seems to match existing infrastructure and 'patterns of organization and thinking', but it would reinforce the institutional lock-in for power supply innovation. This institutional inertia may easily impede individual citizens using this opportunity for their own benefit and to further co-production of power, and in this sense receive due recognition as important actors in DisGenMiGrids.

The significance of the identification of lock-ins for infrastructure more broadly, and of ways to avoid them or address them, is crucial for all decisions that will be significant for deployment of renewables and justice issues within new systems of power supply. As with power supply, desired transport infrastructure also suffers from the lack of social acceptance and obsolete institutions, and it is this rather than technical issues that is holding back implementation (Banister 2008). In transport, overcoming barriers to implementation of V2G infrastructure also requires innovation addressing social as well as technological dimensions. The interconnectedness of all the infrastructures as well as the structure of the sectors behind these infrastructures, combined with the issues of justice as fairness that are associated with the decisions that must be taken, are the perfect examples of increasing complexity in the future systems of power supply.

8 | Framing energy justice in the UK: the nuclear case

CATHERINE BUTLER AND PETER SIMMONS

Introduction

International recognition of climatic change has focused political attention on the need to develop energy systems that significantly reduce carbon dioxide emissions while meeting societal energy needs. Viewed in the broader perspective of sustainability, however, the problem is not simply one of mitigating environmental effects of energy production through a process of socio-technical change but of doing so in ways that are socially just. Nuclear energy at present forms an important part of the United Kingdom's energy policy and is expected to play a significant role in the delivery of low-carbon transitions (DECC 2011). The extent to which nuclear is being pursued with a concern about justice issues embedded holds significant interest for thinking about how 'just' energy systems might be developed. In this chapter, we examine the ways in which justice issues are formulated within political discourse about nuclear energy within the UK. We focus on the ways in which such concerns are represented within the nuclear debate, either explicitly or implicitly. In examining this we seek to shed light on the extent to which nuclear energy systems are likely to be developed in ways that correspond with notions of justice. We anticipate this to be highly contingent on whether aspects of concern within justice literatures are given room and treated as important within policy and political discourse. As we shall see, the UK case provides examples of processes that in broad terms are observable in other national contexts but play out in ways that reflect the specificities of the British context.

The structuring concept for the analysis is that of frames and framing. In very general terms, framing denotes a process of delimiting the (social) world in some way. More specifically, in the analysis of discourse it refers to the application of a frame of reference to a phenomenon, or discursive object, that constructs a particular meaning and significance for it (Gamson and Modigliani 1989). When applied to social and policy problems, framing can not only construct a particular definition of the problem but also, whether explicitly or implicitly, of the kind of solutions that should be adopted. These processes may or may not be strategic, or even intentional, but are fundamentally political in their consequences (see Jasanoff and Wynne 1998; Miller 2000; Bickerstaff et al. 2008). Importantly, how issues are framed has a significant influence on how societies come to understand and approach them, and on which policy approaches come to be seen as appropriate (Stirling 2005; Bickerstaff et al. 2008). The ways in which concerns about equity and justice feature in the discursive framing of energy policy problems, and of particular energy technologies such as nuclear power, can be seen therefore as highly significant for thinking about the development of 'just' energy systems. In focusing on the discursive we undertake an analysis which shifts focus away from the material (e.g. a nuclear facility) and the specifics of place, towards the politics of meaning-making (see Stanley 2009). We view discursive framings as having material consequences in the world through their power to delimit the range of possible outcomes in any given context and enable or constrain ways of thinking, acting, and being in the world.

For our analysis we focus on discourse arising from key political figures and commentators reported within media, key institutions (e.g. the Committee on Radioactive Waste Management – CoRWM), and policy documents which have been important in defining the political frames for nuclear energy (e.g. see DTI 2007). We explore the ways in which ethical and justice issues are treated, applying concepts from the existing justice literature. In the concluding discussion we reflect on questions that remain for policy and decision-making concerning the role of nuclear energy as part of a just energy system in the wider context of global sustainable development. To begin with, it is important to map out the ways in which justice concepts have been elaborated within the academic literature, as well as how they have been developed specifically in the analyses of nuclear energy.

Nuclear energy, ethics and justice: concepts, applications and developments

Central to the literature are the concepts of distribution, participation and recognition, which have been developed and utilized in efforts to make sense of the complex nature of justice issues (Walker 2009). Taken together, these concepts encompass concerns about intra- and intergenerational justice, as well as procedural and epistemic justice (see the Introduction). In what follows we explore how these broadly defined concepts have been applied within analyses of nuclear energy, incorporating reference to some of the conceptual developments in the field pertinent for our purposes.

Within the international context of nuclear energy the literature on justice issues is relatively well developed. In particular questions of distributional and intra-generational justice have been given significant attention. For example, emerging principally from the USA, Canada and Australia, a significant body of work has highlighted how the nuclear production process disproportionately affects indigenous populations (Endres 2009; Stanley 2009; Hoffman 2001). Though there may be acknowledged geological reasons for locating nuclear facilities (particularly for mining) within the lands of indigenous peoples, the gap between the distribution of burdens and benefits associated with nuclear facilities remains markedly large. Writing about the US context, Hoffman (2001: 463), for example, points out that 'whereas the overwhelming majority of nuclear-generated electricity flows to customers east of the Mississippi, the front-end activities, with all their adverse impacts, are largely experienced by residents of Indian country'.

Efforts have been made within the nuclear context to address injustices related to the uneven distribution of goods and bads (e.g. through compensation schemes). These have, however, been scrutinized for the extent to which they can be seen as commensurate with impacts, and for the possibilities they present for creating additional sources of injustice. For example, Hoffman (ibid.: 459) points to a racial divide with regard to the treatment received by different communities in terms of remediation, with white communities seeing 'faster action, better results and stiffer penalties than communities where Blacks, Hispanics and other minorities live'. Consideration of this redirects attention to the structural, social and economic conditions that underpin and relate to environmental injustices.

Endres (2009) contends that issues of distributional injustice are often related not only to the material phenomenon in question (i.e. the presence of a nuclear facility), but are also discursively constructed. Drawing on Makhijani and Hu (1995), Endres uses the concept of *nuclear wastelands* to examine the discursive formation of nuclear distributional injustice, again focusing on the US context. She discusses the historical construction of Native American South-west desert lands as *wastelands* and explores the different ways in which these places are represented by indigenous populations (e.g. as sacred places) and in official documents and wider American discourse (e.g. as desert wastelands). This historical construction of such places as wastelands is argued to have contributed in significant ways to the decisions to use these sites for various nuclear facilities. Endres asserts that with the subsequent degradation of the desert South-west from toxic sites 'it began to turn into a literal wasteland, attracting more and more pollution' (Endres 2009: 927). In this sense, she argues that the dominant discursive construction of the desert South-west as a wasteland has had and continues to have material consequences for land-use policy. This implies the significance of considering how issues are discursively framed within policy and political contexts, as such framings can have these material consequences.

Though these examples of intra-generational justice pertain specifically to indigenous populations within the USA and Canada, such inequities in the share of burdens and benefits are evident throughout the world, both within and between countries (e.g. Banerjee 2000; Karlsson 2009; Hecht 2012). A particular observation in this regard relates to the ways in which benefits from electricity generated by nuclear power are often gleaned by countries or people that are considerably distanced from the negative effects of uranium mining processes. Taebi and Kloosterman (2008: 196) point out that 'the majority of nuclear plants are located in developed countries, while more than 30% of the world's uranium production is coming from developing countries'.

While the nuclear energy justice concerns discussed thus far extend across the various activities and facilities of the nuclear energy life cycle, other intra-generational differences are evident with specific regard to nuclear power *generation* – namely those that arise when consideration is given to the potential for major accidents. Although concern about major accidents had dropped down the political and media agenda in the years since the Chernobyl disaster, the events of 2011 at the Fukushima Daiichi nuclear power plant have prompted a renewed focus on the devastating effects of nuclear accidents. Such accidents raise multiple justice questions; for example, about the health and environmental impacts for local communities; about the displacement of people from their homes and loss of livelihoods; and about the role of compensation. The potential for an accident of this scale, and the devastating implications when it does happen, raises questions regarding how we might think about justice for those living near to nuclear facilities in more general terms. For instance, does the fact that the possibilities exist for such devastation mean that we should consider nuclear power to be inherently unjust?

The impacts of the kinds of *intra*-generational justice issues discussed thus far also intersect with *inter*generational injustices, as multiple generations of people in particular places are subject to residual and repeated injustices over time. For example, in reference to indigenous peoples in the US context, Sharpe summarizes how 'for well over a quarter of a century, uranium dust has been inhaled, ingested, and unknowingly mixed with clay to build structures in the Navajo nation – with radium levels registering 270 times the EPA standard' (2008: 17). In this context, Hoffman points out how existing compensation mechanisms fail 'to address harmful effects suffered by subsequent generations, this despite the fact that the children in uranium-based Indian communities are experiencing some of the highest levels of birth defects and physical traumas in the United States' (2001: 459).

Nuclear waste, particularly the implications of the creation of high-level waste, has formed a central concern in the literature with regard to intergenerational justice. Indeed, as one aspect of the justice debate about nuclear energy, the production of waste has perhaps received the greatest political attention in these terms. The justice concerns associated with waste entail many of the same concerns in terms of harms and burdens but often give greater focus to the impacts on future generations, and the difficulties of accounting for future generations within present decision-making (Adam and Grove 2007). By way of illustration, Shrader-Frechette (2000) points out how future generations cannot give informed consent, arguing that this raises questions about the possibilities for processes that might be considered to deliver procedural justice. In this context, it is interesting to note that, as we will show, in the UK there has been increasing focus on process and procedural justice with regard to waste disposal facilities. In particular, the emergent voluntarism debate, whereby ethical siting such facilities is thought to be made possible through communities volunteering to host them (sometimes in exchange for community benefit packages), has brought procedural justice concerns centre stage. As indicated through Shrader-Frechette's observation regarding the intergenerational issues associated with notions of procedural justice, voluntarism raises its own set of concerns. For example, Gunderson and Rabe (1999: 212), writing about the Canadian experience, point to concerns that existing facility siting processes tend to rely on *single* volunteer communities where there is 'historic conversance with and economic dependence on nuclear energy and research'. This signals a set of concerns around waste siting, which connect with the kinds of distributional justice issues discussed above, whereby communities are subject to repeated and residual injustices.

Examining the Canadian context, Stanley (2009) brings a focus on a further dimension of the justice debate with regard to energy – namely epistemic justice, which refers to a set of concerns about the ways in which knowledge is treated, particularly within decision-making processes. Stanley (ibid.) examines the production and normalization of difference between Aboriginal knowledges and scientific 'expert' knowledge in the processes of nuclear waste management in Canada, highlighting the significance of representations of scale, i.e. Aboriginal knowledge was discursively represented as locked in time and space, while scientific knowledge was produced as objective, universal and placeless.

Thus far the focus has been on unpacking some of the key ways in which justice issues have been examined in the nuclear energy context. Within this and wider academic work there has, however, been a line of conceptual development which has thus far been left implicit. Clearly different justice concepts (e.g. recognition, procedure, distribution, epistemic justice) intersect and there are multiple variations in the characterization of justice issues within different contexts. It has been asserted, however, that these concepts do not provide the requisite depth needed to determine what injustice really means. For example, research examining distributional justice has been critiqued for identifying and signalling difference without explaining why 'socio-environmental inequality mattered and "injustice" was being produced' (Walker 2009: 204). In this context, research has responded to calls to 'consider "the just production of just geographical differences" [in order] to make sense critically of the many, if not infinite, varieties of unevenness that exist' (ibid.: 203, citing Harvey 1996). One response has been to develop a *capabilities* approach that can offer a basis for understanding justice issues in a richer and more satisfactory way. This approach goes beyond a focus solely on distribution and presence of facilities as indicators of injustice, by analysing the extent to which capabilities necessary to function as a healthy community are maintained or re-established in any given context. This represents a more flexible conceptual approach as it draws on everyday social practice, rather than abstract theorizing, in order to capture 'the breadth of what is threatened, what is seen as fair and unfair, and what is valued in a richer and more satisfactory way' (ibid.: 205).

The principles of participation and recognition have also come under critical scrutiny. In particular, questions have been posed about the implicit assumptions with which these well-worn notions can sometimes be weighted (ibid.). For example, in the same way that evidence of spatial-distributional inequity cannot be taken to signal injustice, the delivery of participatory processes and the attainment of recognition equally cannot be taken as indicative of 'justice' (ibid.). The capabilities perspective offers an approach which allows the specificities of different cases and the relevance of justice concerns to be brought into view, allowing a move beyond assumptions regarding what the presence of a facility and processes of participation or recognition mean in any particular place.

We argue that the theoretical construct of capabilities provides means for a deeper, more context-sensitive analysis of justice issues (Schlosberg 2004; Walker 2009). This focus on capabilities as a more flexible conceptual approach that allows for consideration of different forms of justice (e.g. procedural, distributional, intergenerational, epistemic justice) without privileging one over the other (Walker 2009). Here the emphasis is on examining the specific ways in which the capabilities necessary for both individual and community to flourish have been affected by an event, development or process. The work that has been undertaken on justice issues in this sector spans the material components of the process of nuclear power production, from resource extraction to power generation, but also gives insight into the immaterial, including the discursive construction of injustice.

This stock of concepts and research forms the basis for our analysis of nuclear justice discourses within the UK context. Though internationally there are multiple studies examining the treatment of justice issues in the nuclear energy context within policy and political discourse, far less research of this nature has been undertaken within the UK (for a notable exception, see Blowers 2010). In what follows we analyse UK policy and political discourse to reveal the ways in which justice issues have been treated, exploring how issues appear, and what this might mean for the future development of nuclear power in the UK.

Framing 'energy justice' in the nuclear context: exploring the UK case

Our central question in this chapter concerns how justice issues arise within UK policy and political discourse about nuclear energy, or whether the relevant concepts and issues appear at all. Where they do, we ask which aspects of justice concerns (e.g. procedural justice, distributional justice, or a more plural formulation such as that indicated by a capabilities approach) are identifiable within discourse and how are they characterized?

In what follows we examine framings of ethical and justice issues in the UK nuclear debate within the past decade or so. This has been an important period for nuclear energy in the UK, not least because strong policy indications that the UK would not pursue nuclear new build were reversed and policies implemented to bring forward its development. In the same period, following earlier setbacks, government launched a new strategy for developing and implementing a policy for long-term management of higher-activity radioactive wastes. Most recently, the disaster at the Fukushima nuclear power plant in March 2011 aroused concerns around the world about the safety of nuclear power. We follow major developments in the ways that ethical and justice issues have been treated in nuclear energy policy and political debates during this time.

In order to construct our narrative we unpick three key developments in the UK policy context where issues of ethics and justice have formed a part of the issue framings. 1) The ethics of radioactive waste management and the development of the Committee for Radioactive Waste Management; 2) the evolution of public engagement within the nuclear energy context; and 3) the reframing of nuclear energy as 'low carbon' and as central to mitigating climate change. We identify a narrowing of justice concerns within the discourse of UK policy institutions around nuclear energy and consider its implications for the development of a just energy system in the future.

Framing justice in the Committee for Radioactive Waste Management The long-term management of higher-activity radioactive waste has been a contentious issue in the UK for more than thirty years. Despite a policy of geological disposal for most of that time, successive attempts to carry out site investigations provoked opposition in communities identified as potential locations for a facility, resulting in 1997 in the last of a series of failures that left the policy in tatters. The resulting crisis forced recognition within government of the need for a different approach; crucially it created an opening wherein the importance of considering social and ethical issues in the disposal of nuclear waste could be made salient. Even though framed by the government in terms of the need to secure acceptability and legitimacy among the wider public, the possibilities this aim offered made room for a much wider set of concerns to be brought into political discourse.

The space for this wider debate was created, in particular, through the Managing Radioactive Waste Safely (MRWS) initiative, out of which, in 2003, the Committee on Radioactive Waste Management (CoRWM) was established. CoRWM's role was to evaluate the options for long-term management of radioactive waste and to make recommendations to government. Although its role was to advise government on the most appropriate technical option, the Committee's terms of reference mandated it to consider all aspects of the problem and noted that ministers hoped to find among its members skills in 'applying ethical principles to scientific and technical decision-making' (CoRWM 2006: 154). From its inception, therefore, the committee explicitly brought questions about ethics and justice associated with nuclear waste into the public debate: 'Ethical considerations played an important role in both the short-listing of options for radioactive management and, subsequently, in the assessment of the short-listed options' (Blowers 2006: 4).

CoRWM's guiding principles incorporate a conception of justice as fairness (compare Rawls 1958): 'To achieve fairness with respect to procedures, communities and future generations' (Blowers 2006: 29). This principle encompasses concepts of procedural, intra-generational and intergenerational justice. It was accompanied by principles committing CoRWM to 'uphold [...] the public interest by taking public and stakeholder views into account' and to 'secure a safe and sustainable environment' (ibid.). These issues were discussed at length within the Committee and were the subject of an expert workshop on ethics and radioactive waste management in which the challenges posed by each of these ethical principles and the conflicts that may arise between them were considered (ibid.).

This was part of what the Committee characterized as a holistic option evaluation process, which was designed to identify and consider the social and ethical as well as technical complexities associated with the different waste management options. Importantly, this awareness of the ethical dimensions of radioactive waste management and disposal influenced the way in which CoRWM conducted its public and stakeholder engagement process, ensuring that it was open to participation by any interested parties. It also influenced the Committee's deliberations, and these issues were brought to the fore in the recommendations developed by CoRWM to inform the decision-making processes with regard to radioactive waste management in the UK.

CoRWM finally recommended geological disposal as the best available option, with secure interim storage of the wastes until a site for a repository was found and constructed. Although there were disagreements among the Committee members, they concluded on the basis of an integrated appraisal process that geological disposal was the option that was safest and that best met the ethical principles that had been applied. In particular, the Committee noted that there was a very fundamental difference of views in the evidence that they received which was associated with the interpretation of intergenerational justice. These two views were summarized as 'deal with the waste now', a view that emphasizes the responsibilities of the present generation to minimize the burden of risk associated with the waste on future generations, and 'leave it until later', which places greater emphasis on the right of future generations to be free to make their own choices. The Committee concluded that: '[...] there is the view that we should dispose of the wastes as soon as practicable on the grounds that we cannot know what technological needs or powers may be available to our successors. The present generation should remove the burden imposed by its actions from the future. This view ultimately prevailed among the Committee' (CoRWM 2006: 40–1).

In addition to its advice to government about the technical waste management option to adopt, CoRWM also made recommendations about how this should be implemented. The Committee called for a siting process in which communities would be invited to participate on a voluntary basis, subject to confirmation of geological suitability, and would have the right to withdraw from the process up until the construction phase. In addition communities would be eligible for a negotiated package of benefits. From this point the focus turned to processes for addressing ethical as well as technical concerns associated with the voluntary siting of a geological disposal facility.

Following the submission of its recommendations in June 2006, CoRWM's role was reviewed and it was reconstituted with new terms of reference (ToR). Although the word 'ethics' still appears in the ToR, at the end of a long list of potential skills that members might bring to its work, unlike the original ToR, which focused on options appraisal, there is no explicit suggestion of how ethics might be applied. Similarly, although the Committee's role is to provide independent scrutiny and advice to government, its scrutiny of procedures and of community engagement processes as part of the search for a volunteer community is not framed explicitly in terms of a concern with procedural justice. Although some continuity of membership from its earlier existence may ensure that these ethical issues do not disappear entirely from its deliberations, the space initially opened up during the inception of CoRWM for such issues to be aired within political discourse has narrowed.

The period in which CoRWM was operating initially represented one which arose out of a context of public contestation and a crisis of legitimacy with regard to the actions of government. Where the committee meetings designed to address this crisis allowed room for social and ethical concerns to be discussed in wide-ranging terms, the subsequent terms of reference have brought a focus on the procedures for delivering geological disposal. Issues become narrowed to those of voluntarism and due process. Even though the MRWS policy framework has no explicit geographical focus, the search for a single disposal site has tended to involve, for quite pragmatic reasons, communities that have economic ties to the nuclear industry (see Gunderson and Rabe 1999). One consequence has been that the full range of pertinent justice issues is not represented and does not appear to be embedded within the ongoing development of these processes.

Framing justice as procedure and engagement CoRWM provides an unusual example of a policy actor that integrated ethical principles and different forms of justice into its practice, both in its own internal deliberations and in its engagement. As we noted, one prominent feature of CoRWM's practice was the effort to ensure fairness to all in its engagement with stakeholders and citizens. CoRWM was not, however, the only institutional actor to turn to direct engagement. Beginning around 1998, a number of engagement processes emerged in the nuclear sector that were associated with a variety of government bodies and industry organizations, and which focused largely on problems of facility decommissioning and radioactive waste management (Simmons et al. 2006).

Several organizations within the nuclear sector had experienced difficulties in their relations with wider society; these may have stopped short of the crisis faced by Nirex (the former waste management organization whose role has now been taken on by the Nuclear Decommissioning Authority – NDA) and central government over the policy for long-term management of higher-activity waste but they nevertheless called for a different approach. The turn to engagement and deliberation can therefore be seen as a search for legitimacy by government and other policy actors in the face of recurrent conflict and policy failure (ibid.). With this in mind, the question remains to what extent can such developments and the ways in which they are framed be seen to conform to the principle of procedural justice?

As much as the participatory turn was seen by many nuclear sector organizations as politically expedient it also took place within the wider context of a political culture in which active citizenship and local participation in decision-making was being encouraged by successive governments. While this was on the one hand a strategy to address a gradual but measurable decline in the popular legitimacy of democratic institutions, on the other hand it reflected the neoliberal rationality that by that time permeated the thinking and policies of parties of all political hues. This was slowly resulting in changing citizen expectations of public institutions and other large organizations. In this respect the trend towards active public engagement and deliberation can be seen as reflecting a growing sense that citizens, their associations and communities, as well as their formally elected representatives, should not only have a voice but should be more directly involved in decision-making processes that affected their lives.

In this respect it is interesting to note the expression of interest in the MRWS process that was made by three local councils in Cumbria. Though this did not result in a joint decision to volunteer for site investigations, given the history of extremely contentious, even acrimonious, relations during the 1990s between the communities of West Cumbria and Nirex, the fact that a local partnership was established at all indicates that many sceptical, even hostile, representatives of the citizens of West Cumbria saw the new approach as one in which they could consider engaging. This gives some sense of the subtle but significant change that has taken place.

Besides the focus on community voluntarism and the procedures surrounding this, there are other notable processes ongoing in relation to the UK's nuclear energy facilities. Two of the most significant being: (a) the NDA's National Stakeholder Forum and the Site Stakeholder Groups at the nuclear sites that it owns and manages. This acts as the forum through which the NDA engages with the representatives of local citizens about its operational activities and plans for its sites; and (b) the local consultations being carried out by current nuclear power plant operators on plans for new nuclear build at some of the existing nuclear sites (e.g. see EDF Energy 2011).

Despite the pragmatic motivations that may have initiated such responses, engagement processes that genuinely enact the principle of procedural justice, such as those adopted by CoRWM, which were outlined above, can potentially contribute to the creation of a just energy system. Questions remain, however, about the processes that have been enacted within the UK nuclear context and the extent to which these can be seen as commensurate with such principles. Certainly national consultation processes on nuclear energy undertaken by the UK government during 2006 and 2007 were heavily critiqued and subject to a court ruling which declared the processes 'misleading', 'flawed' and 'procedurally unfair' (BBC 2007). The mere presence of an engagement procedure, as noted earlier, is not then sufficient to ensure that the process is inclusive or fair in the way that it operates; and the difference between consultation and engagement is well recognized (Arnstein 1969).

This difference between form and substance can have significant implications for citizens' access to justice. The ability of such processes to deliver on their potential is vulnerable in at least two ways: first, they may be susceptible internally to the imposition of a narrow framing that effectively excludes the perspectives, concerns or needs of less powerful actors (Chilvers and Burgess 2008); and secondly, any advances that are made within such processes may be undermined by external decisions and processes that weaken or nullify their impact on policy, with the additional consequence of stoking cynicism (Mackerron and Berkhout 2009). One trend that has had an impact on the framing of both policy and process, has been the growing prominence of climate change in policy discourse around nuclear energy.

Framing nuclear through climate change: trading off for a just energy system In this final strand of our analysis we explore another way in which issues of ethics and justice figure in UK nuclear policy discourse by examining the framing of nuclear energy as essential to decarbonization. the framing of nuclear energy as essential to decarbonization. Nuclear power has for several years been presented in UK energy policy discourse as a low-carbon form of energy supply that is a necessary part of the solution to climate change (e.g. BERR 2008; DECC 2012). This framing has brought with it a discourse around intergenerational ethics and a particular treatment of these issues in relation to nuclear energy.

In UK policy discourse it is possible to see how intergenerational justice and ethical issues associated with nuclear energy have been quite explicitly posed as a trade-off with those that arise as a consequence of climate change. The UK government's 2007 consultation document on new nuclear build states: 'There are also important ethical issues to consider around whether to create new nuclear waste, including the ethical implications of not allowing nuclear power to play a role, and the risks of failing to meet long-term carbon emissions targets' (DTI 2007: 25).

Within this reframing of nuclear as a solution to climate change, then, it is possible to see how justice concerns are first brought into the debate, and subsequently repositioned as entailing only those inter-generational ethical issues associated with the long-term storage of waste or the broadly defined risks associated with not meeting emission targets. The consultation document goes on to state: 'The Government has taken a preliminary view that *the balance of ethical considerations* does not require ruling out the option of new nuclear power' (ibid.: 25, emphasis added). Here it is possible to see more clearly the second aspect of this framing that is central to justice debates: the notion that ethical issues can be weighed against one another and, crucially, that trade-offs between them can and should be made.

In this framing of justice, the multifarious concerns encompassed within debates about nuclear justice are thus reduced to a simplistic trade-off between different kinds of risks. The important point here is not so much the normative designation of climate change risk as inherently more problematic than the risks of nuclear energy, but that this framing of the problem does not allow room for consideration of the complex and interrelated justice issues that arise with nuclear energy development (see Pralle and Boscarino 2011, who note how this sort of framing can obscure more fundamental issues). Though posed narrowly as a risk–risk trade-off, rather than an explicitly ethical one, the notion of 'trading off' the potential for *negative impacts* from climate change against those from nuclear energy makes it salient in justice terms. This is because, if concerns about justice are fundamen-tally ones about harms being inflicted which reduce an individual's or community's capabilities to function as healthy beings, then talk about negative impacts arising from decisions is, in one way or another, talk about justice.

Though the interest here is in UK political and policy discourse, it is interesting to note that this formulation of the debate runs through numerous accounts within wider public discourse from many other prominent voices. In particular, the Fukushima disaster is notable for having triggered similar framings within media debate about nuclear energy. Mark Lynas, a public figure within sustainability debates, wrote: 'There is no doubt that the explosions and radioactive releases at the stricken Fukushima Daiichi plant represent the worst nuclear disaster since the explosion at the Chernobyl power plant in Ukraine in 1986. However [...] if we abandon nuclear, prepare for a future of catastrophic global warming, imperilling the survival of civilisation and much of the earth's biosphere' (Lynas 2011).

This particular framing, while again not overtly posing a trade-off between justice issues, implicitly brings such matters into view by focusing on particular kinds of negative *impacts*. Although here the focus is on the impacts of nuclear accidents, rather than radioactive waste, once again the whole range of justice concerns relating to nuclear power become subsumed in one overarching meta-narrative. We find a continuation of the trend whereby the debate is treated as one that involves an uncomplicated trade-off between the diverse intra- and intergenerational issues posed by nuclear accidents and the consequences of climate change.

The justice issues that run through but often remain implicit in the risk trade-off discourse linking nuclear and climate change are also at times brought explicitly into the debate by proponents on both sides, with the controversy over the future role of nuclear energy dividing the green lobby. In 2011 British environmentalists George Monbiot and Sir Jonathon Porritt engaged in a heated debate over nuclear power from the pages of their respective blogs (Monbiot 2011; Porritt 2011). Monbiot is a journalist and is one of a number of prominent individuals in the environmental movement to have become convinced of the necessity of nuclear power to combat climate change. Porritt is a former director of Friends of the Earth UK and former chair of the government-appointed Sustainable Development Commission, and remains an equally convinced critic of nuclear power. Monbiot writes: 'The same goes for Jonathon's comments about intergenerational justice. He maintains that the industry's costs will fall on future generations [...] But what about the consequences for intergenerational justice arising from the extra climate change caused by abandoning nuclear power? No one is setting money aside to meet these costs. No one could' (Monbiot 2011).

This brings us to argue that the debate about climate change and nuclear energy can act to subsume ethical and justice concerns in ways that work to obscure important questions about energy system transitions more widely and the range of justice issues that might be important. Where we might expect the debate about climate change mitigation and energy system transitions to open up a space for questions about justice to emerge, we find a narrowing of debate to one of risk–risk trade-offs. As a further identifiable way in which justice issues have appeared within UK policy and political discourse, this represents a narrow framing of the relevant issues, closing down, rather than opening up, possibilities for consideration of energy justice and what this might mean in the UK context and in relation to nuclear energy in particular. This development in the discursive framing of nuclear energy illustrates how decarbonization has been used to re-configure the contours of the justice debate as it relates to nuclear, and draws attention to some of the complexities, interdependencies and tensions which demand consideration by any serious attempt to apply justice principles to global energy production.

Concluding discussion

We have analysed three developments within UK policy discourse to offer insight into how justice issues have been shaped, either implicitly or explicitly, in relation to nuclear energy. Each development has pro-vided an institutional site for analysis, but these discourses and practices are entangled in various ways and are part of the same story about the emerging field of justice debates within UK nuclear policy discourse. In concluding we weave a narrative through our analysis of the different developments we have explored, drawing out the interconnections and examining the ways in which some justice issues have been included while others have been omitted. Crucially, we take up Stirling's (2005) notions of 'closing down' and 'opening up' to explore the wider im-plications of political discourse for fostering or limiting consideration of justice issues. In understanding that which is omitted, left unsaid or unexplored, we offer insight into the contours of the UK political discourse, which we argue holds material consequences for the ways in which nuclear energy has been and will be developed into the future.

In his work on social appraisal and decision-making, Stirling (ibid.) draws a distinction between opening up and closing down in the framing of technology choices or social concerns more generally. Stirling explains opening up as entailing an emphasis on 'revealing to wider policy discourses any open-endedness, contingency and cap-acity for the exercise of agency' (ibid.: 229). The focus is therefore on posing alternatives to emerging recommendations, highlighting neglected issues, including marginalized perspectives, triangulating contending knowledges, and considering ignored uncertainties. By contrast closing down refers to framings which entail cutting through the messy, intractable and conflict-prone diversity of interests and perspectives to develop an authoritative, prescriptive, unitary recom-mendation to inform policy decisions.

An opening up approach, while offering outcomes that Stirling suggests might be 'ambiguous or equivocal in terms of what con-stitutes the best way forward', delivers a process that 'renders those courses of action that are identified as displaying overall good or poor performance all the more robust as a basis for policy' (ibid.: 229). An open approach to framing, either within processes designed explicitly to inform decisions, as was the case in the consultation on radioactive waste management options conducted by the UK's Committee on Radioactive Waste Management as one stage of the Managing Radioactive Waste Safely process (see CoRWM 2006), or within wider political discourse, appears congruent with the kind of process that is required to bring a fuller consideration of justice issues into debate and decision-making about energy systems and proposed low-carbon transitions. Conversely, the existing debate relating to nuclear energy, we argue, acts to close down as it incorporates space for justice concerns only implicitly and principally in terms of procedures that have been viewed by critics as co-optation and pacification of opposition, rather than as the triumph of procedural justice (e.g. Blowers and Sundqvist 2010; Sundqvist and Elam 2010).

Where in the CoRWM process we found examples of justice concerns being addressed explicitly and in more open ways, the frames and terms of reference have since been significantly narrowed. The open framing that was seen by CoRWM's first members as necessary to arrive at a legitimate and acceptable policy for higher activity radioactive wastes is nowhere in evidence in the policy discourse around new nuclear build that subsequently overtook it and effected a narrowing of frame which reduced the ethical issues associated with nuclear energy to a risk-risk trade-off with climate change.

The emergence of heightened global political concern about climate change not only provided a powerful device with which to reframe nuclear power and a moral imperative to legitimize new nuclear build but effectively circumvented the ethical barrier of the UK's unresolved problem of long-term radioactive waste management by mobilizing a superordinate global discourse: in moral terms, climate change effectively trumped radioactive waste, this particular framing itself representing a narrative which closes down through its tendencies to produce only the smallest range of possible outputs, as the problem and solutions are reduced to a choice between enduring one set of (largely pre-framed) risks and associated justice issues or the other.

In the unfolding debate about nuclear new build that gathered pace in the latter part of the 2000s, ethical concerns about nuclear waste that had been central to the objections of many opponents were also, in part, further countered by reference to the progress being made by CoRWM to find an ethically legitimate solution to the problems of waste (see DTI 2007). This use of CoRWM's recommendations within the new build debate was evident even though it was made clear in the report to government that they applied only to waste arising from existing activities. The lasting legacies of the much wider-ranging debates about the justice issues associated with nuclear energy appear to lie only in the lingering risk–risk trade-off framing arising through the locating of nuclear energy as solution to climate change, and in the ongoing concern with voluntarism.

Though there is a high level of emergent and ongoing activity around processes of public engagement and consultation, such as that around voluntarism, this appears again as narrowly focused. Rather than representing governance spaces in which efforts are made to open up the diversity of concerns and perspectives on different approaches to identified issues, they are often restricted to specific concerns, such as changes to local road infrastructure (e.g. see EDF Energy 2011). Though the broader processes we imply might be seen to draw out already slow movement in the development of nuclear facilities, evidence from other countries is indicative of the importance of opening up space for recognition of alternative perspectives. For example, in relation to siting geological waste facilities Gunderson and Rabe (1999) have pointed to the importance of recognizing different approaches (e.g. multiple as opposed to single sites, near-surface disposal) for the attainment of successful siting procedures.

The interconnections between the different developments we have briefly examined here help to provide a picture of the ways in which justice issues have been taken up and wielded in debates about nuclear power. If these are the issues that we find within the UK policy discourse relating to nuclear justice, what then is excluded and what might the effects of this be for envisioning a just energy system and materializing future transitions that are understood as more than purely technological; as imbued with power to reconfigure social life in ways that can produce injustices? As a first point, any development of the policy debate around nuclear in line with the justice literature (i.e. toward a focus on fostering or protecting capabilities) is notably absent. The importance of an approach to energy justice that emphasizes capabilities is that it recognizes the specifics of different social and cultural contexts and allows for consideration of the complexity of justice issues. The ways in which nuclear energy has been dealt with in policy discourse obscure such complexity, potentially making the goal of a just energy system unachievable.

A second issue relates to the way that accidents and the justice issues implied by these have been notably absent from UK debates about nuclear energy development. The major accident at Fukushima provoked national governments around the world to respond in some way. It is notable that in the UK, the events at Fukushima were situated as part of 'learning from experience' (see Butler et al. 2011). This allowed for continued adherence to the 'principle of *continuous improvement*', meaning new nuclear power plant construction would take place concurrently with the development of more safety measures, procedures and knowledge (HM Chief Inspector of Nuclear Installations 2011). This implies a possibility of the elimination of risk and associated justice issues should an accident happen through processes of technological design. Indeed, it may be seen as reflective of a potentially problematic policy logic within the UK for proper consideration of justice concerns; that is, the tendency for issues of harms and capabilities to be reduced to discourses of risk.

Our final point concerns the ways in which an energy justice perspective informed by the notion of capabilities, which takes in the different dimensions of justice across time and space, brings into view a complex picture of the challenges that nuclear energy poses. It forces recognition of how decisions about nuclear energy in the UK have implications not just for communities living near UK facilities, but for populations elsewhere on the globe who are involved in the extraction and refinement of nuclear fuel. A full understanding of nuclear energy justice must therefore encompass consideration of this complex of interrelated issues and their implications. To consider justice issues in a more complete and satisfactory way, then, the perspective must broaden beyond the boundaries of the national and bring into view the injustices that arise across the world in the complex of relationships and interconnections that make up the system of nuclear energy production. This would bring with it a questioning of the imperatives for nuclear energy development, including increasing energy demand. Considering nuclear energy in this more open way would make it possible to see a wide range of approaches and courses of action that could contribute to what might be described as more just decisions, processes and practices in the sector. Centrally, such processes would take in the wider global implications of decisions, including considerations about climate change, while focusing on the specifics of particular cases. We contend that if justice concerns are treated, as they have been, in ways that do not facilitate engagement with the complexity of the issues at hand, processes of energy system development will fail to address such issues in ways commensurate with their implications.

9 | Justice in energy system transitions: the case of carbon capture and storage

DUNCAN MCLAREN, KRISTIAN KRIEGER
AND KAREN BICKERSTAFF

Introduction

The future of energy supply for human societies poses enormous challenges. Easily accessible fossil fuel resources are diminishing and, with burgeoning demand for energy, serious concerns are now being raised about future energy systems and their environmental, economic and social footprints. There is an emerging political consensus that greenhouse gas emissions must be cut dramatically by 2050. Across the developed world there is a substantial and growing body of policies and measures for climate change mitigation, many of which focus on reducing the carbon intensity of systems of energy production and consumption. Such systemic transitions involve complex socio-technical transformations that raise fundamental issues of social justice at multiple scales across nations and generations. A transition towards a low-carbon energy system in the context of climate change mitigation can at first glance be understood as promoting justice, whether as an act of fairness towards future generations or because the climate change problem is underpinned by fundamental spatial and historical injustices (e.g. Shue 1992; Gardiner et al. 2010; Gardiner 2011). However, work exploring the justice dimensions of low-carbon energy systems has raised concerns about the spatial and temporal effects of particular transitional pathways. This existing literature has tended to focus on the located contexts of particular energy system components and the distributional (un)fairness of generation and waste technologies (e.g. Bell et al. 2005). This is not atypical of academic approaches to environmental justice issues, which, as Schlosberg (2007) notes, are strongly rooted in a liberal distributive justice paradigm. Although such 'located' analyses are important in understanding the fairness of particular energy processes, we argue here that this limits our ability to understand justice relations between actors and across time and space. Not only are the conceptual and methodological means to assess justice in a distributional sense – across different time–space horizons (near, far, present, future) – lacking, but an integrated consideration of the ways in which procedural injustices (issues of access to decision-making, respect and recognition) interact to create and exacerbate distributional injustice is also needed.

We argue that there is a strong case for considering both the distributional and procedural justice issues from a 'whole systems' perspective (WSP). It must be recognized that, to date, whole-systems approaches to energy have not generally explored or emphasized justice considerations, being more typically rooted in econometric or technical system modelling work (e.g. Strachan et al. 2009; Ekins and Skea 2009). But a 'just' WSP could helpfully address the ways in which (in)justices are configured across the life cycle of an energy system and how they impact differentially upon stakeholders. Such an approach recognizes energy technologies as part of a complex set of other technologies, physical surroundings, people and procedures (Hughes 1989; Geels 2005), as well as placing value on epistemic diversity and democratic access to (and power to affect) decision-making (Cook and Ferris 2007; Evans et al. 1995; Stasinopoulos et al. 2009).

This chapter develops and applies concepts of whole-system think-ing, with specific attention to experience with carbon capture and storage (CCS), to enrich the conceptualization of energy justice as applied to low-carbon technologies. We begin with a brief review of a small but developing 'energy justice' literature – drawing specifically on social science enquiry centring on nuclear power, onshore wind and more recently CCS. We make the case for a dynamic WSP, reflexively incorporating principles of justice across the full 'system' life cycle and range of stakeholders. We draw on this approach to develop an analysis of how CCS has (and could) generate justice concerns. Finally we draw some conclusions and offer reflections for future research.

Energy justice, participation and instrumentalism

Here we consider how the social science debate about the transi-tion to low-carbon energy systems has engaged with concepts and principles of justice, specifically those relating to procedural issues. In particular we consider how participation has become a key trope in policy and research efforts.

The most systematic engagement with justice concepts and de-bates in energy research relates to the social dimensions of nuclear power systems. Much of this literature has addressed the distributive inequalities associated with particular phases of the nuclear cycle, notably ethical issues associated with the management and disposal of nuclear waste. Justice arguments have tended to centre on distributional outcomes and the direct or indirect targeting of vulnerable groups such as indigenous and economically marginal communities (Blowers and Leroy 1994; Gowda and Easterling 2000).

Attention has also rested on procedural responses to unfair outcomes in the form of policies of community volunteerism and compensation (e.g. Kunreuther and Easterling 1996; Gowda and Easterling 2000; Bickerstaff 2012). It has been suggested that community volunteerism expands opportunities for local publics and stakeholders to participate in siting decisions and that compensation measures offer a corrective to unfair distributional outcomes (Kunreuther and Easterling 1996). But others have contested this view (see Butler and Simmons 2010; Kuhn 1998; Shrader-Frechette and Cooke 2004), for instance, on the grounds that only already disadvantaged communities are likely to volunteer.

To a lesser degree, work has addressed the siting of power stations and the related fairness of distributional outcomes and decision-making (e.g. Aldrich 2005), and the distributional effects of uranium mining and milling (Taebi and Kloosterman 2008; Hoffman 2001). In the US context Endres (2009) uses the concept of 'nuclear colonialism' to describe the unequal distribution of benefits and burdens associated with mining, imposed upon Native American populations (for fuller discussion see Butler and Simmons 2010).

Collectively, these studies do not examine how participation might be delivered across, or with respect to, the whole life cycle. But it seems likely that limited and poor-quality participation in specific life-cycle phases may have contributed not only to breakdowns in trust with respect to communities affected by that specific phase, but also to the emergence of justice impacts and conflicts elsewhere in the life cycle, if only because once a nuclear power station is operating, both mining and waste disposal activities will be required.

Turning, briefly, to social science research addressing opposition to located large-scale renewable energy developments, particularly wind parks (Upreti and Van der Horst 2004; Wolsink 2007), we see similar concerns regarding a lack of effective (and early) participation in siting (and more broadly innovation). These protests can be viewed from a distributive justice perspective using the proximity principle, i.e. the proximity of existing and planned wind farms affects economic values (e.g. of land) (Devine-Wright 2007; Van der Horst 2007). On the other hand, a number of scholars (Bell et al. 2005; Upreti and Van der Horst 2004; Van der Horst 2007) have rejected explanations of resistance based exclusively on spatial-distributive arguments of a NIMBY (not-in-my-backyard) character and pointed to the shortcomings of top-down decision-making processes. This literature echoes strong arguments for enhanced and especially early 'upstream' participation found more widely in new technology development and deployment (Rogers-Hayden and Pidgeon 2007; Stirling 2008). Upstream participation is seen as essential to prevent premature closure of issue-framing and decision options.[1] However, widening participation in the processes whereby problems and solutions are defined may be resisted, as it would challenge a key component of exclusive political power (Markusson, Shackley and Evar 2012).

More broadly, and focusing on energy consumption in general, concerns have notably emerged about the implications of carbon pricing for those most vulnerable groups in society (DTI 2003; Walker and Day 2012) and that access to particular forms of low-carbon generation (for instance solar PV) will be socially regressive because they are preferentially available to homeowners with access to capital (e.g. DECC 2012).

Finally, if we consider recent experience with CCS development and deployment, we see a similar pattern emerging. Conflicts have been characterized as driven by local concerns about health and safety risks relating to CO_2 storage and consequential issues such as liability (e.g. Bradbury et al. 2009; Brunsting et al. 2010). Where risks are distributed spatially or temporally there is a clear dimension of potential injustice. However, perceived and expressed risks have often been framed in research and policy primarily as local issues, with broader procedural concerns – including issues relating to the policy efficacy of CCS and the perpetuation of the fossil fuel industry – categorized as 'secondary' (Hammond and Shackley 2010; Bradbury 2012). Set within the dominant scientific framing of CCS as contributing to climate mitigation, this has helped – unintentionally – to devalue justice concerns at both local and wider scales. Yet some research does underline that the perceived risks themselves are perhaps not central to opposition (e.g. Bradbury et al. 2009), but come to the fore as a result of their perceived imposition through inaccessible or prejudiced decision-making with poor or limited participation opportunities.

In the literature, much of the discussion of participation has focused on the instrumental goal of increasing the social acceptability of a predetermined outcome (i.e. the siting of CCS infrastructures). There has been some discussion of normative and substantive goals; notably the need for recognition of 'plural knowledges' in the governance of CCS (Whitmarsh et al. 2011). Bielicki and Stephens (2008) recognize that where there are conflicts in values, there is little point in communicating technical information alone, if at all. Yet much engagement as routinely practised has started from a position that implicitly devalues public knowledge as inferior or invalid compared with scientific knowledge. Bäckstrand et al. (2011) note the gap between public and scientists' views of CCS, and the predominance of work intended to overcome public acceptance barriers to the adoption of CCS, with an 'agenda to increase public understanding of CCS and so remove barriers to deployment and facilitate implementation of the technology' (p. 277). Such an agenda is based on a 'knowledge gap' approach which avoids wider social and economic issues, and excludes consideration of the fundamental question of 'what is the problem to which CCS is a potential solution?'

Malone et al. (2010) argue that many of the surveys and polls used to gather public views on CCS are of little value, as the participants have 'limited knowledge', and can hold what De Best-Waldhober and Daamen (2006) describe as 'pseudo-opinions'. The authors warn that such approaches risk confirming assumptions built into the framing of questions; and call for the application of deeper and more sophisticated stakeholder engagement tools. As other examples of recent and current engagement (Brunsting et al. 2010; Desbarats et al. 2010) also hint, all too often there is a shared assumption among researchers that there exists an 'objective reality' of low risk, in which the technology is benign, and opposition unreasonable. This perhaps reflects a normative concern informed by a framing of climate change as an issue of international and intergenerational justice. Nonetheless it results in a very partial consideration of justice.

What is clear from this brief review is that the bulk of existing literature on the social dimensions of low-carbon energy technologies has spatially and temporally delimited and separated system components – for the most part concentrating on downstream processes and infrastructures (Butler and Simmons 2010). We also see a recognition (and often critique) of the constrained roles in decision-making that communities (past, present and future) have been afforded. However, a theme running through much of this work is an underlying instrumentalism – a concern with diagnosing the causes of opposition, and from this, articulating modes of participation that will support socially acceptable siting processes and outcomes. As such the policy and research emphasis on (more) participation remains somehow distant from procedural justice issues such as power, voice and access to early decision-making and recognition of difference in fundamental values and beliefs. In what follows we offer an alternative framing of energy justice that is rooted in an analysis of procedural justice challenges across whole systems.

Low-carbon energy systems and embedding principles of procedural justice

In light of the relatively partial treatment of energy justice in the existing literature, we aim in this chapter to explore the utility of a 'whole systems' perspective (WSP). This approach has attracted increasing attention in the scholarly community. A whole-systems perspective, analysing 'the energy system as a whole', is central to the vision of the UK Engineering and Physical Sciences Research Council (EPSRC) and the UK Energy Research Centre (Ekins 2004; DTI 2003).

However, this work has, in general, centred on energy modelling and the socio-techno-economic analysis of the whole UK energy system from supply of fuels for generation of energy through to end use of energy. As such the conventional understanding of a holistic view on energy systems is dominated by the disciplines of economics and engineering, and stimulates technocratic policy approaches (Markusson, Shackley and Evar 2012). Such modelling draws on a long history, with the MARKAL (MARKet ALlocation) model family most common in the UK, having been developed by the International Energy Agency (IEA) since the late 1970s (Strachan et al. 2009). These models are normally 'optimization' models aimed at minimizing the system's cost, and do not typically consider the distribution of costs and benefits. Moreover, such models focus on infrastructure and resources alongside supply and demand, but are limited in their capacities to present and understand the dynamics in, and complexity of, energy systems (Foxon et al. 2010; Keeney and Nair 1975; Roche et al. 2010). But technological systems (such as energy systems) are always also social systems. As Hughes argues, 'technological systems contain messy, complex, problem-solving components. They are both socially constructed and society shaping' (Hughes 1989: 51).

The WSP reflects these insights of energy systems as complex, socio-technological systems. Concretely, a WSP widens the analytical focus in project work in a number of ways. First, one important aspect is the analysis of all stages of the life cycle of a technology, from research and innovation processes to the technology's use in/impact on everyday life (Cook and Ferris 2007; Stasinopoulos et al. 2009).

Secondly, another significant aspect is the recognition that technical processes are embedded and underpinned by socio-economic and political systems (Cook and Ferris 2007; Stasinopoulos et al. 2009).

This embeddedness has led Hitchings (2003) to propose a multilayered model of systems, from the product level to business, industry and political system levels. As a consequence, a WSP necessarily extends beyond a traditionally economics/engineering-driven analysis of energy issues (Foxon et al. 2010) to include further disciplinary perspectives, such as sociology, geography or political science, so as to capture the social processes underlying energy systems (Cook and Ferris 2007; Hitchings 2003; Mao et al. 2010). This has, for example, stimulated growing consideration of energy consumption, and behavioural change as a means of delivering low-carbon energy transitions (Ekins and Skea 2009).

Thirdly, the social embeddedness and need for wider analytical perspective implicit in the WSP also translates into calls for an inclusion of research and stakeholders from a range of disciplines and backgrounds into the project analysis and design (Cook and Ferris 2007; Evans et al. 1995; Stasinopoulos et al. 2009). As Funtowicz and Ravetz (1993: 744) argue: where 'facts are uncertain, values in dispute, stakes high and decisions urgent' the scientific process must be open to scrutiny and the pool of expert voices must be widened. With a WSP researchers can better engage with the complex interests and emergent characteristics of post-normal science. We do, at the same time, recognize the limits to approaching whole systems. A WSP can very easily be no more than an expanded descriptive tool that adds social components and includes all stages of a life cycle, but does little more to extend our conceptualization of energy justice. WSPs can be simplistic and reductionist – assuming systems hold a clear and linear purpose. On the other hand, as Funtowicz and Ravetz (ibid.) point out, complex emergent systems in which components have features such as morality, intentionality, consciousness and/or foresight may lead to irreducible conflicts and uncertainties. With these concerns in mind, our approach is to apply three key whole-systems principles as a device to expand our spatial and temporal conceptualization of energy justice. These principles are:

- A commitment to holism – to make connections between the various (albeit) shifting components of energy systems.
- A recognition of the socio-technical configuration of energy systems.
- The inclusion of otherness; the ambition of widening the peer community.

We argue that these principles can be helpfully realized through a procedural justice lens; one that recognizes that distributional and procedural injustices are often inextricably interlinked. For instance, disadvantaged groups and communities, suffering from poor environmental quality, and potentially poor health as a consequence, are also unlikely to enjoy the capabilities needed to participate effectively in decisions regarding new developments. Schlosberg (2007: 74) powerfully describes the interrelatedness of different conceptions of environmental justice: 'one must have recognition in order to have real participation; one must have participation in order to get equity; further equity would make more participation possible, which would strengthen community functioning, and so on'.

But what do 'fair processes' actually look like? Since this chapter is concerned with the socio-technical energy system, a natural starting point to gain a better understanding of fair processes is to explore the science and technology policy literature. However, this body of literature has made only limited excursions into the territory of fair process. Joss and Brownlea (1999), for instance, suggest aspirational criteria for procedural justice in the development of science and technology policy, including opportunities for social actors to challenge existing, and present alternative, contextual perspectives; safeguards for genuinely symmetric and two-way communication that reflects and integrates different perspectives of participants; the impartial, consistent treatment of all participants in the decision-making process, as well as transparent and accountable decision-making and implementation processes. Abels (2007) has subsequently examined the use made of participatory techniques as tools to promote legitimacy and accountability in technology policy assessment, and concluded that they generally fall well short of claims made for them as a form of deliberative democracy. A more promising venue is the literature on environmental justice (Schlosberg 2007; Walker 1998; Walker and Bulkeley 2006). Insofar as it engages with procedural concerns, the environmental justice literature too tends to focus on participation. But participation alone, *in sensu* the mere involvement of social actors in the decision-making process, is inadequate to ensure procedural justice. Participation does not guarantee access to meaningful information, nor full recognition of the rights and needs of all affected social groups, and in addition procedural justice requires impartiality, consistency and transparency (Maiese 2004) – both within and beyond the process of participation. Capek (1993) identifies activists' calls for accurate information, respectful and unbiased hearings, and democratic participation as fundamental to the 'environmental justice'

TABLE 9.1 Principles of procedural justice

Components	Details
Information	Access to/interpretation of information, with fair notice and bilateral communication at all times
Participation	Participation, with a right to be heard (and if necessary, represented), to refute challenges and engage in the procedures at all stages
Impartiality	Impartiality in the form of an independent judge or panel making (or overseeing the making of) consistent decisions
Accessibility	Accessibility of a venue (a hearing, court or tribunal) which is affordable, timely and treats participants and third parties with courtesy
Objectivity	That decisions and rulings are clearly based on, and can consider the merits of, the issue, and reasons are given and explained for all decisions
Respect and recognition	Respect for and recognition of different backgrounds, cultures and capabilities that those affected might have

Source: Based on McLaren (2012a)

framing. Hunold and Young (1998) argue that in siting hazardous facilities a just participatory decision-making process would be inclusive, provide for engagement throughout the policy process, provide equal resources and access to information to all participants, and deliver authoritative binding decisions through shared decision-making.

In this context, we can also learn from a review of procedures and fairness in other disciplines, in particular legal studies and practice. In general, participation is also a central principle of procedural justice in criminal and civil law in many jurisdictions, and in systems through which civil disputes and infringements of rights may be resolved. Participation is understood as critical in preventing the arbitrary exercise of power and in ensuring legitimacy. To serve these purposes, however, Solum (2004) – writing on legal justice systems but with wider applicability – emphasizes that participation must be genuine, and not instrumental.

Participation therefore is complemented by and associated with other principles that need to be incorporated into the design of procedures. For instance, in international arbitration, participation is associated with a set of rights: right of standing; right of composition of tribunal; right to be heard; right to due deliberation; and the right to a reasoned judgment (Gaffney 1999). Fairly similar procedural justice principles arise from examination of negotiation and mediation procedures within and between businesses. Kumar (1996) suggests: bilateral communication, impartiality, refutability, explanation, familiarity and courtesy. Organizational procedures are perceived to be 'more fair' when affected individuals have an opportunity to either influence the decision process or offer input, particularly through two-way communication (Fearne et al. 2004). The Århus convention of the UN Economic Committee for Europe[2] also makes it clear that participation alone is inadequate, as it clearly defines additional rights to freedom of information, and to access to justice (in the form of access to the courts or some other adequate appeal mechanism).

Table 9.1 provides an overview of these components, linking concepts from legal, business, arbitration and environmental justice.

In some respects these principles could be considered to merely elaborate what is meant by fair participation. But even so, they clarify that participation is not something 'provided' or 'enabled' by a decision-maker: it is something that can be demanded as a right by an affected stakeholder. And it would be illogical to conclude that such stakeholders are somehow limited to those geographically or temporally present persons to whom a decision-maker already has a formal political or other accountability.

With this more comprehensive conception of procedural justice, we can usefully turn to the coverage of both distributional and procedural concerns in the CCS literature.

Applying the WSP framework: justice and CCS

We start this section with a brief overview of the nature (and variety) of CCS infrastructures, and progress in the deployment of the technologies. We then structure the main analysis of procedural justice around the life cycle of CCS research and development, considering research and development, construction and deployment, operation, CO_2 transport, CO_2 storage and decommissioning (see Figure 9.1).

Carbon capture and storage (CCS) technologies are procedures for reducing emissions of carbon dioxide (CO_2) in the burning of fossil fuels.[3] CCS is distinctive to most low-carbon technologies in that the process is essentially divided into three stages – capture, transport and storage. Capture and storage will usually take place in geographically different locations, with transport linking the two. At present CCS technologies remain largely in the research, development and early demonstration stages. There have been numerous demonstration

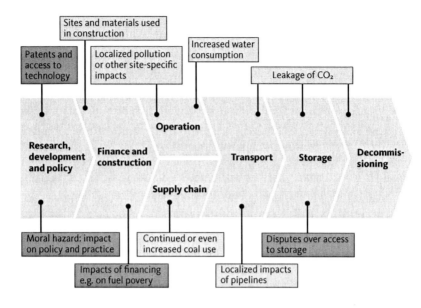

Note: The flags indicate potential impacts: pale ones for mainly local, site-related impacts (both direct and indirect); dark ones for more generic, mainly indirect impacts, such as conflicts over access to and use of carbon storage.

9.1 Potential impacts across the CCS development chain

projects exploring different sections of the CCS chain at smaller scales, with some storage operations having over ten years' operating experience. However, proposals for integrated commercial-scale demonstrations have yet to come to fruition, despite significant levels of government support (Markusson, Shackley and Evar 2012). Since De Coninck et al. (2009) called unsuccessfully for strong international co-operation on demonstration of full-scale integrated CCS systems, very few of the schemes identified then have progressed, and several trial or demonstration-scale proposals have been cancelled or postponed, including all those that were competing for financial support from the UK government in 2010 (Markusson, Shackley and Evar 2012; Global CCS Institute 2012; Watson 2012). Significant technical, economic, political and financial uncertainties remain – yet public and stakeholder contestation over siting, impacts, funding and other issues has already been intense. In 2012 the Global CCS Institute reported just two large-scale integrated CCS projects under construction in the power sector.

CCS is often considered crucial in the long-term carbon abatement strategies of many countries and international organizations (Markusson, Shackley and Evar 2012; Watson 2012). It features heavily in many future scenarios developed by the International Energy Agency (2009) and the Intergovernmental Panel on Climate Change (IPCC 2005). For the UK government, CCS has been described as having 'a key part to play in ensuring that we keep the lights on at the same time as fighting climate change' (Huhne 2011). Watson (2012), in a detailed review of the uncertainties facing CCS, concludes that a comprehensive set of policy interventions to reduce uncertainties at all stages of the life cycle, including resolving storage liabilities, would be required if CCS were to realize its potential.

CCS is set apart from other low-carbon energy technologies by the fact that rather than replacing fossil-fuelled power with a low-carbon source (renewables or nuclear, for example), it enables continued use of fossil fuels with all their other existing implications. Because CCS on power plants is not fully commercially proven, the concept of 'capture readiness' has been suggested by some as an interim policy goal – as a means of ensuring the capability to retrofit capture equipment on to new fossil-fuelled power plants at some future date.

While CCS is seen as vital by some, others claim it is an unattractive option and should not be a part of the transition towards a low-carbon economy (Meadowcroft and Langhelle 2011). A number of projects so far have met some level of opposition – primarily, but not exclusively, with respect to the storage element. Perhaps the most high-profile case of public opposition to CCS concerns the town of Barendrecht in the Netherlands, where public opposition caused a demonstration project, which was planned to store CO_2 in depleted gas fields under the town, to be halted (Brunsting et al. 2011). Similar difficulties have been encountered in Germany (Brunsting et al. 2010).

In the analysis which follows we review the life cycle of CCS, for simplicity dividing it into three main phases – 'research and innovation'; 'development and implementation'; and 'transport and storage' – and explore the procedural justice components associated with each, as well as justice issues that arise beyond the immediate CCS technology life cycle.

The research and innovation process A WSP reminds us that the potential justice implications of CCS do not start only with its deployment in practice but already in the research and innovation process. Moreover, the WSP directs our attention to the political and socio-economic embeddedness of technology development and its effects on a wide range of stakeholders beyond the technology developers and users.

Specifically, the research and innovation process involves at least two potential ethical challenges. The first one is that the promises of CCS may generate a moral hazard for climate mitigation, with consequences for the level and distribution of climate impacts. Secondly, patents in the CCS technologies might be claimed by commercial entities such that their effective deployment relies on wealth transfers from those already unjustly impacted by climate change, to those who benefited economically from causing it.

The potential for moral hazard is especially pertinent in the political sphere (Meadowcroft and Langhelle 2011; Pollak and Wilson 2009). An optimistic and self-reinforcing sociology of expectations among researchers and decision-makers working with an emerging techno- logy can distort policy (Hansson 2012). Decision-makers (in research councils, governments and businesses) may respond to the claimed or predicted climate mitigation potential of CCS by reducing effort dedicated to other forms of emissions abatement. There is already evidence for a policy preference for CCS over other means of reducing emissions in those countries (Meadowcroft and Langhelle 2011) and US states (Pollak and Wilson 2009) which are more dependent on fossil fuels. As CCS development slips behind forecasts, with incidents such as the cancellation of the Longannet CCS trial in the UK, the result of excessive reliance on CCS in policy is to increase the risks of climate change faced by future generations. Such CCS-induced moral hazard would also imply economic costs in terms of reduced employment in the renewable sector, and increased health risk from continued air pollution, among other things (see following subsection).

Patents and intellectual property have fundamental socio-economic distributive implications. A recent study reportedly identified 12,000 patents in CCS technologies mainly held by power generation com- panies and their partners (Evans 2010). There has been no study of the geographical distribution of those patents or the potential justice implications. In economic theory, patents are an essential incentive for the development of new technologies, but by definition they then restrict deployment to those to whom the patent holder grants permits (typically those who can afford high licence fees). Achieving an effective balance between providing incentives for development and avoiding restrictions on fair deployment is non-trivial – as demonstrated by major controversy over generic drugs – and complicated further in climate-related matters. Under the Kyoto Protocol, signatories are obliged to support access to technologies identified as 'necessary' to mitigate climate change. This has caused some controversy in respect of nuclear power, and has yet to be tested with respect to CCS. Access or not to CCS technology could have profound implications for a wide range of stakeholders, especially in developing countries.

The scale and significance of these early-stage implications are difficult to determine in the abstract, but could clearly be global in impact. Effective management also appears challenging. Can fair procedures be introduced into the upstream activity of research and innovation, to provide representation – or proxies – for such diverse stakeholder groups as future generations and the local population in foreign countries? Winskel (2012) – considering a multilevel perspective – suggests that the CCS innovation process (and indeed much current energy system change in response to climate imperatives) is largely driven at the 'regime' level rather than emerging from niches in a decentralized, 'learning by doing' method (which might allow better opportunities for stakeholder engagement). Nonetheless, in the UK there are interesting – if limited – lessons for the management of the publicly funded research phases of technology development emerging from the Research Councils UK's current efforts to identify a framework for 'responsible innovation' in the context of challenging decisions on geo-engineering research (Owen et al. forthcoming). These include the use of public engagement processes – albeit only with current UK publics (Pidgeon et al. 2013) – and the use of independent 'stage-gate' appraisal of the implementation of controversial research proposals (Macnaghten and Owen 2011). Both of these could be construed as emerging 'procedural fairness mechanisms' in which the interests of other stakeholders can be considered at a very early stage.

The development and implementation of CCS facilities In comparison to the research and innovation phase, the development and implementation phase creates a much wider range of direct impacts, potentially affecting a wide variety of groups or individuals. Although these impacts range widely in their likely scale or significance, this further emphasizes the importance of considering the social and environmental embeddedness of technical systems.

First, it is worth briefly considering here the implications of a *failure* by major emitters to install CCS should it become technically feasible. A failure to deploy CCS implies significant setbacks in climate mitigation, as well as increases in air pollution.

While a generic failure to reduce emissions might result in some form of challenge to *governments* failing to set or meet targets, emerging efforts at climate litigation suggest that *companies* responsible for large emissions may potentially face some form of legal challenge for their failure to deploy mitigation technology. If it might be judged unjust to continue exploring for new oil in full knowledge of the potential climate impacts (and regardless of the legality of the activity), would it not be even more unjust to demur from installing a technically feasible means of abating emissions from existing or new power stations? Procedural justice would suggest not only that state decisions about CCS policy, but also company decisions over CCS application, should at least be transparent, participative and impartial in this context.

But at present, we face a situation where it is more likely that a company or government will use the potential of CCS to seek to justify the construction of new fossil-fuelled power capacity. And in these cases, access to justice to challenge such decisions is sorely lacking. One of the few test cases arising in recent years was at Hunterston in Ayrshire, where a partial-CCS coal plant was proposed in 2009. The Scottish government incorporated it into the National Planning Framework with limited consultation in response to lobbying by the developer. This was challenged in the Scottish courts by a local citizen with the backing of several national NGOs. While the court accepted that there was adequate public interest in the case to award a protective costs order, the plaintiff was still exposed to the risk of tens of thousands of pounds in costs, and the court was able to consider only whether the decision to include the proposal in the planning document had been properly made, not whether it imposed injustice on current or future generations. In the event, the court ruled that the limited consultation undertaken by the Scottish government had been adequate to establish the need for the development and rejected the challenge. Subsequently the proposal was withdrawn on commercial grounds, after having attracted over twenty thousand objections at the stage of a full planning application.

Should CCS developments go ahead, there are several potential areas of concern. Once in operation, elevated use of coal might be attributed to CCS as a result of the energy penalty of CCS with associated adverse consequences for the well-being of the local population, as well as potentially employment in the renewable sector. Similarly, the addition of CCS increases water consumption both in the CCS process and in general cooling, affecting water users' access, as well as carrying environmental costs. And we might also attribute to CCS continuing pollution with particulates and other emissions from sustained fossil fuel combustion, while acknowledging that the application of CCS may well require or lead to other consequential improvements in emissions control.

More generally, if we consider climate impacts to otherwise rule out the continued use of coal (as argued by James Hansen et al. 2008, for example), even the continuation of the existing use of coal could be attributed to CCS. The use of coal is of concern for other reasons in addition to climate change. For example, supply of coal through large open-pit mining is controversial in many countries, while in Colombia – one of the cheapest global sources of coal – allegations of human and labour rights abuses in the coal industry are commonplace (ITUC 2012).

Also, dependent on the technology choice, CCS might generate new pollutants of local impact – such as nitrosamines – from the additional plant, even though some recent evidence suggests that the likely levels of emissions and persistence are tolerable (Mulgundmath and Bowden 2011). These issues potentially draw in stakeholders not just locally, but potentially from much farther afield in other locations and countries 'downwind', as well as those affected by coal mining and those with interests in water (such as anglers or farmers).

Similarly, if carbon dioxide storage is combined with enhanced oil recovery (EOR) – a likely scenario, and one already dominating early development in North America (Markusson, Shackley and Evar 2012), then the implications of additional or relocated oil production might be considered as a result of the CCS. EOR not only has potential justice consequences as a result of oil production. Markusson, Shackley and Evar (ibid.) suggest that the different financial incentives involved may also lead to lower standards of monitoring and maintenance of carbon storage in such projects. This potentially brings forward any re-release of stored carbon dioxide with consequences for inter-generational justice.

Other potential implications of the development and operational processes – such as direct effects on valued habitats or landscapes – are also relevant. In comparison with the impacts of other large industrial installations, those of CCS facilities may be further concentrated through clustering. Government strategies for CCS typically suggest the development of facilities in clusters served by a single pipeline. While many industrial facilities benefit from clustering, the drivers in the case of CCS are especially strong. This has the potential to result in elevated cumulative impacts from other pollutants, noise and other local disruption. If, as appears to be the case in many environmental justice analyses, such concentrated clusters are in already disadvantaged locations (Walker 2012), injustice will be exacerbated. At present that seems most likely, with CCS facilities typically proposed in existing industrial locations, with only limited consideration of the optimum location in respect of final storage.

The potential for the site selection process (whether for capture or storage facilities) to lead to inequitable social impacts must also be recognized, especially in the face of clustering. While there are no clear cases yet of CCS site selection exhibiting the social targeting found in nuclear waste storage (summarized by Butler and Simmons 2010) or other locally unwanted land uses (Schlosberg 2007), there is a risk of similar discrimination, especially if developers instrumentally adopt processes of social site characterization, a term coined to describe the process of collecting and incorporating information about local stakeholders and their views (see Markusson, Ishii and Stephens 2012). Brunsting et al. (2011) propose social site characterization as a means of enhancing understanding of affected stakeholders and thus enabling better quality engagement. Bradbury (2012: 72) suggests social characterization is useful 'if environmental justice concerns can be avoided', but it seems almost inevitable that commercial CCS developers would apply such techniques to help identify what they might expect to be more receptive locations.

In this respect, social site characterization shares characteristics with volunteerism, although in the latter case it is left to the community to put itself forward and accept the (collective) risks on the promise of the (often in poorer communities) much-needed benefits in terms of transport, infrastructure and jobs (cf. Blowers and Leroy 1994; Gowda and Easterling 2000). In the absence of a WSP, volunteerism could easily appear to be a just solution – the broader system constraints and incentives for volunteering going unnoticed.

The impacts of CCS on employment are potentially more widespread across the development chain, but perhaps most obvious in the construction and development phase. This chapter is not the place to go into the complexities of determining the employment impacts of a particular development, which are typically contested. However, if CCS enables established fossil-fuelled industries to continue, then it can be expected to sustain employment in existing firms and locations. Insofar as these locations might be otherwise disadvantaged (as are many industrial localities), the distributional benefits might be significant. But as 'just transition' advocates point out, loss of employment in high-carbon activities can potentially be justly compensated by targeted retraining and support (UNEP et al. 2008). Looking even more widely, it could be argued that by enabling continued use of coal, CCS might permit continued economic development and poverty alleviation in countries such as China and India. We can conclude at least that existing and potential employees in both CCS operations and alternative low-carbon energy sources should be considered as stakeholders and be included as participants in the relevant policy and deployment decisions.

Transport and storage Moving along the CCS chain, the most obvious potential issues in both transport and storage concern CO_2 leakage, and the risk of direct health effects, as well as consequent reductions in the effectiveness of the approach for climate mitigation. The routing of pipelines can also be expected to lead to siting controversies from localized impacts and potentially severance effects.

There are parallels with nuclear power at the storage stage insofar as the carbon dioxide must be stored safely for long periods (ideally millennia), and that once CCS has been initiated, the storage facility will be required. These make it important to deal properly with the procedural justice issues at the outset, rather than, as has happened with nuclear, creating the waste in advance of establishing long-term management or storage. However, unlike those for nuclear power, carbon dioxide storage quantities are large, and will be linearly related to the size and length of operation of the CCS process. Thus a decision about a storage facility cannot realistically be delayed until after CCS facilities have begun to operate. On the other hand, in practice a policy of CCS readiness might well lead to such an outcome, with a risk of severe procedural injustices that could arise from an enforced need to establish storage facilities post hoc.

There are also intriguing second-order issues arising in respect of storage, where there are major unknowns. Even though geological storage in disused oil and gas reservoirs, or in saline aquifers, is widely considered plausible – if unpopular, at least under land – proposals for direct oceanic storage of CO_2 have not entirely disappeared. Furthermore, geological storage may yet prove to be practically limited (McLaren 2012a), and without any form of governance for its allocation, disputes could arise between nations and between different interests. Notably, negative emissions technologies (NETs) for the active reduction of atmospheric concentrations of CO_2 could well compete for the same geological reservoirs as CCS (McLaren 2012b).

The potential for bioenergy with CCS (BECCS) to deliver net negative emissions in the future also has implications for such conflicts. Without the development of CCS there will be no BECCS, but with CCS development there will inevitably be a diminution in the carbon storage available for BECCS to utilize. How could decisions on the relative claim of each technology for storage capacity be made justly?

While transport has mainly local implications, storage extends the potential negative justice impacts of CCS to future generations, whether in the form of delayed climate risks or simply extended management costs.

Systemic and indirect impacts Systemic and indirect impacts could arise through other distinct routes. A WSP encourages us to examine these. Here we briefly consider the implications of CCS for the overall levels of energy use, its costs to end users, and the likely mix of technologies for power generation.

As a centralized 'solution' to the problem of carbon dioxide production in power generation, other things being equal, and unlike micro-renewables, CCS might not be expected to trigger behavioural reductions in household energy consumption (Hub Research Consultants 2005). In practice, however, the introduction of CCS is likely to mean more expensive power, and thus some reduction in consumption rates.[4]

The probable impact of rising energy prices as a result of measures to require or incentivize CCS has serious implications for justice. In many countries energy poverty is a concern, with implications for health and capabilities to participate (see Bickerstaff et al., this volume), and increases in energy poverty can be directly related to quantified increases in energy prices. In that context, relevant communities of interest – such as low-income energy consumers (or even energy consumers as a whole) – should be treated as affected groups when measures such as a CCS levy or an emissions performance standard designed to drive CCS adoption are considered, even if the scale of the effect is small relative to other factors influencing energy prices. However, as Walker and Day (2012) have noted, groups vulnerable to fuel poverty are also vulnerable to a lack of recognition, even with respect to that injustice, so here would be doubly disadvantaged.

The implications of CCS for other energy generation technologies will be a complex product of politics, technological synergies, relative costs and deployment practice. In particular, the technologies CCS might displace depend upon the likely place in the merit order taken by CCS-equipped capacity. This is likely to fall somewhere between baseload (competing with nuclear power where that is present), and mid-merit (competing with gas and biomass perhaps). With technological advances, CCS capacity may become easier to ramp up and down, and thus be able to compete with the load-following use of gas or even energy storage. However, the high capital-to-fuel-cost ratio of CCS means that there is an economic driver to operate it close to baseload. Paradoxically, although this then does not directly compete with intermittent renewables such as wind, it may encourage system managers and politicians to cap the total contribution of intermittent renewables at a lower level than is technically feasible with more load-following capacity available.

The justice implications could be equally diverse. Displacement of nuclear power might be generally considered to enhance intergenerational justice, but constraining renewables in favour of a technology with an intergenerational storage burden would harm it.

We end this section by briefly revisiting the procedural justice principles set out in Table 9.1 in order to summarize where CCS development might infringe them and to point to emergent procedural mechanisms which might reduce procedural injustices.

Freedom of information issues could arise at many stages of the development pipeline and with several actors, but are likely to be most severe where the commercial developers of CCS facilities seek to minimize disclosure for commercial reasons and to protect intellectual property. *Participation* is lacking for many stakeholders, not just those remote in time and space, and where it is enabled, typically it is likely to take a very limited form, focused around site selection and approval procedures. However, the emergence of responsible innovation principles to enhance participation in the design and funding of research (Owen et al., forthcoming) is an encouraging sign. *Impartiality* is questionable as most decisions on policy and specific developments are made by politicians subject to the 'sociology of expectations', while vested interests often enjoy privileged access to decision-makers (Markusson, Shackley and Evar 2012). *Accessibility* is limited for most stakeholders. Although interesting precedents are arising in the arena of climate litigation, legal challenges are difficult and expensive to raise – even in countries that are parties to the Århus convention, and particularly problematic where stakeholders from other countries are concerned.

Objectivity has been largely untested in the context of CCS, but in the UK, judicial review cannot be undertaken on the basis of the merits of the case, only its procedural validity. More widely, not all decision-makers routinely provide reasons for decisions, and vested interests are often influential at both policy and development decision stages. *Recognition and respect* are often lacking in the context of CCS.

Remote stakeholders are largely ignored, and local ones often treated as unknowledgeable in participatory processes. These shortcomings are not unique to CCS, but they clearly suggest that in the absence of significantly enhanced procedural justice, just outcomes in the energy system will be unlikely to be realized.

Conclusions

In this chapter, we have identified a number of limitations to the existing energy justice literature, notably a fragmented treatment of energy systems (focusing on particular component parts) and a conceptual framing of justice in distributional terms. From this we have argued a need, and presented an initial framework, for a more comprehensive whole-systems perspective that (i) encompasses a consideration of all phases of energy technology life cycles, (ii) recognizes the social embeddedness of technical systems and (iii) looks to integrate a wider range of disciplinary perspectives and stakeholders into the review and decision-making processes associated with transition pathways. In developing this approach we recognize the fundamental importance of 'fairness' in energy system transitions, highlighting a series of principles of procedural justice based on social science and legal research and practice. We argue that such an integrated approach is fundamental to recognizing public discomfort with energy technologies and effectively addressing the moral causes for this discomfort (where effective addressing does not necessarily mean winning public acceptance).

Our whole-systems perspective (WSP) encourages a review of all phases of the technology life cycle. Our analysis of the CCS case confirms that there is a need for participation *early* in the development of a technology because this is where a range of potentially controversial issues are determined. These can result in technology lock-ins, downstream effects (e.g. need for storage capacity) and higher energy prices, giving rise to procedural and distributive injustices throughout the life cycle of energy technologies and beyond. Political power, which arises at an early stage from defining the problem and its potential solutions (Markusson, Shackley and Evar 2012), is likely to remain concentrated in the hands of political and economic interests as the technology evolves and is deployed. Early participation of a wide range of stakeholders in the decision-making (and implementation) processes regarding nascent technologies such as CCS is challenging and inevitably incomplete, but with meaningful scenarios of the possible role and deployment of the technology (which require a WSP), it is possible to realize (Flynn et al. 2006). The whole-system perspective – by reviewing the entire life cycle and potentially affected groups – also helps identify the extent of under-engaged and under-represented interests, such as communities remote in both space and time.

Secondly, our emphasis on and systematic and interdisciplinary reading of procedural justice enriches the energy justice literature in two ways. On the one hand, we stress the dynamic interactions between procedural and distributive justice issues. On the other hand, our approach engages with the literature on (stakeholder) participation and reviews it from a procedural justice perspective. In much of the participation literature and policy practice, participation revolves around ideas of 'acceptance' and 'project implementation' as benchmarks of success. 'Bolting on' a more deliberative project-level engagement process to an opaque and untrusted development pipeline – which includes research funding decisions, government 'consultations', strategic and project-level environmental assessment and planning decisions – may do little to change the underlying power relations and (perceptions of) injustices. In the UK, consultation, environmental assessment and planning rules have all been challenged repeatedly – sometimes even in the courts – on the grounds that they fall short of procedural fairness owing to prejudice, imbalance and lack of accountability, even to the extent of corruption; but with little if any impact. As a result it is entirely reasonable for Reiner et al. (2011) to note concerns over the perception of developments as centrally imposed, and for Mikunda and Feenstra (2009: 8) to describe the Barendrecht case in the Netherlands as one of 'decide, announce, defend'.

Our application of procedural justice principles highlights that participation on its own is not enough to accomplish fairness in processes, and complementary principles are required upon which procedures need to be based. Principles such as recognition, access, impartiality, consistency, absence of bias would help ensure that communities and their alternative perspectives and different conceptions of knowledge about technologies (Markusson and Shackley 2012; Corry and Riesch 2012), and their different underlying values, are taken into account in order to deliver fair(er) outcomes. This might also translate into a more favourable reception of new technologies by society. For instance, Hammond and Shackley (2010: 6) conclude that 'the sense of empowerment enjoyed by a community – that is, the degree to which it has a "voice" which is heard by the powerful ("those in charge") – has a strong influence over its willingness to embrace unknown technologies'. A rationalist interpretation might be to suggest that where the public trust the authorities to halt something if (the public at large deem) it starts to go wrong, they are more likely to accept a trial (especially if there may also be benefits – economic or environmental – to be obtained). Bielicki and Stephens (2008: 4) argue that 'Risks with high levels of uncertainty need reflective discourse in which people engage with the uncertainty and decide as a group what the proper level of protection should be.'

The CCS case also flags up an issue discussed in the context of nuclear waste, namely how to provide procedural justice for future generations. The justice literature is full of debate over whether future generations are part of our moral community, but has precious little thinking on how, procedurally, we can do them justice. Writers on environmental justice, such as Schlosberg (2007), accept representation rather than participation as a valid approach. Identifying practical and effective ways in which the involvement of representatives or proxies can be given adequate weight in the face of pressing present interests is critical if energy and climate justice are to be delivered.

By being comprehensive and systematic, our approach directs the attention of scholars to aspects of energy system transitions that have been marginal in the emerging literature on energy justice, such as the research and innovation process, the interactions between distributive and procedural justice and different phases of the life cycle and the need for a broader set of process principles to underpin participation. Our approach, however, is relevant not only for scholars but also for an 'ethical' evaluation of policy practice.

If just procedures and decisions are to be delivered in policy and planning for the development and deployment of energy technologies it would seem that current planning changes, in the UK at least, are working against a whole-system understanding of equity. In general, the UK planning system fails to provide adequate appeal rights for communities and NGOs, as well as for developers (as some European systems do).[5] By limiting the scope of public engagement around 'major national infrastructures' to the 'local' dimensions of projects, we see a spatially and temporally constrained reading of justice as 'downstream' participation. While it may be true that instrumentalism (to ensure public acceptance of energy system change) is inevitable (at some scale), we must also find ways to contrast instrumental forms of engagement with those that include full recognition and capabilities to not only participate, but to engage in establishing the terms of participation. This reinforces the argument that participation needs to move 'up' the policy/technology pipeline in an iterative way.

Acknowledgements

We are grateful to the insights we have gained from participants in various InCluESEV-funded workshops, particularly to those who attended and/or presented at the International Workshop on the Governance of Carbon Capture and Storage held in London in 2011.

About the contributors

Charlotte Adams is the business research coordinator for Durham Energy Institute, Durham University. Prior to this she worked in the renewables industry, assessing the feasibility of renewable energy systems and district heating projects. Charlotte's cross-disciplinary research interests include deep geothermal energy and ground source heat, the removal of metals (both contaminating and economic) from waste waters and the potential of mine water and groundwater as a thermal resource, the integration of micro-generation systems into the built environment, the energy efficiency and sustainability of historic buildings, electric vehicles and their potential for symbiosis with the built environment, and micro-generation systems.

Varvara Alimisi is a PhD student at Durham Energy Institute, Durham University. Her research interests include smart grids, complex systems and networks, and artificial intelligence techniques.

Josh Baldwick graduated with a BA in Geography from the University of Birmingham in 2012. His dissertation explored the behavioural aspects of energy consumption in multiple-occupancy student housing.

Sandra Bell is an environmental anthropologist and senior lecturer at the University of Durham. She is currently co-investigator on an industry-regulator-funded project carrying out research on the application of smart grid technology – Customer Led Network Revolution (CLNR). She recently helped to design and launch an innovative, interdisciplinary, taught MSc programme – Energy and Society – based in Durham's Department of Anthropology.

Stefan Bouzarovski is a professor in human geography at the University of Manchester and a visiting professor in economic geography at the University of Gdańsk. He spent most of his academic career at the universities of Oxford, London and Birmingham, in addition to holding visiting university appointments in Prague, Bruges, Berlin, Stockholm, Brisbane and Turin. His main research interests are in social environmental science, political ecology, architecture, urban planning, development, and welfare economics. Stefan has coordinated more than thirty research projects and authored more than sixty publications. The results of his research have been taken up by a number of governments and third-sector organizations, in addition to the European Commission and Parliament.

Catherine Butler is research fellow in environmental sociology at Cardiff University. Her research interests include: energy systems change and everyday life; environmental risk governance; sociocultural dimensions of climate change; environmental justice and ethics; and adaptation and flood risk management. Her recent research looks at the roles of publics and governing institutions in energy system change for low-carbon transitions.

Rosie Day is a lecturer in human geography at the University of Birmingham. She has previously held research fellowships at the Scottish Centre for Research on Social Justice, the University of Glasgow and University College London. Her research interests span environmental justice, environmental risk, energy geographies, environmental health, and ageing. She is a co-investigator at the DEMAND centre – Dynamics of Energy, Mobility and Demand – which is led from Lancaster University.

Malcolm Eames holds a professorial chair in low carbon research, with the Low Carbon Research Institute at the Welsh School of Architecture, Cardiff University, and is the principal investigator for the EPSRC Retrofit 2050 project. His research interests focus on the interface between: science and technology foresight; low-carbon innovation; socio-technological transitions; urban sustainability; and environmental justice. He previously lead the EPSRC's Citizens Science for Sustainability (SuScit) project, co-authored the Sustainable Development Research Network (SDRN) review of evidence on Environment and Social Justice for Defra and was the co-organizer of the ESRC/NERC Addressing Environmental Inequalities trans-disciplinary seminar series.

Sara Fuller is a lecturer in the Department of Environment and Geography, Macquarie University, Australia. Her research explores concepts and practices of justice and democracy in the field of the environment, with an empirical focus on examining the role of NGOs and communities in enacting a low-carbon transition. Before joining Macquarie University, Sara held positions as a postdoctoral fellow at City University of Hong Kong and a research associate at Durham University, UK.

Miriam Hunt is a research assistant at the Welsh School of Architecture. Her work is concerned with understanding the drivers and governance of transitions to sustainability in UK city regions, focusing on the case studies of south-east Wales and Greater Manchester. In particular, it investigates the ways in which retrofitting processes will be constituted and delivered between 2020 and 2050, incorporating social and technical changes in the built environment as part of the EPSRC-funded Retrofit 2050 project. Her research interests lie in sustainable regeneration and regional development, as well as the relationship between regeneration and low-carbon transitions.

Guy Hutchinson is working on his PhD in the use of intelligent agents in power system control. He joined the Centre for Doctoral Training in Energy at Durham Energy Institute after completing his master's in new and renewable energy in 2009. This has involved socio-technical projects on building efficiency and energy use, bridging the anthropological and engineering disciplines, as well as collaborations on science outreach and communication.

Matthew Kitching is an operations executive for the Carbon Trust in London. He graduated from the University of Birmingham with an MSci in geography in 2013. His academic interests centre on energy, specifically tackling issues of efficiency, poverty, security and transitions.

Katharine Knox is a programme manager at the Joseph Rowntree Foundation, where she leads research and policy and practice development work on climate change and social justice. She has also managed work on housing, regeneration, community assets and public spaces for the organization. Prior to this, Katharine worked at the Audit Commission, where she carried out research on the value for money of public services, and at the Refugee Council, delivering communications and research on asylum policy issues.

Kristian Krieger is a research associate in the Department of War Studies at King's College London. His research focuses on the legitimacy of governance in response to climate and other risks and disasters, including questions of how to engage the public and stakeholders in governance, as well as how to make explicit the limitations of governance. He is currently working on the EU-funded project Preparedness and Resilience against CBRN Terrorism using Integrated Concepts and Equipment (PRACTICE). He was recently awarded the Third Giandomenico Majone Prize by the European

Consortium for Political Research for his doctoral research into flood risk governance.

Ankit Kumar is a PhD researcher at the Department of Geography, Durham University. His research looks at the problem of rural electrification in India and tries to understand whether systems such as micro-generation could be plausible solutions. Ankit's wider research interests lie in energy access, energy equity, development and socio-technical transitions.

Duncan McLaren is a part-time PhD student at Lancaster University and also a freelance consultant and researcher. His research interests include climate change, energy and geo-engineering, with a particular focus on issues of justice arising in these areas and the consequences for policy. Among other positions, he currently serves on the UK Energy Research Partnership and the Scientific Advisory Committee of the Research Councils UK Energy Programme. Previously he worked for many years in environmental research and advocacy in the UK and internationally, most recently as chief executive of Friends of the Earth Scotland from 2003 until 2011.

Saska Petrova is a lecturer at the University of Manchester. Her main research interests are in intra-community relations and vulnerabilities as they relate to natural resource management, energy flows, social justice and local governance. Her forthcoming monograph, *Communities in Transition*, situates the findings of this research in the context of broader debates surrounding the relationship between nature and local people. She also has an extensive professional background as a public advocate and consultant for a range of global government institutions and think tanks, including the task force of the Regional Environmental Reconstruction Programme for South East Europe.

Peter Simmons is a member of the Science, Society and Sustainability (3S) research group in the School of Environmental Sciences at the University of East Anglia. His current research includes socio-technical studies of monitoring and of safety demonstration in relation to geological disposal of radioactive waste. His research has involved sociocultural investigations of the construction and management of risk from technological hazards, including relations between expertise, decision-making and citizens. The nuclear sector has been a recent focus, including studies of the experience of communities living near nuclear power stations and of public participation in the radioactive waste policy process.

Philip Taylor is professor of electrical power systems and director of the Newcastle Institute for Research on Sustainability at Newcastle University. His research focuses on the challenges associated with the widespread integration and control of distributed/renewable generation in electrical distribution networks. He has significant industrial experience as an electrical engineer, including a period working in the transmission and distribution projects team at GEC Alsthom. His most recent position was research and development director at Econnect (now Senergy Econnect), a consultancy firm specializing in the grid integration of renewable energy.

Britta Rosenlund Turner is a PhD researcher at the Department of Geography at Durham University and a member of Centre for Doctoral Training at Durham Energy Institute. Her PhD research is concerned with the ways in which solar PV technology is incorporated into everyday life: how the technology and solar electricity is appropriated, used, conserved and made to matter in particular socio-material arrangements in the household.

Maarten Wolsink is an environmental geographer at the University of Amsterdam, and internationally a leading author on the acceptance of energy innovation, introducing the widely applied concept of the three-dimensional unfolding of social acceptance. His research focuses on related domains of environmental policies concerning risk and decision-making on infrastructure, such as waste and water.

Notes

Introduction

1 One example is the Energy Justice Network a grassroots campaigning forum based in the USA, closely connected to environmental justice activism; see www.energy justice.net/.

2 However, following the Hills Review of Fuel Poverty in 2012, the government will now define fuel poverty as a condition of low-income households with high required fuel costs (see DECC 2013).

3 Energy suppliers reward electricity generation using micro-renewable technologies such as solar photovoltaic (PV) panels; the tariff is guaranteed for twenty-five years and is tax free. The aim of the scheme is to expand small-scale generation of electricity so that by 2020 around 2 per cent of the electricity in the UK is generated from this source.

4 Distributional effects can, of course, be identified with direct government investment in other energy technology domains (see McLaren et al., this volume on carbon capture and storage) or with more indirect forms of support (e.g. in the UK through the Renewables Obligation, which places an obligation on electricity suppliers to source an increasing proportion of electricity from renewable sources).

5 Microgrids are small community networks that supply electricity and heat. Microgrids can integrate alternative energy production, such as wind or solar, into the electricity network. The multiple dispersed generation sources and ability to isolate the microgrid from a larger network could provide highly reliable electric power. That network could be made into a smart grid using more sophisticated software and grid computing technologies.

1 Day and Walker

1 Absence is an interesting and somewhat tricky notion for assemblage thinking, as it is more straightforward to trace the elements that are present in an assemblage. We return to this point in the discussion section.

2 Bouzarovski et al.

1 The authors of this report thank the Cheshire Lehmann Fund for their generous support of the background research that led to this study. Additional funding was provided by the Durham Energy Institute, the Ministry of Education of the Czech Republic and the EPSRC via the ADMIER project. We are grateful to Benjamin Hayman and Dr Kathrin Hörschelmann for their contributions in setting the conceptual framework and gathering some of the data that led to this chapter.

2 We understand fuel poverty in wider terms, as a condition when a household lacks socially and

materially necessitated energy services in the home (based on Buzar 2007).

3 Eames and Hunt

1 It should be noted that the precise categorization and definition of system functions varies somewhat between different authors and studies.

6 Adams et al.

1 This work was undertaken as part of the InCluESEV project.

2 The Green Deal is a fund established by the UK government which aims to help fund domestic energy improvements from the annual savings associated with its installation.

9 McLaren et al.

1 Although Stirling (2008) does caution against the use of the term 'upstream' for the inappropriately linear analogy it introduces.

2 www.unece.org/env/pp/treaty text.html.

3 There are several emerging options. Pre-combustion technologies remove carbon from the fuel before it is burnt, while post-combustion technologies scrub carbon dioxide from the flue gases.

4 The elasticity of response to electricity prices is a matter of some debate, and is likely to vary significantly between groups and countries. But in this context we need not delve deeper.

5 Clinch (2006) reviews this debate.

Bibliography

Introduction

Agyeman, J. (2013) *Introducing Just Sustainabilities: Policy, Planning and Practice*, London: Zed Books.

Agyeman, J., R. D. Bullard and B. Evans (eds) (2003) *Just Sustainabilities. Development in an Unequal World*, London: Earthscan.

Alley, W. M. and R. Alley (2013) 'Nuclear waste: too hot to handle?', *New Scientist*, 2904, 18 February.

Bell, D. and F. Rowe (2012) 'Are climate policies fairly made', York: Joseph Rowntree Foundation.

Bell, D., T. Gray, C. Haggett and J. Swaffield (2013) 'Revisiting the "social gap": public opinion and relations of power in the local politics of wind energy', *Environmental Politics*, 22(1): 115–35.

Bickerstaff, K. (2012) '"Because we've got history here": nuclear waste, cooperative siting and the relational geography of a complex issue', *Environment and Planning A*, 44(11): 2611–28.

Bickerstaff, K. and G. Walker (2002) 'Risk, responsibility, and blame: an analysis of vocabularies of motive in air-pollution(ing) discourses', *Environment and Planning A*, 34: 2175–92.

Blowers, A. and P. Leroy (1994) 'Power, politics and environmental inequality: a theoretical and empirical analysis of the process of "peripheralisation"', *Environmental Politics*, 3: 197–228.

Boardman, B. (2010) *Fixing Fuel Poverty: Challenges and Solutions*, London: Earthscan.

Butler, C. and P. Simmons (2010) 'Workshop briefing: whole systems equity analysis of nuclear infrastructures', incluesev.kcl.ac.uk/_media/downloads/2011/03/WP6-Briefing_Note_April-2010.pdf.

DECC (Department of Energy and Climate Change) (2013) *Fuel Poverty: A Framework for Action*, DECC cm 8673.

Fuller, S. and H. Bulkeley (2013) 'Changing countries, changing climates: achieving thermal comfort through adaptation in everyday activities', *Area*, 45(1): 63–9.

Gowda, M. and D. Easterling (2000) 'Voluntary siting and equity: the MRS facility experience in Native America', *Risk Analysis*, 20: 917–30.

Hills, J. (2012) 'Getting the measure of fuel poverty: final report of the Fuel Poverty Review', CASE Report 72, London: Department of Energy and Climate Change.

Horton, T. and N. Doran (2011) 'Climate change and sustainable consumption: what do the public think is fair?', York: Joseph Rowntree Foundation.

Preston, I., V. White, J. Thumim and T. Bridgeman (2013) *Distribution of Carbon Emissions in the UK: Implications for Domestic Energy Policy*, York: Joseph Rowntree Foundation.

Provost, C. (2013) 'Energy poverty deprives 1 billion of adequate healthcare, says report', *Guardian*, www.guardian.co.uk/ global-development/2013/mar/07/ energy-poverty-deprives-billion-adequate-healthcare.

Sen, A. (2009) *The Idea of Justice*, Cambridge, MA: Belknap Press.

Smith, J. (2010) *Biofuels and the Globalization of Risk: The Biggest Change in North–South Relationships since Colonialism?*, London: Zed Books.

Stirling, A. (2005) 'Opening up or closing down: analysis, participation and power in the social appraisal of technology', in I. Scoones and B. Wynne (eds), *Science and Citizens*, London: Zed Books, pp. 218–31.

Stockton, H. and R. Campbell (2011) 'Time to reconsider UK energy and fuel poverty policies?', York: Joseph Rowntree Foundation.

Swyngedouw, E. (2010) 'Apocalypse forever? Post-political populism and the spectre of climate change', *Theory, Culture & Society*, 27(2/3): 213–32.

Walker, G. (2008) 'Decentralised systems and fuel poverty: are there any links or risks?', *Energy Policy*, 36: 4514–17.

Walker, G. and R. Day (2012) 'Fuel poverty as injustice: integrating distribution, recognition and procedure in the struggle for affordable warmth', *Energy Policy*, 49: 69–75.

Wilkinson, P., K. R. Smith, M. Joffe and A. Haines (2007) 'A global perspective on energy: health effects and injustices', *The Lancet*, 370: 965–78.

Wolsink, M. (2007) 'Wind power implementation: the nature of public attitudes: equity and fairness instead of "backyard motives"', *Renewable and Sustainable Energy Review*, 11: 1188–1207.

Wright, F. (2004) 'Old and cold: older people and policies failing to address fuel poverty', *Social Policy and Administration*, 38(5): 488–503.

1 Day and Walker

AGECC (Advisory Group on Energy and Climate Change) (2010) *Energy for a Sustainable Future*, New York: UN Secretary-General's Advisory Group on Energy and Climate Change.

Allen, J. (2011) 'Powerful assemblages?', *Area*, 43(2): 154–7.

Anderson, B. and C. McFarlane (2011) 'Assemblage and geography', *Area*, 43(2): 124–7.

Barratt, P. (2012) 'My Magic Cam: a more-than-representational account of the climbing assemblage', *Area*, 44(1): 46–53.

Barron, C. (ed.) (2003) 'A strong distinction between humans and non-humans is no longer required for research purposes: a debate between Bruno Latour and Steve Fuller', *History of the Human Sciences*, 16(2): 77–99.

Bennet, J. (2004) 'The force of things: steps toward an ecology of matter', *Political Theory*, 32: 347–72.

— (2005) 'The agency of assemblages and the North American blackout', *Public Culture*, 17(3): 445–65.

— (2010) *Vibrant Matter: A Political Ecology of Things*, Durham, NC: Duke University Press.

Bickerstaff, K. and J. Agyeman (2009) 'Assembling justice spaces: the scalar politics of environmental justice in North-East England', *Antipode*, 41(4): 781–806.

Bingham, N. (1996) 'Objections:

from technological determinism towards geographies of relations', *Environment and Planning D: Society and Space*, 14(6): 635–57.

Boardman, B. (2010) *Fixing Fuel Poverty: Challenges and Solutions*, London: Earthscan.

Brenner, N., D. Madden and D. Wachsmuth (2011) 'Assemblage urbanism and the challenges of critical urban theory', *City*, 15(2): 570–6.

Brunner, K. M., M. Spitzer and A. Christanell (2012). 'Experiencing fuel poverty: coping strategies of low-income households in Vienna, Austria', *Energy Policy*, 49: 53–9.

Buzar, S. (2007) 'When homes become prisons: the relational spaces of postsocialist energy poverty', *Environment and Planning A*, 39: 1908–25.

Callon, M (1986) 'Some elements in a sociology of translation: domestication of the scallops and the fishermen of St Brieuc Bay', in J. Law (ed.), *Power, Action and Belief: A New Sociology of Knowledge?*, London: Routledge, pp. 196–223.

Castree, N. (2002) 'False antitheses? Marxism, nature and actor-networks', *Antipode*, 34(1): 111–46.

Clark, N. (2011) *Inhuman Nature: Sociable Life on a Dynamic Planet*, London: Sage.

Davies, A. D. (2012) 'Assemblage and social movements: Tibet support groups and the spatialities of political organisation', *Transactions of the Institute of British Geographers*, 37: 273–86.

De Landa, M. (2006) *A New Philosophy of Society: Assemblage Theory and Social Complexity*, New York: Continuum.

Deleuze, G. and F. Guattari (1987) *A Thousand Plateaus: Capitalism and Schizophrenia*, Minneapolis: University of Minnesota Press.

Dovey, K. (2011) 'Uprooting critical urbanism', *City*, 15(3/4): 347–54.

Edensor, T. (2011) 'Entangled agencies, material networks and repair in a building assemblage: the mutable stone of St Ann's church, Manchester', *Transactions of the Institute of British Geographers*, 36(2): 238–52.

Farías, I. (2009) 'Introduction', in I. Farías and T. Bender (eds), *Urban Assemblages: How Actor-Network Theory Changes Urban Studies*, Abingdon: Routledge.

Friel, S. (2007) 'Housing, fuel poverty and health: a pan-European analysis', *Health Sociology Review*, 16: 195–7.

Harrison, C. and J. Popke (2011) '"Because you got to have heat": the networked assemblage of energy poverty in eastern North Carolina', *Annals of the Association of American Geographers*, 101(4): 949–61.

Healy, J. D. (2003) 'Excess winter mortality in Europe: a cross country analysis identifying key risk factors', *Journal of Epidemiology and Community Health*, 57(10): 784–9.

Hills, J. (2012) 'Getting the measure of fuel poverty: final report of the Fuel Poverty Review', CASE Report 72, London: Department of Energy and Climate Change.

Hinchliffe, S. (2007) *Geographies of Nature: Societies, Environments, Ecologies*, London: Sage.

Jacobs, J. M. (2012) 'Urban geographies I: still thinking cities relationally', *Progress in Human Geography*, 36(3): 412–22.

Kirsch, S. and D. Mitchell (2004) 'The nature of things: dead labor, nonhuman actors, and the persistence of Marxism', *Antipode*, 36(4): 687–705.

Latour, B. (1993) *We Have Never been Modern*, New York: Harvester Wheatsheaf.

— (2004) *Politics of Nature: How to Bring the Sciences into Democracy*, Cambridge, MA: Harvard University Press.

— (2005) *Reassembling the Social: An Introduction to Actor Network Theory*, Oxford: Oxford University Press.

Law, J. (1992) 'Notes on the theory of the actor-network: ordering, strategy and heterogeneity', *Systems Practice*, 5(4): 379–93.

Madden, D. J. (2010) 'Urban ANTs: a review essay', *Qualitative Sociology*, 33: 583–9.

Marcus, G. E. and E. Saka (2006) 'Assemblage', *Theory, Culture & Society*, 23(2/3): 101–9.

Marston, S. A., J. P. Jones and K. Woodward (2005) 'Human geography without scale', *Transactions of the Institute of British Geographers*, 30(4): 416–32.

McFarlane, C. (2011a) 'Assemblage and critical urbanism', *City*, 15(2): 204–24.

— (2011b) 'On context: assemblage, political economy and structure', *City*, 15(3/4): 375–88.

McFarlane, C. and B. Anderson (2011) 'Thinking with assemblage', *Area*, 43(2): 162–4.

OFGEM (2011) 'Prepayment meters: a scourge penalising the poor', www.energychoices.co.uk/prepayment-meters-a-scourge-penalising-the-poor.html, accessed 16 February 2011.

O'Sullivan, C., P. L. Howden-Chapman and G. Fougere (2011) 'Making the connection: the relationship between fuel poverty, electricity disconnection, and prepayment metering', *Energy Policy*, 39: 733–41.

Pachauri, S. and D. Spreng (2011) 'Measuring and monitoring energy poverty', *Energy Policy*, 39: 7497–504.

Powells, G. D. (2009) 'Complexity, entanglement, and overflow in the new carbon economy: the case of the UK's Energy Efficiency Commitment', *Environment and Planning A*, 41(10): 2342–56.

Rankin, K. (2011) 'Assemblage and the politics of thick description', *City*, 15(2): 204–24.

Simone, A.-M. (2011) 'The surfacing of urban life', *City*, 15(3/4): 355–64.

Simshauser, P., T. Nelson and T. Doan (2011) 'The boomerang paradox, part I: how a nation's wealth is creating fuel poverty', *Electricity Journal*, 24(1): 72–91.

Tirado Herrero, S. and D. Ürge-Vorsatz (2012) 'Trapped in the heat: a post-communist type of fuel poverty', *Energy Policy*, 49: 60–8.

Tonkiss, F. (2011) 'Template urbanism: four points about assemblage', *City*, 15(3/4): 584–8.

Walker, G. and R. Day (2012) 'Fuel poverty as injustice: integrating distribution, recognition and procedure in the struggle for affordable warmth', *Energy Policy*, 49: 69–75.

Walker, G., R. Whittle, W. Medd and M. Walker (2011) 'Assembling the flood: producing spaces of bad water in the city of Hull', *Environment and Planning A*, 43: 2304–20.

Whatmore, S. (1999) 'Hybrid geographies', in D. Massey, J. Allen and P. Sarre (eds), *Human Geography Today*, Cambridge: Polity Press, pp. 22–39.

Whatmore, S. and L. Thorne

(1997) 'Nourishing networks', in D. Goodman and M. Watts (eds), *Globalising Food*, London: Routledge, pp. 287–304.

Wilkinson, P., K. R. Smith, M. Joffe and A. Haines (2007) 'A global perspective on energy: health effects and injustices', *The Lancet*, 370: 965–78.

Wright, F. (2004) 'Old and cold: older people and policies failing to address fuel poverty', *Social Policy & Administration*, 38(5): 488–503.

2 Bouzarovski et al.

Baker, W., G. Starling and D. Gordon (2003) *Predicting Fuel Poverty at the Local Level: Final Report on the Development of the Fuel Poverty Indicator*, Bristol: Centre for Sustainable Energy.

Boardman, B. (2010) *Fixing Fuel Poverty: Challenges and Solutions*, London: Earthscan.

Buzar, S. (2007) *Energy Poverty in Eastern Europe: Hidden Geographies of Deprivation*, Aldershot: Ashgate.

Clugston, R. M. and W. Calder (1999) 'Critical dimensions of sustainability in higher education', in W. L. Filho (ed.), *Sustainability and University Life*, New York: Peter Lang.

Harrington, B. E., B. Heyman, N. Merleau-Ponty, H. Stockton, N. Ritchie and A. Heyman (2005) 'Keeping warm and staying well: findings from the qualitative arm of the Warm Homes Project', *Health and Social Care in the Community*, 13: 259–67.

Healy, J. D. and J. P. Clinch (2004) 'Quantifying the severity of fuel poverty, its relationship with poor housing and reasons for non-investment in energy-saving measures in Ireland', *Energy Policy*, 32: 207–20.

Honneth, A. (2004) 'Recognition and justice: outline of a plural theory of justice', *Acta Sociologica*, 47: 351–64.

Humphrey, R. and P. McCarthy (1997) 'High debt and poor housing: a taxing life for contemporary students', *Youth and Policy*, 56: 55–64.

Katz, C. (2004) *Growing Up Global: Economic Restructuring and Children's Everyday Lives*, Minneapolis: University of Minnesota Press.

Meola, C. and G. M. Carlomagno (2004) 'Recent advances in the use of infrared thermography', *Measurement Science and Technology*, 15: 27–58.

Nicholson, L. and F. Wasoff (1989) *Students' Experience of Private Rented Housing in Edinburgh*, Student Accommodation Service, University of Edinburgh, Edinburgh.

Rudge, J. and F. Nicol (eds) (1999) *Cutting the Cost of Cold: Affordable Warmth for Healthier Homes*, London: E. & F. N. Spon.

Rugg, J., D. Rhodes and A. Jones (2000) *The Nature and Impact of Student Demand on Housing Markets*, York: York Publishing Services for the Joseph Rowntree Foundation.

Shortt, N. K. and J. Rugkasa (2007) '"The walls were so damp and cold". Fuel poverty and ill health in Northern Ireland: results from a housing intervention', *Health and Place*, 13(1): 99–110.

Slater, T. (2002) *Edgbaston: A History*, Chichester: Phillimore.

Smith, D. P. and L. Holt (2007) 'Studentification and "apprentice" gentrifiers within Britain's provincial towns and cities: extending the meaning of gentrification', *Environment and Planning A*, 39: 142–61.

Walker, G. and R. Day (2012) 'Fuel poverty as injustice: integrating distribution, recognition and procedure in the struggle for affordable warmth', *Energy Policy*, 49: 67–75.

3 Eames and Hunt

Asheim, B. and L. Coenen (2006) 'Contextualising regional innovation systems in a globalising learning economy: on knowledge bases and institutional frameworks', *Journal of Technology Transfer*, 31(1): 163–73.

Bergek, A. and S. Jacobsson (2003) 'The emergence of a growth industry: a comparative analysis of the German, Dutch and Swedish wind turbine industries', in S. Metcalfe and U. Cantner (eds), *Change, Transformation and Development*, Heidelberg: Physica-Verlag, pp. 197–227.

Bergek, A. et al. (2008) 'Analysing the functional dynamics of technological innovation systems: a scheme of analysis', *Research Policy*, 37(3): 407–29.

Berkhout, F., A. Smith and A. Stirling (2004) 'Socio-technical regimes and transition contexts', in B. Elzen, F. W. Geels and K. Green (eds), *System Innovation and the Transition to Sustainability: Theory, evidence and policy*, Camberley: Edward Elgar.

Breukers, S., M. Hisschemöller, E. Cuppen and R. Suurs (2013) 'Analysing the past and exploring the future of sustainable biomass. Participatory stakeholder dialogue and technological innovation systems research', *Technological Forecasting and Social Change*, forthcoming.

Coenen, L. and F. Diaz Lopez (2010) 'Comparing systems approaches to innovation and technological change for sustainable and competitive economies: an explorative study into conceptual commonalities, differences and complementarities', *Journal of Cleaner Production*, 18(18): 1149–60.

Dewald, U. and B. Truffer (2012) 'The local sources of market formation: explaining regional growth differentials in German photovoltaic markets', *European Planning Studies*, 20(3): 397–419.

Doloreux, D. and S. Parto (2005) 'Regional innovation systems: current discourse and unresolved issues', *Technology in Society*, 27(2): 133–53.

Eames, M. and C. de Laurentis (2012) 'A multi-scale model of low carbon innovation systems', Presented at IST 2012 – 3rd International Conference on Sustainability Transitions: 'Sustainability transitions: navigating theories and challenging realities', Technical University of Denmark (DTU), Lyngby, Denmark, 29–31 August.

Eames, M. and W. McDowall (2010) 'Sustainability, foresight and contested futures: exploring visions and pathways in the transition to a hydrogen economy', *Technology Analysis and Strategic Management*, 22(6): 671–92, www.informaworld.com/smpp/275617794~20311173/title~db =all~content=t713447357~tab= issueslist~branches.

Eames, M. and J. Mortensen (2011) 'Community foresight for urban sustainability: insights from the Citizens Science for Sustainability (SuScit) project', *Technology Forecasting and Social Change*, 78(5): 769–84.

Elzen, B., F. W. Geels and K. Green (2004) 'Transitions to sustainability: lessons learned and remaining challenges', in B. Elzen, F. W. Geels and K. Green (eds), *System Innovation and the Transition to Sustainability*, Cheltenham: Edward Elgar, pp. 282–300.

Elzen, B., F. W. Geels, P. S. Hofman and K. Green (2004) 'Sociotechnical scenarios as a tool for transition policy – an example from the traffic and transport domain', in B. Elzen, F. W. Geels and K. Green (eds), *System Innovation and the Transition to Sustainability*, Cheltenham: Edward Elgar, pp. 251–81.

Foxon, T. J. (2013) 'Transition Pathways for a UK low carbon electricity future', *Energy Policy*, 52(1): 10–24.

Freeman, C. (1987) *Technology Policy and Economic Performance: Lessons from Japan*, London: Pinter.

Geels, F. W. (2002) 'Technological transitions as evolutionary reconfiguration process: a multi-level perspective and a case-study', *Research Policy*, 31(8): 1257–74.

— (2005a) *Technological Transitions and System Innovations: A Coevolutionary and Socio-Technical Analysis*, Cheltenham: Edward Elgar.

— (2005b) 'Processes and patterns in transitions and system innovations: refining the coevolutionary multi-level perspective', *Technological Forecasting and Social Change*, 72(6): 681–96.

— (2011) 'The multi-level perspective on sustainability transitions: responses to seven criticisms', *Environmental Innovation and Societal Transitions*, 1(1): 24–40.

Geels, F. W. and J. Schot (2007) 'Typology of sociotechnical transition pathways', *Research Policy*, 36(3): 399–417.

Geels, F. W., A. Monaghan, M. Eames and F. Steward (2008) 'The feasibility of systems thinking in sustainable consumption and production policy: a report to the Department for Environment, Food and Rural Affairs', Brunel University, London: Defra.

Godoe, H. and S. Nygaard (2006) 'System failure, innovation policy and patents: fuel cells and related hydrogen technology in Norway 1990–2002', *Energy Policy*, 34(13): 1697–708.

Guruswamy, L. (2011) 'Energy poverty', *Annual Review of Environment and Resources*, 36: 139–61.

Hekkert, M. et al. (2007) 'Functions of innovation systems: a new approach for analysing technological change', *Technological Forecasting and Social Change*, 74(4): 413–32.

Hendricks, C. (2008) 'On inclusion and network governance: the democratic disconnect of Dutch energy transitions', *Public Administration*, 86(4): 1009–31.

Kemp, R. and D. Loorbach (2006) 'Transition management: a reflexive governance approach', in J.-P. Voss, D. Bauknecht and R. Kemp (eds), *Reflexive Governance for Sustainable Development*, Cheltenham: Edward Elgar, pp. 103–30.

Kemp, R., D. Loorbach and J. Rotmans (2006) 'Transition Management as a model for managing processes of co-evolution towards sustainable development', in M. M. Andersen and A. Tukker (eds), *Perspectives on Radical Change to Sustainable Consumption and Production (SCP)*,

Proceedings of the Workshop of the Sustainable Consumption Research Exchange (SCORE) Network, pp. 459–77.

Lawhon, M. and J. Murphy (2011) 'Socio-technical regimes and sustainability transitions: insights from political ecology', *Progress in Human Geography*, pp. 1–25.

Lundvall, B.-A. (1992) *National Systems of Innovation: Towards a theory of innovation and interactive learning*, London: Pinter.

Markard, J. and B. Truffer (2008) 'Technological innovation systems and the multi-level perspective: towards an integrated framework', *Research Policy*, 37(4): 596–615.

Markard, J., R. Raven and B. Truffer (2012) 'Sustainability transitions: an emerging field of research and its prospects', *Research Policy*, 41(6): 955–67.

Markard, J., M. Stadelmann and B. Truffer (2009) 'Prospective analysis of technological innovation systems: identifying technological and organizational development options for Biogas in Switzerland', *Research Policy*, 38(4): 655–67.

Meadowcroft, J. (2011) 'Engaging with the politics of sustainability transitions', *Environmental Innovation and Societal Transitions*, 1(1): 70–5.

Moulaert, F. and F. Sekia (2003) 'Territorial innovation models: a critical survey', *Regional Studies*, 37(3): 289–302.

Nelson, R. R. (ed.) (1993) *National Systems of Innovation: A comparative study*, Oxford: Oxford University Press.

Raven, R. and G. Verbong (2007) 'Multi-regime interactions in the Dutch energy sector. The case

of combined heat and power technologies in the Netherlands 1970–2000', *Technology Analysis & Strategic Management*, 19(4): 1–18.

Rotmans, J. and D. Loorbach (2008) 'Transition management: reflexive governance of societal complexity through searching, learning and experimenting', in J. van der Bergh and F. Bruisma (eds), *Managing the Transition to Renewable Energy*, Cheltenham: Edward Elgar.

Shove, E. and G. Walker (2007) 'Caution! Transitions ahead: politics, practice, and sustainable transition management', *Environment and Planning A*, 39: 763–70.

Smith, A. et al. (2010) 'Innovation studies and sustainability transitions: the allure of the multi-level perspective and its challenges', *Research Policy*, 39(4): 435–48.

Stirling, A. (2006) 'Precaution, foresight and sustainability: reflection and reflexivity in the governance of science and technology', in J.-P. Voss, D. Bauknecht and R. Kemp (eds), *Reflexive Governance for Sustainable Development*, Cheltenham: Edward Elgar, pp. 225–72.

Truffer, B. and L. Coenen (2012) 'Environmental innovation and sustainability transitions in regional studies', *Regional Studies*, 46(1): 1–21.

Truffer, B., J. P. Voss and K. Konrad (2008) 'Mapping expectations for system transformations: lessons from sustainability foresight in German utility sectors', *Technological Forecasting and Social Change*, 75(9): 1360–72.

Verbong, G. and F. W. Geels (2007) 'The ongoing energy transition: lessons from a socio-technical, multi-level analysis of the Dutch

electricity system (1960–2004)',
Energy Policy, 35(2): 1025–37.

Walker, G. and M. Eames (2006)
'Environmental inequalities:
crosscutting themes for the
trans-disciplinary seminar series
on environmental inequalities
2006–8', Discussion paper,
Lancaster University, geography.
lancs.ac.uk/EnvJustice/eiseminars
/downloads/ei_discussion.pdf.

Werenfels, I. and K. Westphal (2010)
'Solar power from North Africa:
framework and prospects', SWP
Research Paper for the German
Institute for International and
Security Affairs, Berlin: SWP.

4 Fuller and Bulkeley

Adger, W. N. (2001) 'Scales of governance and environmental justice
for adaptation and mitigation of
climate change', *Journal of International Development*, 13: 921–31.

Aylett, A. (2010) 'Conflict, collaboration and climate change:
participatory democracy and
urban environmental struggles
in Durban, South Africa',
*International Journal of Urban and
Regional Research*, 34(3): 478–95.

Bell, D. and F. Rowe (2012) *Are Climate Policies Fairly Made?*, York:
Joseph Rowntree Foundation.

British Gas (2012) 'Welcome to Green
Streets', www.britishgas.co.uk/
smarter-living/save-energy/green-
streets.html, accessed 31 August
2012.

Büchs, M., N. Bardsley and S. Duwe
(2011) 'Who bears the brunt?
Distributional effects of climate
change mitigation policies', *Critical Social Policy*, 31(2): 285–307.

Bulkeley, H. and S. Fuller (2012)
*Social Justice and Low Carbon
Communities*, York: Joseph
Rowntree Foundation.

Caney, S. (2005) 'Cosmopolitan
justice, responsibility, and global
climate change', *Leiden Journal of
International Law*, 18: 747–75.

Cowell, R., G. Bristow and M. Mun-
day (2011) 'Acceptance, acceptability and environmental justice:
the role of community benefits
in wind energy development',
*Journal of Environmental Planning
and Management*, 54(4): 539–57.

DECC (2009) *The Low Carbon Communities Challenge 2010–2012
Application Form*, London: Department for Energy and Climate
Change.

— (2010) *The Low Carbon Communities Challenge: Supporting people,
projects and partnerships for a low
carbon future*, London: Department for Energy and Climate
Change.

DEFRA (2009) *Adapting to Climate
Change – UK Climate Projections*,
London: DEFRA.

Energy Saving Trust (2010) *Helping
People Save Money*, London:
Energy Saving Trust.

Foresight Sustainable Energy Management and the Built Environment Project (2008) *Final Project
Report*, London: Government
Office for Science.

FPEEG and PRASEG (2011) *Inquiry
into Social Justice in the Low Carbon Economy*, London: FPEEG/
PRASEG.

Fraser, N. (1997) *Justice Interrupts:
Critical Reflections on the 'Post-
socialist' Condition*, New York:
Routledge.

Greater London Authority (2009) *Low
Carbon Zones: Candidate Zone
Prospectus*.

Harris, P. G. (2010) 'Misplaced ethics
of climate change: political vs.
environmental geography', *Ethics,
Place & Environment*, 13(2): 215–22.

Heiskanen, E., M. Johnson, S. Robinson, E. Vadovics and M. Saastamoinen (2010) 'Low-carbon communities as a context for individual behavioural change', *Energy Policy*, 38: 7586–95.

Hinshelwood, E. (2001) 'Power to the people: community-led wind energy – obstacles and opportunities in a South Wales Valley', *Community Development Journal*, 36: 95–110.

HM Government (2009) *The UK Low Carbon Transition Plan: National strategy for climate and energy.*

Hoffman, S. M. and A. High-Pippert (2010) 'From private lives to collective action: recruitment and participation incentives for a community energy program', *Energy Policy*, 38(12): 7567–74.

Hopkins, R. and P. Lipman (2009) 'Who we are and what we do', Totnes: Transition Network.

Larsen, K., U. Gunnarsson-Östling and E. Westholm (2011) 'Environmental scenarios and local-global level of community engagement: environmental justice, jams, institutions and innovation', *Futures*, 43(4): 413–23.

Levermore, G., D. Chow, P. Jones and D. Lister (2004) 'Accuracy of modelled extremes of temperature and climate change and its implications for the built environment in the UK', Tyndall Centre for Climate Change Research Technical Report 14.

Low Carbon Communities Network (2008) *End of Year Report.*

McGeehin, M. A. and M. Mirabelli (2001) 'The potential impacts of climate variability and change on temperature-related morbidity and mortality in the United States', *Environmental Health Perspectives*, 109(Suppl. 2): 185–9.

Middlemiss, L. and B. D. Parrish (2010) 'Building capacity for low-carbon communities: the role of grassroots initiatives', *Energy Policy*, 38(12): 7559–66.

Moloney, S., R. E. Horne and J. Fien (2010) 'Transitioning to low carbon communities – from behaviour change to systemic change: lessons from Australia', *Energy Policy*, 38: 7614–23.

Mulugetta, Y., T. Jackson and D. van der Horst (2010) 'Carbon reduction at community scale', *Energy Policy*, 38(12): 7541–5.

O'Brien, G. and A. Hope (2010) 'Localism and energy: negotiating approaches to embedding resilience in energy systems', *Energy Policy*, 38(12): 7550–8.

Paavola, J. and W. N. Adger (2006) 'Fair adaptation to climate change', *Ecological Economics*, 56(4): 594–609.

Peters, M., S. Fudge and S. Sinclair (2010) 'Mobilising community action towards a low-carbon future: opportunities and challenges for local government in the UK', *Energy Policy*, 38(12): 7596–603.

Pilli-Sihvola, K., P. Aatola, M. Ollikainen and H. Tuomenvirta (2010) 'Climate change and electricity consumption – witnessing increasing or decreasing use and costs?', *Energy Policy*, 38: 2409–19.

Pout, C. and E. R. Hitchin (2009) 'Future environmental impacts of room air-conditioners in Europe', *Building Research and Information*, 37: 358–68.

Roberts, S. (2008) 'Energy, equity and the future of the fuel poor', *Energy Policy*, 36: 4471–4.

Seyfang, G. (2010) 'Community action for sustainable housing:

building a low-carbon future',
Energy Policy, 38(12): 7624–33.

Shrader-Frechette, K. (2002) *Environmental Justice: Creating Equality, Reclaiming Democracy*, Oxford: Oxford University Press.

Stockton, H. and R. Campbell (2012) *Time to Reconsider UK Energy and Fuel Poverty Policies?*, York: Joseph Rowntree Foundation.

Swyngedouw, E. and N. C. Heynen (2003) 'Urban political ecology, justice and the politics of scale', *Antipode*, 35(5): 898–918.

Sze, J. and J. K. London (2008) 'Environmental justice at the crossroads', *Sociology Compass*, 2(4): 1331–54.

Transition Network (2012) *About Transition Network*, www.transitionnetwork.org/about, accessed 31 August 2012.

Vaze, P. and S. Tindale (2011) *Repowering Communities: Small-scale Solutions for Large-scale Energy Problems*, London: Earthscan.

Walker, G. (2008) 'Decentralised systems and fuel poverty: are there any links or risks?', *Energy Policy*, 36(12): 4514–17.

— (2011) 'The Role for "community" in carbon governance', *Interdisciplinary Reviews Climate Change*, 2: 777–82.

Walker, G. and N. Cass (2007) 'Carbon reduction, "the public" and renewable energy: engaging with socio-technical configurations', *Area*, 39(4): 458–69.

Walker, G. and R. Day (2012) 'Fuel poverty as injustice: integrating distribution, recognition and procedure in the struggle for affordable warmth', *Energy Policy*, 49: 69–75.

Walker, G. and P. Devine-Wright (2008) 'Community renewable energy: what should it mean?', *Energy Policy*, 36(2): 497–500.

Walker, G., S. Hunter, P. Devine-Wright, B. Evans and H. Fay (2007) 'Harnessing community energies: explaining and evaluating community-based localism in renewable energy policy in the UK', *Global Environmental Politics*, 7(2): 64–82.

Whitmarsh, L., G. Seyfang and S. O'Neill (2011) 'Public engagement with carbon and climate change: to what extent is the public "carbon capable"?', *Global Environmental Change*, 21: 56–65.

Wolf, J., K. Brown and D. Conway (2009) 'Ecological citizenship and climate change: perceptions and practice', *Environmental Politics*, 18(4): 503–21.

Young, I. M. (1990) *Justice and the Politics of Difference*, Princeton, NJ: Princeton University Press.

Zhang, X., G. P. Q. Shen, J. Feng and Y. Wu (2013) 'Delivering a low-carbon community in China: technology vs. strategy?', *Habitat International*, 37: 130–7.

5 Knox

Bell, D. and F. Rowe (2012) *Are Climate Policies Fairly Made?*, York: Joseph Rowntree Foundation.

Bulkeley, H. and S. Fuller (2012) *Low Carbon Communities and Social Justice*, York: Joseph Rowntree Foundation.

Cowell, R. et al. (2012) *Wind Energy and Justice for Disadvantaged Communities*, York: Joseph Rowntree Foundation.

DECC (Department of Energy and Climate Change) (2013a) *Fuel Poverty: A Framework for Action*, DECC cm 8673.

— (2013b) *Onshore Wind Call for Evidence: Government Response to*

Part A (Community Engagement and Benefits) and Part B (Costs), London: DECC.

Dresner, S. et al. (2013) *Designing Carbon Taxation to Protect Low Income Households*, York: Joseph Rowntree Foundation.

Druckman A. et al. (2011) *Sustainable Income Standards: Towards a greener minimum*, York: Joseph Rowntree Foundation.

Ekins, P. and M. Lockwood (2011) *Tackling Fuel Poverty during the Transition to a Low Carbon Economy*, York: Joseph Rowntree Foundation.

Financial Inclusion Centre (2011) *Report 1: Debt and household incomes*, London: Financial Inclusion Centre.

Horton, T. and N. Doran (2011) *Climate Change and Sustainable Consumption: What do the public think is fair?*, York: Joseph Rowntree Foundation.

Lindley, S. et al. (2011) *Climate Change, Justice and Vulnerability*, York: Joseph Rowntree Foundation.

O'Neill, J. and M. O'Neill (2012) *Social Justice and the Future of Flood Insurance*, York: Joseph Rowntree Foundation.

Preston, I. et al. (2013) *Distribution of Carbon Emissions in the UK: Implications for domestic energy policy*, York: Joseph Rowntree Foundation.

Stockton, H. and R. Campbell (2011) *Time to Reconsider UK Energy and Fuel Poverty Policies?*, York: Joseph Rowntree Foundation.

United Nations (1992) *UN Framework Convention on Climate Change (UNFCCC)*, New York: United Nations.

See also JRF's website and related topic page: www.jrf.org.uk/topic/climate-change

6 Adams et al.

Adams, C., P. Taylor and S. Bell (2012) 'Equity dimensions of micro-generation: a whole systems approach', *Journal of Renewable and Sustainable Energy*, 4.

Afgan, N. H. and M. G. Carvalho (2002) 'Multi-criteria assessment of new and renewable energy power plants', *Energy*, 27(8).

Allen, S. R., G. P. Hammond, H. A. Harajli, M. C. McManus and A. B. Winnett (2010) 'Integrated appraisal of a solar hot water system', *Energy*, 35(3).

Bahaj, A. S., P. A. B. James and M. F. Jentsch (2007) 'Photovoltaics: added value of architectural integration', *Proceedings of ICE: Energy*, 160(2).

Bergman, N. and N. Eyre (2011) 'What role for micro-generation in a shift to a low carbon domestic energy sector in the UK?', *Energy Efficiency*, 4(3).

Bergman, N., J. Barton, R. Blanchard, N. Brandon, D. Brett, A. Hawkes, C. Jardine, N. Kelly, M. Leach, A. Peacock, I. Staffel and B. Woodman (2009) 'Maximising energy savings from domestic microgeneration: a cultural and behavioural analysis', *IOP Conference Series, Earth and Environmental Science*, 6(19).

Brashear, T. G., C. M. Brooks and J. S. Boles (2004) 'Distributive and procedural justice in a sales force context. Scale development and validation', *Journal of Business Research*, 57(1).

Burton, J. and K. Hubacek (2007) 'Is small beautiful? A multicriteria assessment of small-scale energy technology applications in local governments', *Energy Policy*, 35(12).

Claussen, E. and L. McNeilly (1998)

'Equity and global climate change: the complex elements of global fairness', Pew Centre on Global Climate Change, Arlington.

Climate Change Act (2008) London: The Stationery Office.

Dalton, G. J., D. A. Lockington and T. E. Baldock (2008) 'Feasibility analysis of stand-alone renewable energy supply options for a large hotel', *Renewable Energy*, 33(7).

DCLG (Department for Communities and Local Government) (2011) *English Housing Survey: Headline report 2009–10*, London.

DECC (Department of Energy and Climate Change) (2010) *The Green Deal: Energy savings for homes and business*, London.

Diakoulaki, D., A. Zervos, J. Sarafidis and S. Mirasgedis (2001) 'Cost benefit analysis for solar water heating systems', *Energy Conversion and Management*, 42(14).

DTI (Department of Trade and Industry) (2006) *Our Energy Challenge. Power from the People*, London.

Energy Saving Trust, Econnect, Element Energy (2005) *Potential for Micro-generation: Study and analysis full report*, London: Energy Saving Trust.

European Commission (EC) (2007) *Energy Mix Fact Sheet*, Greece: Europa.

Fukushima, Y., Y. Kikuchi, Y. Kajikawa, M. Kubota, T. Nakagaki, M. Matsukata, Y. Kato and M. Koyama (2011) 'Tackling power outages in Japan: the earthquake compels a swift transformation of the power supply', *Journal of Chemical Engineering of Japan*, 44(6).

House of Commons (2012) 'Note 39', Select Committee on Energy, London.

Ikeme, J. (2003) 'Equity, environmental justice and sustainability: incomplete approaches in climate change politics', *Global Environmental Change*, 13(3).

Leenheer, J., M. de Nooij and O. Sheikh (2011) 'Own power: motives of having electricity without the energy company', *Energy Policy*, 39(9).

Lovins, A. B. (2002) *Small is Profitable*, Snowmass, CO: Rocky Mt Inst.

Madlener, R., K. Kowalski and S. Stagl (2007) 'New ways for the integrated appraisal of national energy scenarios: the case of renewable energy use in Austria', *Energy Policy*, 35(12).

Matsuura, M., H. Shiroyama and T. Suzuki (2010) 'Sustainable energy and environmental policy-making in Japan', *Technology and Society Magazine, IEEE*, 29(3).

Meadows, D. H. (2009) *Thinking in Systems: A primer*, London: Earthscan.

More Micro-grids Project, TF3 (2009) 'Experimental validation of islanding mode of operation', *Deliverable DF2, Report on field tests for islanded mode (Kythnos Test site)*, Greece, www.microgrids.eu.

Morozumi, S. (2007) 'Micro-grid demonstration projects in Japan', IEEE Power Conversion Conference, Nagoya.

Ofgem (2011) *Updated Household Energy Bills Explained*, Factsheet 97, London.

Oikonomou, V., A. Flamos, M. Gargiulo, G. Giannakidis, A. Kanudia, E. Spijker and S. Grafakos (2011) 'Linking least-cost energy system costs models with MCA: an assessment of the EU renewable energy targets and supporting policies', *Energy Policy*, 39(5).

ONS (Office for National Statistics) (2010) *Super Output Area Mid-year Population Estimates for England and Wales, Mid 2009*, London.

Owen, G. (2008) 'Towards an equitable climate change policy for the UK: the costs and benefits for low income households of UK climate change policy', Eaga Working Paper, Wolverhampton.

Pratt, J., P. Gordon and D. Plamping (1999) *Working Whole Systems*, London: Radcliffe Publishing, King's Fund..

Rankine, R. K., J. P. Chick and G. P. Harrison (2006) 'Energy and carbon audit of a rooftop wind turbine', *Proceedings of the Institute of Mechanical Engineering, Part A: Journal of Power and Energy*, 220(7).

Roberts, S. and J. Thumim (2006) *A Rough Guide to Individual Carbon Trading. The Ideas, Issues and Next Steps*, Report to Defra, Bristol: Centre for Sustainable Energy.

Skarvelis-Kazakos, S., L. M. Cipcigan and N. Jenkins (2009) 'Micro-generation for 2050: life-cycle carbon footprint of micro-generation sources', Universities Power Engineering Conference (UPEC), 2009 Proceedings of the 44th International Conference, Glasgow, 1–4 September.

Staffell, I. and A. Ingram (2010) 'Life cycle assessment of an alkaline fuel cell CHP system', *International Journal of Hydrogen Energy*, 35(6).

Stockton, H. and R. Campbell (2011) *Time to Reconsider UK Energy and Fuel Poverty Policies*, York: Joseph Rowntree Foundation.

UK Energy Act (2004) London: The Stationery Office.

US EIA (Energy Information Administration) (2011) *Japan Energy Data, Statistics and Analysis – Oil, Gas, Electricity, Coal*, Washington, DC.

Walker, G. (2008a) 'Community renewable energy: what should it mean?', *Energy Policy*, 38(6).

— (2008b) 'Decentralised systems and fuel poverty: are there any links or risks?', *Energy Policy*, 36(12).

Walker, G. and H. Bulkeley (2006) 'Geographies of environmental justice', *Geoforum*, 37.

Walker, G. and N. Cass (2007) 'Carbon reduction, "the public" and renewable energy: engaging with socio-technical configurations', *Area*, 39(4).

7 Wolsink

Ackermann, T., G. Andersson and L. Söder (2001) 'Distributed Generation: a definition', *Electric Power Systems Research*, 57: 195–204.

Andersen, P. H., J. A. Mathews and M. Rask (2009) 'Integrating private transport into renewable energy policy: the strategy of creating intelligent recharging grids for electric vehicles', *Energy Policy*, 37: 2481–6.

Bagliani, M., E. Dansero and M. Puttilli (2010) 'Territory and energy sustainability: the challenge of renewable energy sources', *Journal of Environmental Planning and Management*, 53: 447–57.

Banister, D. (2008) 'The sustainable mobility paradigm', *Transport Policy*, 15: 73–80.

Breukers, S. and M. Wolsink (2007) 'Wind power implementation in changing institutional landscapes: an international comparison', *Energy Policy*, 35(5): 2737–50.

Brown, H. E., S. Suryanarayanan and

G. T. Heydt (2010) 'Some characteristics of emerging distribution systems considering the Smart Grid initiative', *Electricity Journal*, 23: 64–75.

Capek, S. M. (1993) 'The environmental justice frame: a conceptual discussion and an application', *Social Problems*, 40: 5–24.

Cowell, R. and S. Owens (2006) 'Governing space: planning reform and the politics of sustainability', *Environment and Planning C*, 24: 403–21.

Darby, S. J. and E. McKenna (2012) 'Social implications of residential demand response in cool temperate climates', *Energy Policy*, 49: 759–69.

Devine-Wright, P. (2009) 'Rethinking NIMBYism: the role of place attachment and place identity in explaining place-protective action', *Journal of Community & Applied Social Psychology*, 19(6): 426–41.

Devine-Wright, P. and H. Devine-Wright (2006) 'Social representations of intermittency and the shaping of public support for wind energy in the UK', *International Journal of Global Energy Issues*, 25: 243–56.

Dietz, T., E. Ostrom and P. Stern (2003) 'The struggle to govern the commons', *Science*, 302: 1907–12.

Fischlein, M., J. Larson, D. M. Hall et al. (2010) 'Policy stakeholders and deployment of wind power in the sub-national context: a comparison of four U.S. states', *Energy Policy*, 38: 4429–39.

Fraser, N. (2000) 'Rethinking recognition', *New Left Review*, 3: 107–20.

Geels, F. W. (2004) 'From sectoral systems of innovation to sociotechnical systems. Insights about dynamics and change from sociology and institutional theory', *Research Policy*, 33: 897–920.

Green, II, R. C., L. Wang and M. Alam (2011) 'The impact of plug-in hybrid electric vehicles on distributed networks: a review and outlook', *Renewable and Sustainable Energy Reviews*, 15: 544–53.

Hammons, T. J. (2008) 'Integrating renewable energy sources into European grids', *Electrical Power and Energy Systems*, 30: 462–75.

Harvey, D. (1996) *Justice, Nature, and the Geography of Difference*, Oxford: Blackwell.

Honneth, A. (1992) 'Integrity and disrespect: principles of morality based on the theory of recognition', *Political Theory*, 20: 187–201.

Houthakker, H. S. (1951) 'Electricity tariffs in theory and practice', *Economic Journal*, 61: 1–25.

Jacobsson, S. and A. Bergek (2004) 'Transforming the energy sector: the evolution of technological systems in renewable energy technology', *Industrial and Corporate Change*, 13(5): 815–49.

Jacobsson, S. and A. Johnson (2000) 'The diffusion of renewable energy technology: an analytical framework and key issues for research', *Energy Policy*, 28: 625–40.

Lehmann, P., F. Creutzig, M.-H. Ehlers, N. Friedrichsen, C. Heuson, L. Hirth and R. Pietzcker (2012) 'Carbon lock-out: advancing renewable energy policy in Europe', *Energies*, 5: 323–54.

Lund, H. (2010) 'The implementation of renewable energy systems. Lessons learned from the Danish case', *Energy*, 35: 4003–9.

Lund, H. and W. Kempton (2008) 'Integration of renewable energy into the transport and electricity sectors through V2G', *Energy Policy*, 36(9): 3578–87.

Lund, H., A. N. Andersen, P. A. Ostergaard, B. V. Mathiesen and D. Connolly (2012) 'From electricity smart grids to smart energy systems – a market operation based approach and understanding', *Energy*, 42: 96–102.

MacKay, D. J. C. (2009) *Sustainable Energy – without the hot air*, Cambridge: UIT.

Marris, E. (2008) 'Upgrading the grid', *Nature*, 454: 570–3.

North, D. (1990) *Institutions, Institutional Change and Economic Performance*, Cambridge: Cambridge University Press.

Ostrom, E. (1999) 'Coping with tragedies of the commons', *Annual Review of Political Science*, 2: 493–535.

— (2010) 'A long polycentric journey', *Annual Review of Political Science*, 13: 1–23.

Ostrom, E., J. Burger, C. Field, R. Norgaard and D. Policansky (1999) 'Revisiting the commons: local lessons, global challenges', *Science*, 284: 278–82.

Paavola, J. (2007) 'Institutions and environmental governance: a reconceptualization', *Ecological Economics*, 63: 93–103.

Pero, L. and T. Smith (2008) 'Institutional credibility and leadership: critical challenges for community-based natural resource governance in rural and remote Australia', *Regional Environmental Change*, 8(1): 15–29.

Rawls, J. (1972) *A Theory of Justice*, Oxford: Oxford University Press.

— (2001) *Justice as Fairness: A restatement*, Cambridge, MA: Belknap Press.

Ribot, J. C. and N. L. Peluso (2003) 'A theory of access', *Rural Sociology*, 68: 153–81.

Sauter, R. and J. Watson (2007) 'Strategies for the deployment of micro-generation: implications for social acceptance', *Energy Policy*, 35: 2770–9.

Schlager, E. and E. Ostrom (1992) 'Property rights regimes and natural resources – a conceptual analysis', *Land Economics*, 68(3): 249–62.

Schlosberg, D. (2004) 'Reconceiving environmental justice: global movements and political theories', *Environmental Politics*, 13: 517–40.

Shove, E. (2010) 'Beyond the ABC: climate change policy and theories of social change', *Environment and Planning A*, 42(6): 1273–85.

Smith, P. D. and M. H. McDonaugh (2001) 'Beyond public participation: fairness in natural resource decision making', *Society and Natural Resources*, 14: 239–49.

Sovacool, B. K. (2009) 'The intermittency of wind, solar, and renewable electricity generators: technical barrier or rhetorical excuse', *Utilities Policy*, 17: 288–96.

Sovacool, B. K. and P. Lakshmi Ratan (2012) 'Conceptualizing the acceptance of wind and solar electricity', *Renewable and Sustainable Energy Reviews*, 16: 5268–79.

Thelen, K. (1999) 'Historical institutionalism in comparative politics', *Annual Review of Political Science*, 2: 369–404.

Toke, D., S. Breukers and M. Wolsink (2008) 'Wind power deployment outcomes: how can we account for the differences?', *Renewable and Sustainable Energy Reviews*, 12(4): 1129–47.

Unruh, G. (2002) 'Escaping carbon lock-in', *Energy Policy*, 30: 317–25.

Vermeylen, S. (2010) 'Resource rights and the evolution of renewable energy technologies', *Renewable Energy*, 35: 2399–405.

Walker, G. (2011) 'The role for "community" in carbon governance', Wiley Interdisciplinary Reviews, *Climate Change*, 2: 777–82.

Walker, G. and P. Devine-Wright (2008) 'Community renewable energy: what should it mean?', *Energy Policy*, 36: 497–50.

Walker, G., P. Devine-Wright, S. Hunter, H. High and B. Evans (2010) 'Trust and community: exploring the meanings, contexts and dynamics of community renewable energy', *Energy Policy*, 38: 2655–63.

Walker, W. (2000) 'Entrapment in large technology systems: institutional commitment and power relations', *Research Policy*, 29: 833–46.

Wolsink, M. (2003) 'Reshaping the Dutch planning system: a learning process?', *Environment and Planning A*, 35: 705–23.

— (2012a) 'The research agenda on social acceptance of distributed generation in smart grids: renewable as common pool resources', *Renewable and Sustainable Energy Reviews*, 16: 822–35.

— (2012b) 'Wind power: basic challenge concerning social acceptance', in R. A. Meyers (ed.), *Encyclopedia of Sustainability Science and Technology*, vol. 17, Springer, pp. 12218–54.

— (2013) 'The next phase in social acceptance of renewable innovation', *IDE Quarterly*, 5(1): 10–13.

Wüstenhagen, R., M. Wolsink and M. J. Bürer (2007) 'Social acceptance of renewable energy innovation: an introduction to the concept', *Energy Policy*, 35(5): 2683–91.

Young, I. M. (1990) *Justice and the Politics of Difference*, Princeton, NJ: Princeton University Press.

8 Butler and Simmons

Adam, B. and C. Grove (2007) *Future Matters: Action, Knowledge, Ethics*, Leiden: Brill.

Arnstein, S. R. (1969) 'A ladder of citizen participation', *Journal of the American Institute of Planners*, 35(4): 216–24.

Banerjee, S. B. (2000) 'Whose land is it anyway? National interest, indigenous stakeholders, and colonial discourses: the case of the Jabiluka uranium mine', *Organization & Environment*, 13(1): 3–38.

BBC (2007) 'Nuclear review was "misleading"', *BBC News Online*, 15 February, news.bbc.co.uk/1/hi/uk_politics/6364281.stm.

BERR (Department for Business, Enterprise and Regulatory Reform) (2008) *Meeting the Energy Challenge: A White Paper on Nuclear Power*, London, Department for Business, Enterprise and Regulatory Reform.

Bickerstaff, K., I. Lorenzoni, N. F. Pidgeon, W. Poortinga and P. Simmons (2008) 'Reframing nuclear power in the UK energy debate: nuclear power, climate change mitigation and radioactive waste', *Public Understanding of Science*, 17: 145–69.

Blowers, A. (2006) *Ethics and Decision-making for Radioactive Waste: A Report for CoRWM edited by Andrew Blowers*, CoRWM, corwm. decc.gov.uk/assets/corwm/pre-nov%202007%20doc%20archive/plenary%20papers/2006/11-12%20april%202006/1692%20-%20ethics%20report%20draft.pdf.

— (2010) 'Why dump on us? Power,

pragmatism and the periphery in the siting of new nuclear reactors in the UK', *Journal of Integrative Environmental Sciences*, 7(3): 157–73.

Blowers, A. and G. Sundqvist (2010) 'Radioactive waste management – technocratic dominance in an age of participation', *Journal of Integrative Environmental Sciences*, 7(3): 149–55.

Butler, C., K. A. Parkhill and N. Pidgeon (2011) 'Nuclear pwer after Japan: the social dimensions', *Environment: Science and Policy for Sustainable Development*, 53(6): 3–14.

Chilvers, J. and J. Burgess (2008) 'Power relations: the politics of risk and procedure in nuclear waste governance', *Environment and Planning A*, 40(8): 1881–900.

CoWRM (Committee for Radioactive Waste Management) (2006) *Managing Our Radioactive Waste Safely: CoRWM's Recommendations to Government*, CoRWM Doc 700, corwm.decc.gov.uk/assets/corwm/post-nov%2007%20doc%20store/documents/reports%20 to %20 government/nov%20 and %20dec%202007/700%20-%20corwm%20july%202006%20 recommendations%20to%20 government.pdf.

Davey, E. (2013) 'Cumbria County Council voted to withdraw from the process to find a host community for an underground radioactive waste disposal facility', Press release, www.gov.uk/government/news/energy-secretary-responds-to-cumbria-nuclear-waste-vote.

DECC (Department of Energy and Climate Change) (2011) *The Carbon Plan: Delivering our Low Carbon Future*, London: Department of Energy and Climate Change.

— (2012) *National Policy Statement for Nuclear Power Generation*, London: Department of Energy and Climate Change

DTI (Department of Trade and Industry) (2007) *The Future of Nuclear Power: The Role of Nuclear Power in a Low Carbon UK Economy*, Consultation Document, London: DTI, May.

EDF Energy (2011) *Proposed Nuclear Development: Hinkley C: Pre-application Consultation*, hinkleypoint. edfenergyconsultation.info/public-documents/j24bridgwater-highways-consultation/.

Endres, D. (2009) 'From wasteland to waste site: the role of discourse in nuclear power's environmental injustices', *Local Environment: The International Journal of Justice and Sustainability*, 14(10): 917–37.

Gamson, A. W. and A. Modigliani (1989) 'Media discourse and public opinion on nuclear power: a constructionist approach', *American Journal of Sociology*, 95(1): 1–37.

Gunderson, W. C. and B. G. Rabe (1999) 'Voluntarism and its limits: Canada's search for radioactive waste-siting candidates', *Canadian Public Administration/Administration Publique du Canada*, 42(2): 193–214.

Hayward, T. (2005) *Constitutional Environmental Rights*, Oxford: Oxford University Press.

Hecht, G. (2012) *Being Nuclear: Africans and the Global Uranium Trade*, Cambridge, MA: MIT Press.

HM Chief Inspector of Nuclear Installations (2011) 'Japanese earthquake and tsunami: implications for the UK nuclear industry', Final report, Bootle: Office for Nuclear Regulation.

Hoffman, S. M. (2001) 'Negotiating eternity: energy policy, environmental justice, and the politics of nuclear waste', *Bulletin of Science, Technology & Society*, 21(6): 456–72.

Jasanoff, S. and B. Wynne (1998) *Science and Decision Making (STS) in Human Choice and Climate Change: The Societal Framework*, vol. 1, Columbus, OH: Battelle Press.

Karlsson, B. G. (2009) 'Nuclear lives: uranium mining, indigenous peoples, and development in India', *Economic and Political Weekly*, 44(34): 43–9.

Kunreuther, H. and D. Easterling (1996) 'The role of compensation in siting hazardous facilities', *Journal of Policy Analysis and Management*, 15(4): 601–22.

Lynas, M. (2011) 'Fukushima's lessons in climate change', *New Statesman*, 17 March, www.newstatesman.com/asia/2011/03/nuclear-power-lynas-japan.

Mackerron, G. and F. Berkhout (2009) 'Learning to listen: institutional change and legitimation in UK radioactive waste policy', *Journal of Risk Research*, 12(7/8): 989–1008.

Makhijani, A. and H. Hu (1995) 'Methodology', in A. Makhijani, H. Hu and K. Yih (eds), *Nuclear Wastelands: A Global Guide to Nuclear Weapons Production and Its Health and Environmental Effects*, Cambridge, MA: MIT Press.

Miller, C. (2000) 'The dynamics of framing environmental values and policy: four models of societal processes', *Environmental Values*, 9: 211–33.

Monbiot, G. (2011) 'The moral case for nuclear power', *Monbiot.com*, 8 August, www.monbiot.com/2011/08/08/the-moral-case-for-nuclear-power/.

Porritt, J. (2011) 'Why George Monbiot is completely wrong about nuclear power', *JonathonPorritt.com*, 26 July, www.jonathonporritt.com/blog/why-george-monbiot-completely-wrong-nuclear-power.

Pralle, S. and J. Boscarino (2011) 'Framing trade-offs: the politics of nuclear power and wind energy in the age of global climate change', *Review of Policy Research*, 28(4): 323–46.

Rawls, J. (1958) 'Justice as fairness', *Philosophical Review*, 67(2): 164–94.

RCEP (Royal Commission on Environmental Pollution) (1976) *Nuclear Power and the Environment*, London: HMSO.

Sarewitz, D. (2004) 'How science makes environmental controversies worse', *Environmental Science & Policy*, 7(5): 385–403.

Schlosberg, D. (2004) 'Reconceiving environmental justice: global movements and political theories', *Environmental Politics*, 13(3): 517–40.

Sharpe, V. A. (2008) 'Policy and politics: "clean" nuclear energy? Global warming, public health and justice', *Hastings Center Report*, 38(4): 16–18.

Shrader-Frechette, K. (2000) 'Duties to future generations, proxy consent, intra- and intergenerational equity: the case of nuclear waste', *Risk Analysis: An International Journal*, 20(6): 771–8.

Simmons, P., K. Bickerstaff and J. Walls (2006) *Country Report – United Kingdom*, Report to CARL Project on Stakeholder Involvement in Radioactive Waste Management, webhost.ua.ac.be/carlresearch/docs/20070723141722BSCN.pdf.

Stanley, A. (2009) 'Just space or spatial justice? Difference, discourse, and environmental justice', *Local Environment: The International Journal of Justice and Sustainability*, 14(10): 999–1014.

Stirling, A. (2005) 'Opening up or closing down: analysis, participation and power in the social appraisal of technology', in I. Scoones and B. Wynne (eds), *Science and Citizens: Globalisation and the Challenge of Engagement*, London: Zed Books.

— (2009) 'Sustainable energy: the challenge of choice', in I. Scrase and G. Mackerron, *Energy for the Future: A New Agenda*, Basingstoke: Palgrave Macmillan.

Sundqvist, G. and M. Elam (2010) 'Public involvement designed to circumvent public concern? The "participatory turn" in European nuclear activities', *Risk, Hazards & Crisis in Public Policy*, 1(4): 203–29.

Taebi, B. and J. L. Kloosterman (2008) 'To recycle or not to recycle? An intergenerational approach to nuclear fuel cycles', *Science & Engineering Ethics*, 14(2): 177–200.

Walker, G. (2009) 'Environmental justice and normative thinking', *Antipode*, 41(1): 203–5.

Young, I. M. (1990) *Justice and the Politics of Difference*, Princeton, NJ: Princeton University Press.

9 McLaren et al.

Abels, G. (2007) 'Citizen involvement in public policy-making: does it improve democratic legitimacy and accountability? The case of pTA', *Interdisciplinary Information Sciences*, 13(1): 103–16.

Aldrich, D. (2005) 'Review: controversial project siting: state policy instruments and flexibility', *Comparative Politics*, 38: 103–23.

Bäckstrand, K., J. Meadowcraft and M. Oppenheimer (2011) 'Editorial: The politics and policy of carbon capture and storage: framing an emergent technology', *Global Environmental Change*, 21: 275–81.

Bell, D., T. Gray and C. Haggett (2005) 'The "social gap" in wind farm siting decisions: explanations and policy responses', *Environmental Politics*, 14: 460–77.

Bergmans, A., M. Elam, D. Kos, M. Polič, P. Simmons, G. Sundqvist and J. Walls (2008) 'Wanting the unwanted: effects of public and stakeholder involvement in the long-term management of radioactive waste and the siting of repository facilities', Final Report, CARL Project, webhost.ua.ac.be/carlresearch/docs/20080222112500ZGYI.pdf.

Bickerstaff, K. (2012) '"Because we've got history here": nuclear waste, cooperative siting, and the relational geography of a complex issue', *Environment and Planning A*, 44(11): 2611–28.

Bielicki, J. M. and J. C. Stephens (2008) 'Public perception of carbon capture and storage technology: workshop report', Energy Technology Innovation Policy research group of the Belfer Center for Science and International Affairs at Harvard University's John F. Kennedy School of Government, Cambridge, MA.

Blowers, A. and P. Leroy (1994) 'Power, politics and environmental inequality: a theoretical and empirical analysis of the process of "peripheralisation"', *Environmental Politics*, 3(2): 197–228.

Bradbury, J., I. Ray, T. Peterson, S. Wade, G. Wong-Parodi and A. Feldpausch (2009) 'The role of social factors in shaping public perceptions of CCS: results of multi-state focus group interviews in the US', *Energy Procedia*, 1: 4665–72.

Bradbury, J. A. (2012) 'Public understanding of and engagement with CCS', in N. Markusson, S. Shackley and B. Evar (eds), *The Social Dynamics of Carbon Capture and Storage*, London: Earthscan, pp. 45–73.

Brunsting, S., M. de Best-Waldhober, C. F. J. Feenstra and T. Mikunda (2011) 'Stakeholder participation practices and onshore CCS: lessons from the Dutch CCS case Barendrecht', *Energy Procedia*, 4: 6376–83.

Brunsting, S., J. Desbarats, M. de Best-Waldhober, E. Duetschke, C. Oltra, P. Upham and H. Riesch (2010) 'The public and CCS: the importance of communication and participation in the context of local realities', *Energy Procedia*, 4: 6241–7.

Butler, C. and P. Simmons (2010) 'Workshop briefing: whole systems equity analysis of nuclear infrastructures', Interdisciplinary Cluster for Energy Systems, Equity and Vulnerability (InCluESEV). Copy available from the authors.

Capek, S. M. (1993) 'The environmental justice frame: a conceptual discussion and an application', *Social Problems*, 40(1): 5–24.

Clinch, J. P. (2006) 'Third party rights of appeal: enhancing democracy or hindering progress?', *Planning Theory & Practice*, 7(3): 327–50.

Cook, S. and T. Ferris (2007) 'Re-evaluating systems engineering as a framework for tackling systems issues', *Systems Research and Behavioural Science*, 24: 169–81.

Corry, O. and H. Riesch (2012)

'Beyond "for and against": environmental NGO evaluations of CCS as a climate change solution', in N. Markusson, S. Shackley and B. Evar (eds), *The Social Dynamics of Carbon Capture and Storage*, London: Earthscan, pp. 91–108.

De Best-Waldhober, M. and D. Daamen (2006) 'Public perceptions and preferences regarding large scale implementation of six CO_2 capture and storage technologies. Well-informed and well-considered opinions versus uninformed pseudo-opinions of the Dutch public', Centre for Energy and Environmental Studies, Leiden University, for NWO/ SenterNovem Project 'Transition to sustainable use of fossil fuels'.

De Coninck, H., J. C. Stephens and B. Metz (2009) 'Global learning on carbon capture and storage: a call for strong international cooperation on CCS demonstration', *Energy Policy*, 37(6): 2161–5.

DECC (Department of Energy and Climate Change) (2012) *Annual Report on Fuel Poverty Statistics*, London: HM Government.

Desbarats, J., P. Upham, H. Riesch, D. Reiner, S. Brunsting, M. de Best-Waldhober, E. Duetschke, C. Oltra, R. Sala and C. McLachlan (2010) 'Review of the public participation practices for CCS and non-CCS projects in Europe. Near CO_2 WP1', Institute for European Environmental Policy.

Devine-Wright, P. (2007) 'Energy citizenship: psychological aspects of evolution in sustainable energy technologies', in J. Murphy (ed.), *Framing the Present, Shaping the Future: Contemporary Governance of Sustainable Technologies*, London: Earthscan, pp. 63–86.

Dobson, A. (1998) *Justice and the*

Environment: Conceptions of Environmental Sustainability and Dimensions of Social Justice, Oxford: OUP.

DTI (Department of Trade and Industry) (2003) *Our Energy Future – Creating a Low Carbon Future*, London: Department of Trade and Industry.

Ekins, P. (2004) 'Step changes for decarbonising the energy system: research needs for renewables, energy efficiency, and nuclear power', *Energy Policy*, 32: 1891–904.

Ekins, P. and J. Skea (2009) 'Making the transition to a secure and low-carbon energy system: synthesis report', UKERC 2050 Report, www.ukerc. ac.uk/ Downloads/PDF/U/UKERC Energy2050/0906UKERC 2050.pdf.

Endres, D. (2009) 'From wasteland to waste site: the role of discourse in nuclear power's environmental injustices', *Local Environment*, 14: 417–36.

Evans, K., K. Aubry, M. Hawkins, T. A. Curley and T. Porter-O'Grady (1995) 'Whole systems shared governance: a model for the integrated health system', *Journal of Nursing Administration*, 25: 18–27.

Evans, V. (2010) 'Beware infringing CCS patents', *Utility Week*, www.utility week.co.uk/news/ news_story.asp?id= 121337&title= Beware+infringing+CCS+patents.

Evar, B. and S. Shackley (2012) 'Technology management in the face of scientific uncertainty', in N. Markusson, S. Shackley and B. Evar (eds), *The Social Dynamics of Carbon Capture and Storage*, London: Earthscan, pp. 172–87.

Fearne, A., R. Duffy and S. Hornibrook (2004) 'Measuring distributive and procedural

justice in buyer/supplier relationships: an empirical study of UK supermarket supply chains', Presented at the 88th Seminar of the European Association of Agricultural Economics, Retailing and Producer–Retailer Relationships in Food Chains, Paris, 5/6 May.

Flynn, R., P. Bellaby and M. Ricci (2006) 'Risk perception of an emergent technology: the case of hydrogen energy', Forum, *Qualitative Social Research*, 7(1): www. qualitative-research.net/index. php/fqs/article/viewArticle/58.

Forbes, S. M., F. Almendra and M. S. Ziegler (2010) *CCS and Community Engagement. Guidelines for Community Engagement in Carbon Dioxide Capture, Transport, and Storage Projects*, Washington, DC: World Resources Institute.

Foxon, T., G. Hammond and P. Pearson (2010) 'Developing transition pathways for a low carbon electricity system in the UK', *Technology Forecasting and Social Change*, 77: 1203–13.

Funtowicz, S. O. and J. Ravetz (1993) 'Science for the post-normal age', *Futures*, 25(7): 739–57.

Gaffney, J. (1999) 'Due process in the World Trade Organisation: the need for procedural justice in the dispute settlement system', *American University International Law Review*, 14: 1173–221.

Gardiner, S. M. (2011) 'Climate justice', in J. Dryzek, D. Schlosberg and R. Norgaard (eds), *Oxford Handbook of Climate Change and Society*, Oxford: OUP.

Gardiner, S. M., S. Caney, D. Jamieson and H. Shue (eds) (2010) *Climate Ethics: Essential Readings*, Oxford: OUP.

Geels, F. (2005) *Technological Transitions and System Innovations: A Co-evolutionary and Sociotechnical Analysis*, Cheltenham: Edward Elgar.

Global CCS Institute (2012) 'Global status of large-scale integrated CCS projects', June 2012 update, cdn.globalccsinstitute.com/sites/default/files/publications/41146/globalstatusoflargescaleintegratedprojectsjune2012update.pdf.

Gowda, M. and D. Easterling (2000) 'Voluntary siting and equity: the MRS facility experience in Native America', *Risk Analysis*, 20: 917–30.

Hammond, J. and S. Shackley (2010) 'Towards a public communication and engagement strategy for carbon dioxide capture and storage projects in Scotland', Scottish Centre for Carbon Capture Working Paper 2010-08.

Hansen, J., M. Sato, P. Kharecha, D. Beerling, R. Berner, V. Masson-Delmotte, M. Pagani, M. Raymo, D. L. Royer and J. C. Zachos (2008) 'Target atmospheric CO_2: where should humanity aim?', *Open Atmospheric Science Journal*, 2: 217–31.

Hansson, A. (2012) 'Colonizing the future: the case of CCS', in N. Markusson, S. Shackley and B. Evar (eds), *The Social Dynamics of Carbon Capture and Storage*, London: Routledge, pp. 74–90.

Hitchings, D. (2003) *Advanced Systems Thinking, Engineering and Management*, Boston, MA: Artech House.

Hoffman, S. (2001) 'Negotiating eternity: energy policy, environmental justice, and the politics of nuclear waste', *Bulletin of Science, Technology and Society*, 21: 456–72.

Hub Research Consultants (2005) *Seeing the Light: The Impact of Micro-generation on the Way We Use Energy: Qualitative Research Findings*, On behalf of the Sustainable Consumption Roundtable for the Sustainable Development Commission, London.

Hughes, T. P. (1989) *American Genesis: A Century of Invention and Technological Enthusiasm 1870–1970*, New York: Penguin.

Huhne, C. (2011) cited in 'Scottish-Power welcomes Chris Huhne MP to visit carbon capture prototype at Longannet power station', Press release, www.scottishpower.com/PressReleases_2118.htm.

Hunold, C. and I. M. Young (1998) 'Justice, democracy and hazardous siting', *Political Studies*, 46: 82–99.

International Energy Agency (2009) 'Technology roadmap: Carbon Capture and Storage', www.iea.org/publications/freepublications/publication/CCS_Roadmap.pdf.

IPCC (Intergovernmental Panel on Climate Change) (2005) *IPCC Special Report on Carbon Dioxide Capture and Storage*, Prepared by Working Group III of the Intergovernmental Panel on Climate Change (ed. B. Metz, O. Davidson, H. C. de Coninck, M. Loos and L. A. Meyer), Cambridge: Cambridge University Press.

ITUC (International Trade Union Confederation) (2012) 'Annual survey of violations of trade union rights 2012', survey.ituc-csi.org/Colombia.html?lang=en#tabs-5.

Joss, S. and A. Brownlea (1999) 'Considering the concept of procedural justice for public policy and decision-making in science and technology', *Science and Public Policy*, 26(5): 321–30.

Keeney, R. L. and K. Nair (1975) 'Decision analysis for the siting of nuclear power plants: the relevance of multiattribute utility theory', *Proceedings of the IEEE*, 63: 494–501.

Kuhn, R. G. (1998) 'Social and political issues in siting a nuclear-fuel waste disposal facility in Ontario, Canada', *Canadian Geographer*, 42(1): 14–28.

Kumar, N. (1996) 'The power of trust in manufacturer–retailer relationships', *Harvard Business Review*, 74: 92–106.

Kunreuther, H. and D. Easterling (1996) 'The role of compensation in siting hazardous facilities', *Journal of Policy Analysis and Management*, 15(4): 601–22.

Macnaghten, P. and R. Owen (2011) 'Good governance for geo-engineering', *Nature*, 479: 293.

Maiese, M. (2004) 'Procedural justice', in G. Burgess and H. Burgess (eds), *Beyond Intractability*, Boulder, CO: Conflict Research Consortium, University of Colorado, www. beyondintractability.org/essay/ procedural_justice/.

Malone, E. L., J. J. Dooley and J. A. Bradbury (2010) 'Moving from misinformation derived from public attitude surveys on carbon dioxide capture and storage towards realistic stakeholder involvement', *International Journal of Greenhouse Gas Control*, 4: 419–25.

Mao, H., H. Yang, Z. Hu and S. Wang (2010) 'Research on whole-system dynamic meteorology model for IATE', *Acta Metrologica Sinica*, 31: 241–4.

Markusson, N. and S. Shackley (2012) 'Introduction to Part 1: Perceptions and representations', in N. Markusson, S. Shackley and B. Evar (eds), *The Social Dynamics of Carbon Capture and Storage*, London: Earthscan, pp. 33–44.

Markusson, N., I. Ishii and J. C. Stephens (2012). 'Learning in CCS demonstration projects', in N. Markusson, S. Shackley and B. Evar (eds), *The Social Dynamics of Carbon Capture and Storage*, London: Earthscan, pp. 222–44.

Markusson, N., S. Shackley and B. Evar (2012) 'Conclusions', in N. Markusson, S. Shackley and B. Evar (eds), *The Social Dynamics of Carbon Capture and Storage*, London: Earthscan, pp. 245–73.

McLaren, D. (2012a) 'Procedural justice in carbon capture and storage', *Energy & Environment*, 23(2/3): 345–64.

— (2012b) 'A comparative global assessment of potential negative emissions technologies', *Process Safety and Environmental Protection*, dx.doi.org/10.1016/j.psep. 2012.10.005.

Meadowcroft, J. and O. Langhelle (2011) *Caching the Carbon: The Politics and Policy of Carbon Capture and Storage*, London: Edward Elgar.

Michanek, G. and P. Soderholm (2009) 'Licensing of nuclear power plants: the case of Sweden in international comparison', *Energy Policy*, 37: 4086–97.

Mikunda, T. and F. Feenstra (2009) 'Effective communication strategies to engage the public and stakeholders around CCS projects: a review of country experiences', Workshop report ECN-O-10-039, Energy Research Centre of the Netherlands.

Mulgundmath, V. P. and S. Bowden (2011) 'Plant product development: post-combustion CO_2 capture process emissions', Doosan Power Systems for Ayrshire Power Ltd, PP-11-014.

Newell, P. (2005) 'Race, class and the global politics of environmental inequality', *Global Environmental Politics*, 5: 70–94.

Okereke, C. (2006) 'Global environmental sustainability: intragenerational equity and conceptions of justice in multilateral environmental regimes', *Geoforum*, 37: 725–38.

Owen, R., P. M. Macnaghten, J. S. Stilgoe, E. Fisher, M. Gorman and D. H. Guston (forthcoming) 'A framework for responsible innovation', in R. Owen, M. Heintz and J. Bessant (eds), *Responsible Innovation: Concepts and Practice*, London: Wiley.

Patel, Z. (2006) 'Of questionable value: the role of practitioners in building sustainable cities', *Geoforum*, 37: 682–94.

Pidgeon, N., K. Parkhill, A. Corner and N. Vaughan (2013) 'Deliberating stratospheric aerosols for climate geoengineering: the case of the UK SPICE project', *Nature Climate Change*, doi: 10.1038/NCLIMATE1807.

Pollak, M. F. and E. J. Wilson (2009) 'Regulating geologic sequestration in the United States: early rules take divergent approaches', *Environmental Science and Technology*, 43(9): 3035–41.

Reiner, D., H. Riesch and C. K. Chyong (2011) 'Opinion shaping factors towards CCS and local CCS projects: public and stakeholder survey and focus groups', Near CO_2 Project Report (WP2), Judge Business School, Cambridge, www.communicationnearco2.eu/file

admin/communicationnearco2/user/docs/W2.1_Report_Final.pdf.

Roche, M. Y., S. Mourato, M. Fischedick, K. Pietzner and P. Viebahn (2010) 'Public attitudes towards and demand for hydrogen and fuel cell vehicles: a review of the evidence and methodological implications', *Energy Policy*, 38: 5301–10.

Rogers-Hayden, T. and N. F. Pidgeon (2007) 'Moving engagement "upstream"? Nanotechnologies and the Royal Society and Royal Academy of Engineering inquiry', *Public Understanding of Science*, 16: 346–64.

Schlosberg, D. (2007) *Defining Environmental Justice – Theories, Movements, and Nature*, Oxford: OUP.

Sharpe, V. (2008) '"Clean" nuclear energy?: global warming, public health, and justice', Hastings Center Report 38, pp. 16–18.

Shrader-Frechette, K. (2000) 'Duties to future generations, proxy consent, intra- and intergenerational equity: the case of nuclear waste', *Risk Analysis*, 20: 771–8.

Shrader-Frechette, K. and R. Cooke (2004) 'Ethics and choosing appropriate means to an end: problems with coal mine and nuclear workplace safety', *Risk Analysis*, 24(1): 147–56.

Shue, H. (1992) 'The uavoidability of justice', in A. Hurrell and B. Kingsbury (eds), *The International Politics of the Environment: Actors, Interests, and Institutions*, Oxford: OUP, pp. 373–97.

Solum, L. B. (2004) 'Procedural justice', bepress Legal Series Working Paper 141, law.bepress.com/expresso/eps/141.

Stanley, A. (2009) 'Just space or spatial justice? Difference, discourse, and environmental justice', *Local Environment*, 14: 999–1014.

Stasinopoulos, P., M. H. Smith, K. Hargroves and C. Desha (2009) *Whole System Design: An Integrated Approach to Sustainable Engineering*, London: Earthscan.

Stirling, A. (2008) '"Opening up" and "closing down": power, participation, and pluralism in the social appraisal of technology', *Science, Technology, & Human Values*, 33(2): 262–94.

Strachan, N., S. Pye and R. Kanna (2009) 'The iterative contribution and relevance of modelling to UK energy policy', *Energy Policy*, 37: 817–30.

Taebi, B. and J. Kloosterman (2008) 'To recycle or not to recycle? An intergenerational approach to nuclear fuel cycles', *Science and Engineering Ethics*, 14: 177–200.

UNEP, ILO, IOE and ITUC (2008) 'Green jobs: towards decent work in a sustainable, low-carbon world', www.unep.org/labour_ environment/features/greenjobs. asp.

Upreti, B. and D. van der Horst (2004) 'National renewable energy policy and local opposition in the UK: the failed development of a biomass electricity plant', *Biomass and Bioenergy*, 26: 61–9.

USEPA (US Environmental Protection Agency) (1998) *Final guidance for incorporating environmental justice concerns in EPA's NEPA compliance analyses*, Washington, DC: US Environmental Protection Agency.

Van der Horst, D. (2007) 'NIMBY or not? Exploring the relevance of location and the politics of voiced opinions in renewable energy siting controversies', *Energy Policy*, 35: 2705–14.

Vergragt, P. J., N. Markusson and H. Karlsson (2011) 'Carbon capture and storage, bioenergy with carbon capture and storage, and the escape from the fossil-fuel lock-in', *Global Environmental Change*, 21(2): 282–92.

Walker, G. (1998) 'Environmental justice and the politics of risk', *Town and Country Planning*, 67: 358–9.

Walker, G. (2012) *Environmental Justice: Concepts, Evidence and Politics*, London: Routledge.

Walker, G. and H. Bulkeley (2006) 'Geographies of environmental justice', *Geoforum*, 37: 655–9.

Walker, G. and R. Day (2012) 'Fuel poverty as injustice: integrating distribution, recognition and procedure in the struggle for affordable warmth', *Energy Policy*, 49: 69–75.

Walker, G., K. Burningham, J. Fielding, G. Smith, D. Thrush and H. Fay (2006) 'Addressing environmental inequalities: flood risk', Science Report SC020061/ SR1, Environment Agency, Bristol.

Watson, J. (ed.) (2012) 'Carbon capture and storage: realising the potential', Report for UKERC, UKERC/RR/ESY/CCS/2012/001.

Whitmarsh, L., P. Upham, W. Poortinga, C. McLachlan, A. Darnton, P. Devine-Wright, C. Demski and F. Sherry-Brennan (2011) 'Public attitudes, understanding, and engagement in relation to low-carbon energy: a selective review of academic and non-academic literatures', Report for RCUK Energy Programme, Research Councils UK, Swindon.

Winskel, M. (2012) 'CCS: a disruptive technology for innovation theory', in N. Markusson, S. Shackley and B. Evar (eds), *The*

Social Dynamics of Carbon Capture and Storage, London: Routledge, pp. 199–221.

Wolsink, M. (2007) 'Wind power implementation: the nature of public attitudes: equity and fairness instead of "backyard motives"', *Renewable and Sustainable Energy Review*, 11: 1188–207.

Index

Aboriginal knowledge, 144
access, 177, 179; definition of, 127; in renewable energy, 134
accountability, 94
actants, 17
Actor Network Theory, 17, 28
actors: diversity of (in energy vulnerability situations, 26; in renewable energy, 11); omitted from energy decisions, 57
affordable energy, 61, 62, 66
agencement, 16
agency, 21–2; distributed, 22
air conditioning: in USA, 63; need for, 3; possible trigger for energy vulnerability, 63
air pollution, 118, 172
air travel, emissions associated with, 82–3
allocative justice, 12
alternatives, 28; in assemblage discourse, 25–6
ARTEMIS project (Austria), 93
Ashden Awards, 70, 74, 75
assemblage: and energy vulnerability, 19–26; concept of, 14–29 *passim* (criticism of, 19; features of, 19–26; in analysis of cities, 29); heterogeneity of components of, 17; temporal synchronicity in, 25; time-space of, 18
assembling of associations, 17
austerity, limitations imposed by, 86
Australia, 61

back-up systems for technological failure, 27
Barendrecht, Netherlands, opposition to CCS project in, 169, 179
bedroom, heating data for, 37

behavioural change, 89, 112, 114, 164
Bell, D., 4, 6, 87–9
Bioenergy with CCS (BECCS), 175–6
biofuels, 8; production of, 48; technologies of, 57
biogas energy production, 110
biomass district heating, 112
Bournbrook (Birmingham), 31–45 *passim*
British Gas, Green Streets programme, 71, 75
buying rather than renting, 43

Canada, community volunteering in, 144
capabilities, concept of, 13, 145, 157
capacity-building in communities, 74, 76
capture readiness, concept of, 169
carbon, oceanic storage of, 175
Carbon Capture and Storage (CCS), 5, 6, 8, 9, 13, 49, 50, 158–80; clustering of facilities, 173–4; criticism of, 169; development and implementation of, 171–5; discussion of, 167–78; failure to install, 171; freedom of information, 177; generative of new pollutants, 173; impact on employment, 174; implications for other energy technologies, 176–7; increases water consumption, 172; life cycle of, 169–71; policy preference for, 170; research and innovation process, 169–71; systemic and indirect impacts of, 176–7; transport and storage of, 175–6
carbon emissions, 79, 104; differential distribution of,

81; embedded in products, 87; non-equality of, 65; of residential sector, 85; of UK, 91; reduction of, 87, 89, 91, 92, 95, 98, 112, 139, 167
carbon footprint associated with food consumption, 89
carbon intensity, reduction of *see* decarbonization
carbon price floor mechanism, 86
carbon pricing, 161
central heating systems, 21–2
centralization/decentralization, 136, 176
Centre for Sustainable Energy (CSE), 82–4, 85, 86, 87
change, radical, resistance to, 50–1
Chernobyl disaster, 142, 152
Child Well-being Index (CWI), 34
China, 61
classroom, as assemblage, 17–18
Climate Challenge Fund, 71, 73
climate change, 1, 48, 49, 53, 61, 62–5; and energy justice, 79–90; complexity of policy process, 67; distribution of impacts, 95; factor in nuclear energy debate, 73, 151–4; mitigation of, 4, 6, 139, 146, 153, 161, 171–2 (costs of, 1, 3, 66, 80, 83–4; distributive burdens of, 73; moral hazard in, 170)
Climate Change Act (2008) (UK), 79, 85
climate litigation, 171–2
coal, use of, 172–3, 174
cold, 44; acceptance of, 38–9, 41; endurance of, morally wrong, 62; health impacts of, 39–40, 45
collective action perspective, 126–8
Colombia, coal mining in, 173
Committee for Radioactive Waste Management (CoRWM), 140, 146–51, 155–6
Committee on Climate Change, 79
commodification of carbon, 4
Common Pool Resource management, 117
common pool resources, 12–13, 116–38, 132–5, 137

community, 123, 126–8; as mechanism for behaviour change, 69; as site for appropriate technology, 61; as site for climate mitigation, 69; as site for renewable energy technologies, 69; benefits from wind farms, 88; composition of, 132; concept of, 69; definition of, 75, 133; empowerment of, 179; matched to energy system, 131–2; volunteering to host nuclear waste, 143–4
compensation mechanisms, 143, 160
compliance rules, 135
condensation, 35
Constructive Conflict Methodology, 57
consumers, role in establishing renewables capacity, 126
consumption of energy, politics of, 2–4
cooling systems, 24, 63
cost–benefit analysis, 92
Cowell, Richard, 88
Cumbria, nuclear industry in, 150

dams, displacement of peoples, 47
debt, 25, 84; coping with, 27
decarbonization: of energy systems, 1, 6, 114, 151, 168 (aspect of nuclear energy debate, 154; Japanese approach to, 110); of everyday life, 3
decentralized governance of energy usage, 50
decentring the human as subject, 17
'decide, announce, defend' approach, 179
decision-making, streamlining of, 130
Deleuze, Gilles, 16–18, 22
demand: management of, 136, 137; reduction of, 49
Demand-Side Management, 125
demos, constitution of, 4
Department of Energy and Climate Change (UK), 79
Desertec programme, 59

distributed generation (DG), 66, 116, 121; beliefs about, 123; ownership and control of assets of, 133

distributed generation microgrids (DisGenMiGrids), 10, 117, 122, 124, 125, 126, 128, 132–3, 135, 136; as socio-technical systems, 123; characteristics of, 121; for all, 129–32; regulation of, 128

distribution, 144; concept of, 140

distributive justice, 11, 48, 64, 65–7, 68, 71–4, 78, 80, 82–7, 130, 158, 160, 179; intra-generational, 141

diversification of energy resources, 118

diversity of situations of fuel poverty, 26

dominant groups, power of, 48

double glazing, 35, 42

draught proofing, 33

dynamic understandings of fuel poverty, 27

dynamics and flux of assemblages, 24–5

earthquakes, 112

ecological footprints of communities, 65, 74

efficiency of energy usage, 30, 31, 83, 85, 135; improvement of, 66; of housing stock, 41, 42, 45 (in rented properties, 33) *see also* inefficient heating systems

electric vehicles, 104, 107, 117, 122, 132, 137, 138

electricity bills, calculation of, 12

embeddedness of technical systems, 163–4

empowerment, 94

Energy Act (2011) (UK), 33

energy bills: in student housing, 40; increased to drive investment, 87; of wealthy and poor households, 83; portion allocated to environmental costs, 104; reduction of, 85; sharing of, 44

energy blackouts, 79

energy certificates, 42

energy companies, 134, 170; projects initiated by, 127

Energy Company Obligation, 84, 85

energy consumption, reduction of, 89, 176; mandatory, 111

energy diaries, keeping of, 35, 37, 38

energy efficiency *see* efficiency of energy usage

energy injustice, 2; scale, scope and production of, 7

energy justice, 1–13, 14, 52, 57; achievement of, 6–8; and climate change, 79–90; and low-carbon transition, 61–78; complexity of, 8; conceived relationally, 8; concept of, 47, 78 (contested, 48); in context of climate change, 61, 62–5; in relation to nuclear energy, 146–54; in sustainability transitions research, 46, 59; in UK, 139–57; literature regarding, 159, 178; use of term, 2; viewed relationally, 11

energy literacy, promotion of, 102

energy market, reforms of, 119

energy poverty *see* fuel poverty

energy research, need for, 9

Energy Research Centre (UK), 163

Energy Saving Trust, 91

energy security, 8, 14, 66, 92, 108; of UK, 79

energy systems, 6, 11, 46; complexity of injustice issues, 2

energy technologies, complexity of, 46

energy underclass, 5

energy vulnerability, 2, 7, 8, 9–10, 15, 63, 68; among urban young adults, 30–45; as assemblage, 12, 14–29; concept of, 16; interacting elements of, 11; recognition of, 44; spatially dynamic view of, 11; use of term, 3

Engineering and Physical Science Research Council (EPSRC), 163

enhanced oil recovery (EOR), 173

entities, 26; in energy vulnerability discourse, 20

environmental justice, 64, 94, 128, 129, 133, 158, 165, 174, 180; literature regarding, 165
epistemic justice, 144
equity, 93, 98, 129–30, 140, 165; in context of micro-generation, 94–5 *see also* fairness
equity assessment tool (EAT), 91, 95–9, 109, 114–15
ethics: of nuclear waste disposal, 151–2; use of word, 148
European Union (EU): Emissions Trading Scheme, 104; energy efficiency directives, 135; targets for greenhouse gas emissions, 1

Fabians study of climate change, 89
fairness, 5, 13, 48, 79, 88, 89, 90, 128–9, 130, 165, 178; of microgrid benefits, 116–38 *see also* equity
Feed-in-Tariffs (FiTs), 5, 26, 63, 84, 93, 95, 102, 104, 108, 110, 111, 113, 114; benefits of, 107
flooding, 81
fossil fuels, 46, 48, 49, 50, 79, 92, 108, 114, 158, 161, 169, 172, 174; extraction of, impact on indigenous peoples, 47
framing, concept of, 139–40
freedom of information, 177
free-riding, problem of, 3, 89, 135
fuel poverty, 2–4, 61, 66, 74, 84, 85, 86, 87, 95, 103, 112, 176; as geographical assemblage, 20; concept of, 2, 39 (in UK, 23–4; rooted in UK experience, 14, 30; definition of, 85; estimates of, 99; in rural areas, 104; measurements of, 27; relational account of, 23; residents' experiences of, 37–40
Fukushima disaster, 108–9, 111, 142, 146, 152–3, 157
Fuller, S., 21–2

Gaidourmadra, island of Kythnos, Greece, 105, 114
Geels, F., 51, 52
gender relations, 46

geography: of resources, 59; of transitions, 52–3, 58, 60
geothermal energy production, 111
Global CCS Institute, 168
governance, reflexive, 54
Greece, as case study, 105–8
Green Communities scheme (UK), 71, 76
Green Deal, 33–4, 84, 85, 103, 104, 113
greenhouse gases: reducing emissions of, 64, 137, 158; right to emit, 1
Guattari, Félix, 16–18, 22

harmonization of regulatory platforms, 135
harms in households, diversity of, 24
health consequences, 165
heat pumps, 104
heating of homes: during the day, 39; refusal to use, 37, 38
heating systems, 42 *see also* inefficient heating systems
heatwaves, 81
homeowners, preferential treatment of, 161
hot water systems, 33
housework, transformation of, 46
housing career paths, 43
housing shortages, 27
housing stock: age and condition of, 30, 102, 104; improvements to fabric of, 113; low-carbon, 102
Hunterston (Ayrshire), CCS project proposed, 172
hydropower schemes, displacement of peoples, 47

impartiality, 177, 179
inclusion, 151
indigenous peoples, affected by nuclear energy projects, 141, 143
inefficient heating systems, 24, 27
informed consent, 143
injustice, production of, 8, 9–10
innovation: definition of, 123; dynamic patterns of, 50; studies of, 47

innovation systems, territorial, 58–9
institutional change, acceptance of, 124–6
institutional obstacles to renewable energy, 116–18
institutional variety, need for, 13
insulation, 33, 35, 43; in lofts, 42
insurance: against flooding, 81; for micro-generation equipment, 112
interdisciplinary approaches, 60, 93, 95–6, 164, 178, 179
Interdisciplinary Cluster on Energy Systems, Equity and Vulnerability (InCluESEV), 1, 3, 6, 16
intergenerational justice, 142, 147, 148, 151, 152, 153, 172, 177, 180
Intergovernmental Panel on Climate Change (IPCC), 169
International Energy Agency (IEA), 163, 169
intra-generational justice, 141, 142, 147

Japan, case study of, 108–12
Joseph Rowntree Foundation (JRF), 7; Climate Change and Social Justice (CCSJ) programme, 3, 9, 79–90 (details of, 80–1)
Junior Climate Challenge Fund, 75
Just Sustainabilities, 2
justice, 6–8, 9; as fairness, 128–9, 147; claims for, 48; concept of, 62, 77; framed as procedure and engagement, 149–5; in Carbon Capture and Storage, 158–80; in case of nuclear energy, 140–5; in demand response, 137; principles of, 128 see also distributive justice, intergenerational justice, intra-generational justice, nuclear justice, procedural justice and social justice
justice assemblages, socio-material complexity of, 10

knowledges, plural, recognition of, 161 see also Aboriginal knowledge
Kyotango (Japan): micro-grid project, 109; typhoon, 110, 112

Kyoto Protocol on climate change, 170

landlords: implicated in energy consumption, 40–4; observance of energy efficiency standards, 33; of student housing, 32; power of, 44; private, and energy efficiency, 114; tenants' relationships with, 31 see also Registered Social Landlords
Landlord's Energy Saving Allowance (LESA), 33, 45
landscape, symbolic meaning of, 132
landscape level of transitions, 51
Latour, B., 21–2
leaking ceilings, 41
letting agencies: non-responsiveness of, 41; power of, 44
liability for risks, 161
life cycle analysis, 92
living-rooms, heating data for, 37
local forms of knowledge, 55
lock-ins, institutional, 117, 119, 138
London Low Carbon Zones programme, 71–5
Longannet (UK), CCS trial project in, 170
low-carbon communities, in UK, emergence of, 69–70
Low Carbon Communities Challenge (UK), 71, 73, 74, 75
Low Carbon Communities Network, 73, 74, 75
low-carbon community programmes, 12; distribution of risks, 71; justice dimensions of, 70–7 see also London Low Carbon Zones programme
low-carbon policy objectives, social and equity in, 2
low-carbon systems, geographical space for, 122
Low Carbon Transition Plan (UK), 69–70
low-carbon transitions, 4–6, 8, 47, 48, 49, 56, 59, 79, 86, 90, 118, 133, 153, 158, 159, 164; costs and benefits

of, 58; in UK, 61–78; justice aspects of, 7

Lynas, Mark, 152–3

Managing Radioactive Waste Safely (MRWS), 147, 150, 155

marginalized groups: engagement with, 60; recognition of, 66, 77; voice of, 6

Market Allocation (MARKAL), 163

market regulation of energy use, 10

Mediterranean Solar Plan, 59

messiness and variety, 12, 27; in assemblages, 23–4; in energy debate, 10; of political change, 54; of technological systems, 163

metering, smart, 121, 124, 129, 135, 136; control of, 134

microgeneration, 5, 6, 10, 26, 49, 70; capital funding for, 112; costs and benefits of, 128; fairness of, 116–38; in rented properties, 103; subsidization of, 104; thermal, 113; UK definition of, 91–2; whole-systems approach to, 91–115

microgrid systems, 7, 10, 12; benefits of, 106; optimization of, 137; smart, in relation to distributed generation, 118

'milieu', 22

mitigation see climate change, mitigation of

Monbiot, George, 153

moral hazard, in climate mitigation, 170

mould, 35

Multi Level Perspective framework, 47, 51–3; criticism of, 52, 54

multi-criteria decision analysis, 92

National Innovation Systems (NIS), 55, 58

natural resources, local repercussions of, 59

Navajo nation, impacted by uranium dust, 143

negative emissions technologies (NETs), 175

negative impacts: of nuclear energy, narrative of, 153; trading of, 152

neighbouring consumers, energy sharing with, 134

neoliberalism, place-specific contingency of, 23

NESTA Big Green Challenge, 70, 73, 75

Netherlands, transition in energy system of, 52, 53–4

networks of entities, 19–21

New Energy and Industrial Technology Development Organization (NEDO), 108–10

niche level of transitions, 51

Nirex organization, 149, 150

non-human entities: in energy vulnerability discourse, 20; taking account of, 17

North American blackout, 21

Nuclear Decommissioning Authority (NDA), 149; National Stakeholder Forum, 150

nuclear energy, 6, 9, 13, 48, 49, 50, 105, 108, 109, 113, 159–60, 177, 180; accidents in production process, 142, 156 see also Chernobyl disaster and Fukushima disaster; effect on indigenous populations, 141–2; ethics and justice of, 140–5; in the UK, 139–57 (political discourse on, 7, 145); reframing of (as low-carbon option, 139, 146, 151; in climate change debate, 151, 155); research into, 11; siting of plants, 62

nuclear justice, 156, 157

nuclear waste, 141–2, 143, 146–51, 175; disposal of (ethics of, 146, 147, 151–2; geological disposal of, 148); management of, 155–6, 159–60

nuclear wastelands, concept of, 141–2

objectivity, in context of CCS, 177

oil crisis (1974), 118

opening up and closing down, 154–5

openness of decision-making processes, 130

opposition to outcomes, 160, 162; in
Barendrecht CCS project, 169
otherness, inclusion of, 164
ownership of assets in energy
systems, 129

participation, 5, 13, 55, 57, 74, 80,
87, 88, 94, 127, 129, 130, 145, 148,
161, 162, 165, 166, 171, 177, 179,
180; concept of, 140; early, need
for, 178; engagement of nuclear
industry in, 150; false, 162;
inadequate on its own, 167;
obstacles to, 68; right to, 67;
to promote legitimacy and
accountability, 165
participatory stakeholder dialogue
process, 57
patents, in CSS technologies, 170
path dependency, 119, 131
personal carbon emissions, 114;
allowances, 104
petrochemical plants, siting of, 62
photovoltaic systems, 93, 105, 108,
109, 110, 114, 134, 161
political power, concentration of, 178
Porritt, Jonathon, 153
precautionary foresight, 54–5
pre-payment meters, 21
principle of generalized symmetry, 21
procedural justice, 11, 48, 64, 67–8,
74–7, 80, 82, 87–9, 129, 134, 143,
162, 165, 166, 178; embedding
principles of, 163–7
property, as bundle of rights, 128
property rights, in common pool
systems, 127
proportionality, principle of, 4, 87–8
proximity principle, 160
pseudo-opinions, 162
public acceptance, 124–5, 147, 179

Q methodology, 57

Rafina, Attica, Greece, 105
Rawls, J., 128
recognition, 4, 13, 65–8, 71–7, 78,
80, 131, 134, 144, 145, 165, 177,

179; concept of, 140; of energy
vulnerability, 44; of marginalized
groups, 77; reducing energy
demand, 79
regime level of transitions, 51
Regional Innovation Systems (RIS), 58
Registered Social Landlords (RSLs),
99, 102
regulation, 134–5
remediation, 143; racial divide in,
141 see also climate change,
mitigation of
renewable energy, 12, 69–70, 108, 109,
111, 113, 116–38, 169; geography of,
59; integration of, 119; opposition
to sitings of, 160; stagnant
deployment of, 125
rented accommodation, 43; fuel
poverty in, 30–1; private sector,
99, 103
Research Council (UK), 1, 171
responsibility, 65–8, 71–7, 78;
common but differentiated, 82–3;
for carbon emissions, 82; for
contribution to climate change,
81 (distribution of, 95)
retrofit work, on housing, 85, 87
rights, 65–8, 71–7, 78, 79, 165; sets of,
166–7
roofs, loss of heat through, 35
Rowe, F., 4, 6, 87–8
rural locations, energy bills in, 102;
fuel poverty in, 104

scale, flattening of, 23
second-hand goods, buying of, 83
security of energy supply see energy
security
self-governance, 116, 118, 131; need
for, 13
Selly Oak (Birmingham), 34
siting: of carbon capture and
storage facilities, 161, 174, 175;
of energy production facilities,
146; of hazardous facilities,
162, 166 (disputes over, 62); of
nuclear waste facilities, 148, 156,
159–60; of power generation, risks

associated with, 4; 'social site characterization', 174
smart grids, 7, 49, 116; definition of, 119–22; innovation in, 122–4; IT in, 137
smart metering *see* metering, smart
social justice, 79, 86
societal change, evolutionary nature of, 50
solar energy, 59; from deserts, 122; obstacles to, 127 *see also* photovoltaic systems
space and place, 22–3, 58; for energy generation, use of, 122; of transitions, 52
spatial planning decisions, 130
stage-gate appraisal, 171
standard of living, sustainable minimum, 89
standardization, 134–5
Stirling, A., 154
storage capacity, 118
students: ghettoization of, 32–3; housing needs of, 31–3 (as niche market, 32); second-year experiences of, 41–2
subsidies, 26; environmentally perverse, 86; for energy technologies, 63
subtractability, 117
success of energy assemblages, 28
sun, right to capture, 134
sustainability, 139; contested concept, 48, 54; issues of fairness arising from, 3; of energy systems, 1–2; of lifestyles, 74; of sustainable technologies, 55–6; of transitions, theory of, 49–59
SWOT analysis, 97
Swyngedouw, Erik, 4
system failure, concept of, 56

tariffs, variability of, 136
taxation: carbon taxes, 87; changes to, 86; of energy flows, 137
Technological Innovation System (TIS) framework, 47, 51, 55–7; criticism of, 57

technology, appropriate, 93
thermal camera imaging, 35
trading-off of risks, 152, 153, 156
'transition arena', 53, 55
Transition Management, 47, 51, 53–5
Transition Network, 74
Transition Towns movement, 50, 70
transitions, 4–6; concept of, 47; cost and benefits of, 60; dynamic patterns of, 50; management of, 8; power and negotiation dynamics in, 52; theory of, 49–59
transparency, 94
travel, by sustainable means, 89
trust/distrust, 130–1

under-consumption of energy, 3
United Kingdom (UK): climate change projections for, 63; concept of fuel poverty in, 2; energy justice in, 139–57; fuel mix of, 91; housing needs of young adults in, 31–4; low-carbon community programmes in, 61–78; monitoring of fuel-poor households, 22 *see also* low-carbon communities, in UK
United Nations Economic Committee for Europe, 167
United Nations Framework Convention on Climate Change, 82
United States of America (USA), energy vulnerability initiatives in, 22
universal credit, 86
uranium: hazards of dust, 143; mining, distributional effects of, 160; production of, 142
urbanization, 46

VAT, on energy bills, 86
vehicle-to-grid (V2G) energy transfers, 135, 137
voice, 81, 88, 150, 162, 179; absent voices, 8
voluntarism, 143, 149, 156, 160, 174
vulnerability, concept of, 16

Warm Front, 104

Warm Home Discount, 84

wealthy households, carbon emissions of, 82

whole systems perspective (WSP), 91–115, 159, 163–4, 176, 178–9; application of, 167–78; complexity of, 164; desirability of, 93–4

wind, right to capture, 134

wind energy, 112; deployment policies for, 118; obstacles to, 127; offshore farms, 49, 111, 122; onshore farms, 6, 88, 111, 159; opposition to sitings of, 160

windows: condition of, 43; ill-fitting, 35 *see also* double glazing

winter fuel payments, 104

wood biomass fuel, 25

young adults: energy vulnerability of, 7, 9; housing needs of, 31–4; urban, energy vulnerability among, 30–45

young people, low-carbon projects run by, 75